OGDEN RAILS

*A History of Railroads in Ogden, Utah
From 1869 To Today*

by Don Strack

Produced in association with:
Golden Spike Chapter
Railway & Locomotive Historical Society
Ogden, Utah

Acknowledgments

This book was made possible by a grant from the George S. and Delores Dore Eccles Foundation. The generous funding provided for research and acquisition of photographs, along with actual production and printing. Many thanks to the Foundation for its support. All proceeds from the sale of this book will go toward preservation of Utah's railroad history by the Utah State Railroad Museum at Ogden Union Station.

The initial idea for this project came from Michael Burdett, Chairman of the Golden Spike Chapter of the Railway & Locomotive Historical Society. Mike's guiding vision has been most helpful throughout. Thank you, Mike.

Concept of the project took solid form after numerous discussions between the author and Mark Hemphill, and between the author and Paul Withers. These two individuals each graciously lent their expertise and extensive background in publishing and printing. On several occasions, Mark especially added to the author's enthusiasm to see this project through to completion. Thanks to both of you.

Initial research took place at Union Pacific's headquarters in Omaha, Neb., and at Southern Pacific's headquarters in San Francisco. At UP, Don Snoddy was most helpful in identifying much important information. At SP, Mike Furtney was able to point the author in the right direction, and assisted in identifying company records that proved to be very useful.

Union Pacific Railroad had in its archives numerous maps of Ogden, showing the yard as it has developed over time, and many of those maps are presented here. Thanks to Don Snoddy at UP for providing those maps. The large fold-out map included with this book comes from the collection of Ogden Union Station, and shows the complete yard at its peak, missing only the Southern Pacific and Rio Grande roundhouses. The interurban terminal map and streetcar route map were produced by Shay Stark. Shay is possibly the premier historian of Utah's electric railroads, and his participation here is most appreciated.

The photographs presented here come from numerous and varied sources. The most significant source has been the highly illustrative photos of Emil Albrecht, from the collection of James Watson. Emil Albrecht grew up and spent his entire life in Logan, Utah. He began taking pictures in the mid-1930s and continued until his death in November 1988 at age 78. He traveled throughout Utah and neighboring states, capturing railroading as he saw it. Emil was an artist who saw the world as a collection of details; he used his camera to record those details. When the author contacted Jim about the availability of Emil's photos, he was surprised to receive a very definite 'yes.' Over the next six to nine months, prints of Emil's valuable negatives continued to arrive, as Jim took time from his busy schedule to spend countless hours in the darkroom. Jim's acquaintance with Bill Gibson added several photographs from Bill's father (William A. Gibson, Sr.) to the effort. Thank you, Jim; your help has made this book much, more than originally envisioned.

Gordon Cardall, a former Bamberger engineer and avid historian of electric railroading in Utah, graciously made his own photographic collection available. His photos, and his excellent memory, have been most helpful. The unexpected availability of photographic images from John Humiston, taken during his visit to Utah in June 1940, have added much to the depth of coverage. Mrs. Kenneth (Doris) Knowles graciously made her late husband's extensive collection of Ogden Union Stock Yards data and photographs available. Many thanks go to her family, and Scott Laughter for putting the author in touch with Mrs. Knowles. Other photographs came from D. B. Harrop; A. J. "Jack" Wolff; Utah State Historical Society; LDS Church Archives; Utah State University; California State Railroad Museum; Colorado State Historical Society; Wyoming State Museum; and Ogden Union Station Museum.

Many authors today can set their words to paper with the help of a desktop computer and word processing software. But even those words need the help of an experienced editor. For this project, Dan Cupper, of Dan Cupper & Associates in Harrisburg, Pa., lent his considerable expertise. His editing efforts have made the author's words much more readable. Of course, any mistakes are solely those of the author.

After numerous discussions with, and bids from, local and out-of-state printers, service bureaus, and graphic artists, Withers Publishing was selected for the final production and printing effort. Paul Withers has on several occasions shown his exemplary competence and capability, and it is an honor to have him associated with this project. Paul has proven to be a good friend and a willing mentor. Thank you, Paul.

The author wishes to thank his wife Joanne and daughter Gina for their immeasurable patience over the past two years as this project came to completion. ☆

Front cover, *Majestic Mount Ogden seems a fitting backdrop for Union Pacific Big Boy 4010 as it waits to be serviced at UP's Ogden coaling tower.* (Union Pacific Museum Collection)

Title Page, *Union Pacific 0-6-0 4740 simmers beside the Ogden roundhouse, while Big Boy 4018 and 2-8-2 MacArthur-type number 2015 await their next assignment. Number 2015 was regularly assigned to the Park City Local, between Ogden and Park City.* (Union Pacific Museum Collection, Negative 15407)

Back cover, *Ogden's first Union Station, completed in 1889, was an important example of Romanesque architecture. As was popular with many other public buildings during the same era at the turn-of-the-century, Union Station is the subject of this colorized post card.* (Union Pacific Museum Collection)

First Edition, First Printing - April 1997
Page design and layout by Withers Publishing, Halifax, Pennsylvania
Printed and bound by Paulhamus Litho, Montoursville, Pennsylvania
Manufactured entirely in the United States of America

Additional copies of this book are available for $24.95 (dealer inquiries invited), plus $5.00 shipping, from the author at:
Don Strack, 1212 North 225 West, Centerville, Utah 84014-1104

Golden Spike Chapter
Railway & Locomotive Historical Society
Ogden Union Station, Room 212
Ogden, Utah 84401

The "Sacramento-type" train sheds completed in 1928 at Ogden's Union Station remained in place until April 1969. They were removed during a general cleanup of the station and yard in preparation for the national celebration in May 1969 of the 100th anniversary of the driving of the Golden Spike. Their design and construction detail is evident here as the Montana-bound Butte Special *arrives at the depot during the mid-1950s. (Ogden Union Station Collection)*

Table of Contents

Introduction

Ogden, Utah, has been known for many years as the "Crossroads of the West" As one looks at a map of the western United States, the reason is obvious, especially if it's a railroad map that pre-dates today's publicly funded highway system. The construction of railways through Ogden made it a geographical crossroads, and it remained so right through most of the 20th Century, up until merger mania began to sweep the nation's western railroads during the late 1970s and through the 1990s. With the merger of Union Pacific Railroad and Western Pacific Railroad in 1982, UP's connection to the San Francisco Bay area was no longer Southern Pacific at Ogden, but instead, SP's much smaller competitor, Western Pacific, through Salt Lake City. With the merger, the traffic patterns of rail cars through the Ogden rail yards changed forever. The number of trains moving through Ogden fell dramatically when Southern Pacific began diverting many more cars to its own east-west route through the Southwest and Texas. Still more changes are on the horizon with the September 1996 merger of Union Pacific and Southern Pacific.

From the day the first rails entered Ogden in 1869, railroads have played an important and insepa-rable part in the city's economy and its sense of who it was. Before the improved highway system came during the late 1940s and early 1950s, railroads and Ogden rode the economic roller coaster together — when the nation's railroads hit rocky ground, so did the city. But even with the highways and their never-ending truck, bus, and private auto competition, nearly everyone in Ogden either worked for the railroad, or knew someone who did. Working for the railroad meant that you had an important job, that you made good wages, and that you were contribut-ing your part. Boys dreamed of being a railroad engineer. During much of this century, railroads were an everyday part of life. Before World War II, many people in Ogden didn't own a car, or owned only one car, and rode the streetcars downtown, or rode the electric trains of the Bamberger to Salt Lake, or the Utah Idaho Central to Logan. When the family traveled, it went by train to visit relatives in Seattle, or California, or somewhere in the Midwest. "Travel By Train." "Workin' On The Railroad." These two phrases summarize what many local residents thought of railroads, and what many residents today remem-ber of railroads. This, then, is the story of railroads and railroading in and around Ogden, Utah. ✩

Until the completion of a through route to Los Angeles in 1905, and the construction of Salt Lake City's Union Station in 1908, Ogden's depot was the focus of railroad passenger service in Utah. This 1904 view shows Union Station from its northeast corner.
(J. E. Stimson, LDS Church Archives)

1. Union Pacific Rails Come to Ogden

On March 8, 1869, railroad rails came to Ogden for the first time. The celebration of the first rails was reported in the Ogden and Salt Lake City newspapers, speculating as to the significance of the event. While it was big news locally, it was just one chapter in an unfolding drama of national significance, the construction of the transcontinental line that would help unify a recently divided nation and become part of the healing from the wounds of the bloody Civil War that had ended just four years before. The building of the transcontinental Pacific Railroad during the 1860s would be a public works project so massive that it would not be matched for another 40 years, with the completion of the Panama Canal.

The story of the building of the Central Pacific and the Union Pacific has been told many times, and by many people. However, a brief review of Union Pacific's start is in order here. Chartered by the Pacific Railway Act of 1862, the Union Pacific Rail Road was organized in Boston on October 29, 1863. Track laying began at Omaha during July 1865 and was completed to Fremont, Nebraska Territory, by January 1866. A year later, in January 1867, tracks had been completed to North Platte, Neb., and 11 months later, trains were running into Cheyenne, Wyo. UP track-laying crews pushed the tracks across Wyoming rapidly after reaching Cheyenne during mid-November 1867. By December 4, 1868, the crews reached across the new Wyoming Territory to Evanston.

During the last week of December 1868, tracks formally entered Utah Territory at Echo Summit near present-day Wahsatch, at the head of Echo Canyon. A tunnel was still under construction that would take the trains under the summit, but until it was finished, the summit was crossed using a pair of temporary switchback tracks. Within two weeks, on January 15, 1869, the line was completed down Echo Canyon to the settlement of Echo City, where Echo Creek joined the Weber River. Seven days later, on January 22nd, the rails were laid to a point that was 1,000 miles from the starting point at Omaha. A 90-foot-high pine tree was

Union Pacific's Ogden roundhouse at the height of steam operations. The 135-foot turntable was one of four on Union Pacific (and the largest locomotive turntables ever built). The other three were at Green River, Laramie, and Cheyenne, Wyoming. These four locations were the maintenance centers for UP's 25-locomotive fleet of 4-8-8-4 Big Boy engines, designed and purchased specifically to conquer the 65-mile grade from Ogden to Wahsatch at the top of Echo Canyon without additional helper locomotives. (Union Pacific Museum Collection, Negative 15387)

well established within about 30 feet of that point and it immediately became known as "Thousand Mile Tree," which remained as a landmark to passing trains until its removal in September 1900. That same point today is actually 960 railroad miles from Omaha, due to many right-of-way realignments carried out over the years. To commemorate the Thousand Mile Tree, in 1982 Union Pacific planted a new tree and erected a commemorative sign at the original 1,000 mile point. It has grown to about 15 feet high and is visible from Interstate Highway 84 near Union Pacific's tracks, between Devils Slide and Henefer.

As the company's track-laying crews were speeding across Wyoming, Union Pacific in May 1868 contracted with Brigham Young, as president of The Church of Jesus Christ of Latter Day Saints (the Mormons), to build the roadbed and grade from the top of Echo Summit to Great Salt Lake. The scope of construction was later extended 80 miles west to the top of Promontory Summit. As part of the contract, UP agreed to provide free transportation from Omaha for the contractor's men, tools, and teams, and to provide, at cost, all tools and materials necessary for the construction. Subcontractors for Brigham Young included his sons Joseph A. Young, Brigham Young Jr., and John W. Young, along with John Sharp, Brigham Young's close friend, business associate, and personal attorney. The $2,125,000 grading contract was signed on May 21, 1868 at the Continental Hotel in Salt Lake City, between Brigham Young, and, for Union Pacific, Samuel Reed.

UP completed construction to the mouth of Weber Canyon by February 28, 1869, laying ties and rails on the grade completed by the Mormons. The tent town that sprang up at the end of track was called Uintah, which became the stage stop for Salt Lake City and points south. Uintah was closer to Salt Lake City than Ogden and remained the principle stop for Salt Lake City-bound passengers, at least until the Utah Central was completed in January 1870.

Within a week of reaching Uintah, the graders had completed the seven miles of line into Ogden, and on March 8, 1869, Union Pacific operated the first train into the city. In anticipation, a week before, on February 27, 1869, the Ogden City Council had voted, "that a public demonstration be made on the arrival of the U. P. R. R. cars at Ogden City. That the Marshal request Brother Pugh and the band turn out the flags

to be hoisted. The artillery to fire a salute. The schools to march in procession, and the citizens to assemble and welcome it." The total cost of the March 8 celebration was later pegged at $66.45. Author Wesley Griswold, in his book, *A Work Of Giants*, described Ogden at the time: ". . .Ogden was growing up. There was no longer a local bounty on wolves, and for two years now, farmers had been forbidden to let their livestock roam at will among the populace. Ogden had 1,500 citizens, and most of them turned out to welcome the first locomotive, which puffed into their midst at 11:20 a.m." Meanwhile, the track layers kept pressing west, and a month later, on April 8, 1869, the tracks were completed another 27 miles to Corinne.

With the completion of Union Pacific west through Ogden to Corinne, a problem of duplicate rights-of-way became apparent. UP had pushed work as far west as Monument Point, at the far north end of Great Salt Lake, while Central Pacific, building east from its California terminus at Sacramento, had completed work in Weber Canyon. The amount of government land turned over to the two companies through the land grants from the Pacific Railway Act of 1862, and its amendment of 1864, depended on the distance that each company completed, so they were each building partial, parallel grades in hopes of snaring as much land-grant property as possible, together with the very lucrative government bonds. The parallel grades, at times only 100 feet apart, were not continuous, but were instead situated at many of the strategic points along the surveyed routes. The two companies soon realized that a meeting point must be designated to avoid additional expenditures on unneeded right-of-way. In early March 1869, U. S. President Ulysses S. Grant told his friend, UP Chief Engineer Grenville M. Dodge, that if the two companies couldn't agree on a meeting point, Congress would do it for them.

On April 8, 1869, Central Pacific president Collis P. Huntington and UP's Dodge met at Samuel Hooper's house in Washington, D.C., where negotiations between the archrivals lasted well into the night. In the April 9 compromise agreement known as the Treaty of Hooper's House, the companies agreed to meet at "the summit of Promontory Point," at the crest of the Promontory Mountains. The summit was roughly equidistant between opposing track-laying crews who were rushing headlong toward each other in what has been called "the race to Promontory." As historian

Side by side, Union Pacific and Southern Pacific steam switchers, UP 533 and SP 2810, leased to Ogden Union Railway & Depot Co., switch the depot company's freight yard at Ogden. August 25, 1947.
(Emil Albrecht, James W. Watson collection)

Wallace Farnham states in his essay, *Shadows From The Gilded Age*, "The race to Promontory, it turns out, was really a race to Ogden, and it ended at neither Promontory nor Ogden but in Sam Hooper's parlor in Washington."

In addition to fixing the meeting point at Promontory, the agreement stated that a permanent junction between the two roads would be "within eight miles of Ogden." Union Pacific was to complete its line from the new junction west to Promontory, with Central Pacific reimbursing UP the cost of construction. CP would receive the government bonds for the tracks completed by Union Pacific. The junction, originally called "City of Bear River," was named Bonneville by Union Pacific upon construction, and the name remained when Central Pacific purchased the line six months later. Utah Northern (today's UP) later completed its parallel narrow-gauge line in 1874 and called the same point Hot Springs.

On the next day, April 10, Congress passed a nonbinding joint resolution that accepted the previous day's agreed-to terminus. Congress also accepted that the two roads would actually meet at Promontory. According to the *San Francisco Bulletin*, the Congressional resolution read, "Resolved, that the common terminal of the Union Pacific and Central Pacific shall be at or near Ogden; and the Union Pacific Railroad Company shall build, and the Central Pacific Railroad Company shall pay for and own, the railroad from the terminus aforesaid to Promontory Summit, at which point the rails shall meet and connect and form one continuous line." With the meeting point finally decided on, CP halted construction at Blue Cut, at the eastern slope of the Promontory Mountains (near today's Thiokol facility), and UP halted construction at Monument Point, at the far north end of Great Salt Lake. Central Pacific actually reached Promontory on April 30, 1869, then transferred its construction forces back along the line to improve some of the stretches of track that had been rushed into operation. Union Pacific was still six miles away awaiting completion of a large trestle and rock cut. To save time, UP crews began laying track on both sides of the trestle and rock cut, including installing a siding and a wye turning track at Promontory. UP track was completed to

Promontory on May 8. On May 9, Dodge telegraphed the railroad's directors in Boston that the road was completed to Promontory Summit, "1,085 miles and 4,680 feet from the initial point" at Omaha.

The ceremony for the completion of the transcontinental railroad at Promontory was set to take place on May 8, 1869, but the UP party was delayed in its arrival until the morning of May 10. In the 100 days between the end of the previous December and the first week in April, UP crews had completed the 91 miles of railroad from the head of Echo Canyon at Wahsatch, to Corinne, passing through Ogden in early March - a furious pace, especially if one considers the ruggedness of Echo and Weber canyons, and the fierce Utah winters.

Since the "Great Event," much has been made by various writers about Brigham Young not attending the Golden Spike ceremony at Promontory. Many have speculated that he felt snubbed by the railroads' decision to build the transcontinental line around the northern end of Great Salt Lake instead of through Salt Lake City, and around the southern end of the lake. Union Pacific's chief engineer, Dodge, explained it in August 1868, saying, "The northern route was shorter by 76 miles, had less ascent and descent, less elevation to overcome, less curvature, and the total cost was $2,500,000 less. There was more running water, more timber, and better land for agriculture for grazing." In an effort to placate Young, Dodge promised to build a branch to Salt Lake City.

Dodge himself stated that he had originally intended to head due west from Ogden across the Bear River Bay arm of the lake, to Promontory Point, then north along the west slope of the Promontory Mountains to Monument Point at the north end, then west from there. The lake proved to be deeper than first thought, and Dodge was forced to build north around Bear River Bay, through Corinne, and over Promontory Summit, 700 feet above the level of the lake.

Research has shown that the Mormon leader understood both the engineering and cost-of-construction for the final route. But he still favored the southern route, wanting the railroad to go through Salt Lake City, the largest city between Denver and San Francisco. Brigham Young was disappointed and dissatisfied that UP's main line would bypass Salt

In 1941, the original 100-foot turntable at Ogden was replaced by the 135-foot version. The original Ogden 100-foot table was supposedly moved to Lynndyl, Utah, where it replaced an older 90-foot table. The four 135-foot turntables built by UP were needed to turn the road's famous Big Boy locomotives, and were the world's largest railroad turntables. This view shows just how big the turntables were – they could easily accommodate two smaller locomotives. Switcher 4904 was one of 34 built for a UP Pacific Northwest subsidiary, Oregon-Washington Railway and Navigation Co., and among 298 other 0-6-0 steam switchers. The other locomotive, UP 591, a 2-8-0 Consolidation type, was one of 101 built for the Oregon Short Line, and among 542 Consolidations built for UP and its subsidiaries between 1888 and 1910. Both locomotives are fine examples of the Harriman Common Standard designs used by Union Pacific, Southern Pacific, and other Harriman roads.
(Union Pacific Museum Collection, Negative 68-201)

7

During World War II, America's women went to work doing the jobs of men who were in uniform. Here, in 1942, one of Union Pacific's hundreds of women in shop service does her share by turning Big Boy 4007 on the Ogden turntable. *(Union Pacific Museum Collection, Negative 14612)*

Lake City, but when Central Pacific informed him that it too would take the northern route, Young acceded and offered all the help that he could. In addition to surveying the southern route, CP even considered building a bridge across the lake. In June 1868, a party of surveyors took depth soundings and found that the lake at its deepest was 38 feet rather than the previously estimated 11 feet. A route across the lake would have to wait for another 30 years and the construction of the Lucin Cutoff. In the meantime, CP chose the northern route, which actually extends not just from the northern shore of Great Salt Lake, but 219 miles west from Ogden to [Humboldt] Wells, Nevada, with its gateway to the westward flowing Humboldt River.

The August 16, 1868, issue of Salt Lake City's *Deseret Evening News* reported Brigham Young's acceptance of the final route, quoting him: "The railroad might or might not come through Salt Lake City, but either way, it's all right because God rules and He will have things as he pleases; we can act, but He will over-rule." Brigham Young may have been willing to accept the change in route as an unimportant point. While the last-spike event was important to the nation, it was UP's connection to the east that was most important to Young and the residents of Utah Territory, and that connection was made on March 8, 1869 when Union Pacific rails reached Ogden. Although he did not participate in the last-spike ceremony at Promontory, Brigham Young later attended the ground breaking of three local roads that all connected with the transcontinental line: Utah Central, Utah Southern, and Utah Northern.

Young grasped the importance of a railroad to the East as early as 1852 when a resolution or "memorial" was passed by the first session of the Utah Territorial Legislature, asking for a railroad between the Mississippi or Missouri Rivers and the Pacific Coast. Another memorial was voted in a mass meeting held in Salt Lake City on January 3, 1854, and passed by the third session of the same legislature, asking that the Pacific Railway pass through Salt Lake City. Brigham Young felt so strongly about the need for a railroad

that he was among the first subscribers of Union Pacific stock after the company's organization in 1863, and when he was asked to be a director of the new company in 1865, he immediately accepted. As will be discussed later, within a week of the last-spike ceremony at Promontory, Young broke ground for a rail connection between Ogden and Salt Lake City, thereby giving the territory's largest city and economic center the low-cost railroad transportation it so badly needed.

The completion of the transcontinental railroad allowed immigrants to travel to Utah, the new "Zion," more quickly and more cheaply than before. Previously, new Mormon church members bound for Utah from places as distant as Great Britain and Europe came by way of seaports along the East and Gulf coasts, traveling by eastern railroads, riverboats, and wagons to Independence and other points on the Missouri River, then by wagon and handcart to Utah. As railroad construction progressed across the prairie during 1867 and 1868, immigrants began their wagon journeys to Salt Lake City from each successive end of track. The completed transcontinental railroad shortened the trip across the prairie from months to just days. The first company of new members of the LDS Church to come to Utah completely by rail, a group of 300 from Wales, arrived in Omaha on June 23, 1869. The party boarded UP cars, arriving in Ogden four days later on the evening of Sunday, June 27. Their arrival brought to a close the era of difficult wagon and hand cart crossings of the plains required of earlier travelers to Utah. Historians have designated the coming of the railroad as the end of Utah's pioneer era.

Some of the first items shipped into Utah from the East by rail were pieces of manufactured furniture that arrived in mid-June 1869 at Ogden, where they moved by ox team to Salt Lake City. The shipment was sponsored by Henry Dinwoodey, who later imported machinery to make furniture from native woods, with his newly established Dinwoodey Furniture Manufacturing Co.

The earliest locally generated freight for the railroad was mining traffic. Uintah, the tent town located at the mouth of Weber Canyon, was closer to Salt Lake City than was Ogden, and became the transshipment point for 100-pound sacks of galena (a combined silver and lead ore), shipped to San Francisco by the Walker brothers, local store and mine owners, and later, bankers. Much of this ore came from their silver mines in the Cottonwood canyons in the Wasatch range, and in Ophir Canyon on the western side of the Oquirrh range, and was carried to Uintah by wagon. During just one month in 1869, the Walker brothers shipped 4,000 tons of ore over the Central Pacific and Union Pacific railroads, or 400 carloads of the then-current 10-ton capacity rail cars. (The equivalent of 16 full trains, considering the average train length of 25 cars.) The large initial tonnage was likely due to stockpiling in anticipation of the coming of low-cost railroad transportation. As active as the Walker brothers were, the distinction of making the first rail shipment of ore from Utah mines went to the Woodhull brothers when they loaded, also at Uintah, a shipment of Utah ore onto rail cars bound for California, on June 25, 1869. In that first shipment, they sent 10 tons of ore from the Monitor and Magnet Mine (later known as the Emma Mine) in Little Cottonwood Canyon, consigned to Thomas H. Selby

Reduction Works in San Francisco. This first shipment was followed in the fall of 1869 by others from the same mine, bound for the same destination. Later shipments from the Emma Mine went to James Lewis & Co. of Liverpool, England, and were smelted at Swansea, Wales. The completion of the Utah Central between Ogden and Salt Lake City in early January 1870 allowed the Woodhull interests to ship their mined galena ore from Salt Lake City. The first such through shipment left Salt Lake City on January 12, 1870, just two days after the Utah Central's completion ceremony. This shipment consisted of an entire carload of ore, about 10 tons. The rising star of the Woodhull brothers becoming Utah's first mining magnates abruptly fell when S. D. Woodhull, one of the brothers, was shot on August 13, 1870, in Little Cottonwood Canyon in a dispute over a mining claim. He died the next day.

With the completion of the transcontinental line in May 1869, Union Pacific and Central Pacific began negotiations over ownership of the trackage between Ogden and Promontory. While neither road wanted the "middle of nowhere" junction just completed at Promontory, UP favored a point as far west as possible in order to control the traffic of Utah and the Great Basin region, and therefore the freight rates. A junction at Corinne would be the ideal place to transfer wagon-load shipments of supplies bound for, and ores coming from the rapidly expanding Idaho and Montana mining districts. CP, which favored Ogden as the junction point, could see that if the junction was at Corinne, it would suffer from lack of access to Ogden and the lucrative Utah traffic that an interchange with the new Utah Central line to Salt Lake City would provide. If CP did not reach Ogden, UP would control the freight traffic between Utah and San Francisco. Forgetting or ignoring that the two companies had already agreed to a terminus "eight miles west of Ogden," the local press made much of the "battle" between Ogden and Corinne for designation as the final junction point, and the economic gain that would follow. Published barbs in the press aside, it was the projected construction of the Utah Central between Ogden and Salt Lake City, and the influence of Brigham Young in the form of his designating land in

Ogden for specific use as railroad yards, at no apparent cost to the two companies, that eventually led to Ogden becoming the actual point of interchange.

Finally, in September 1869, an agreement was reached, clarifying the junction "eight miles west of Ogden," agreed to in April. In March 1869, Union Pacific had surveyed the site, named it Bonneville, and attempted to sell building lots. Response was mediocre at best, and the effort was abandoned. For reasons unknown today, the intended junction at Bonneville (today known as Hot Springs) was bypassed. Instead, a point just five miles west of Ogden was chosen and in November 1869, CP purchased from UP the track between Promontory and the new point of compromise, near present-day Harrisville, where the two companies planned to build a junction and terminal, called, appropriately, Junction City. This location was more closely defined as a point "five miles west of Utah Central crossing." (Railroad directions are always east, for eastbound, or west, for westbound, regardless of the actual compass direction.) This site was within the limits set by the April 1869 agreement, and was likely chosen due to its flatness and the availability of water from wells. Union Pacific retained ownership of the five miles of tracks from Ogden to the new junction for the purposes of the government bonds, again in accordance with the April agreement. Central Pacific paid $2.8 million for the 47.5 miles of UP tracks in the form of CP first mortgage bonds and government securities, and leased the final five miles into Ogden from UP for a period of 999 years. The two railroads continued to exchange freight and passengers at Promontory from May to December 1869. At that time, with the completion of the Utah Central, together with the sale of UP's line to CP the previous month, they agreed to temporarily move the exchange point to Ogden, pending completion of the terminal at Junction City.

The agreement of September 1869 was confirmed on May 6, 1870, when a Joint Resolution of the U. S. Congress fixed the junction at the same point, five miles west of Ogden as that already agreed to by the railroads. Between 1870 and 1874, work progressed on plans for a common terminal at Junction City. The completion of the narrow-gauge Utah Northern between Logan and Ogden in February 1874, however,

Union Pacific 4015 rides the turntable while being serviced at Ogden's large roundhouse. Note that the coal pile in the tender is heaped, denoting that this Big Boy locomotive is about to take another eastbound up the famous Wahsatch grade. The first Big Boys, arguably the largest and most powerful steam locomotives ever built, were delivered in September 1941 and remained a common sight in the Ogden yards until their retirement in 1959. (Union Pacific Museum Collection, Negative 14611-A)

forced the two roads to reconsider, and in May 1874, five years after the completion of the transcontinental railroad, the two railroads agreed to Ogden as the junction point and they each commenced construction of significant improvements in the new terminal.

A map of Ogden dated 1874 shows a combination of both Union Pacific and Central Pacific facilities. When the Utah Central was completed in 1870, it crossed the transcontinental line at a point midway between Fourth and Fifth streets, about 1,000 feet west of Wall Avenue (about midway along today's 24th Street Viaduct, about even with the old Southern Pacific shops). The Utah Central crossing became the point of division between Central Pacific and Union Pacific. CP's freight yard was located north of the Utah Central crossing, and the UP freight yard was on the south side. The common passenger depot and a common small turntable serving separate, single-stall enginehouses, were also located on the south side. Both companies had car shops and enginehouses located off the original turntable; Central Pacific's enginehouse included an interior water tank. That original turntable, which appears to be only 40 feet in diameter, was located between Fifth and Sixth streets

(25th and 26th streets today), about midway between the west side of the tracks and the Weber River. The same 1874 map also shows a Utah Central depot and enginehouse adjacent to Wall Street, at Fifth Street, along with a separate Utah Northern narrow-gauge depot and stub-ended yard located on Wall Street between Fourth and Fifth streets.

Despite this change in plans, the five miles of tracks from Ogden along the original Central Pacific route remained in UP ownership, with CP leasing the line. When CP's successor, Southern Pacific, abandoned its original route around the north side of the Great Salt Lake, known as its Promontory Branch, in 1942, the road also officially abandoned its line north from Ogden to Corinne, although SP trains had been using Union Pacific's tracks between Ogden and Corinne since 1903. (In 1903, UP completed its Malad Branch, north from Corinne, along with a four-mile connection between UP's line at Brigham City and the CP line just east of Corinne.) Union Pacific retained its original five mile segment north from Ogden, and the trackage was later used as a spur for the War Department's Utah General Depot (today known as Defense Depot Ogden), built during World War II. ☆

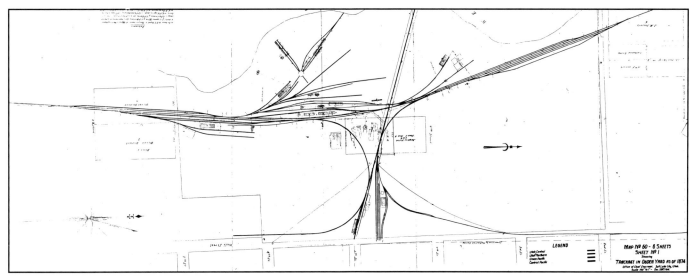

Ogden yard in 1874, after the completion of the narrow-gauge Utah Northern. At left is the Union Pacific yard. Just left of the Utah Central crossing is the UP passenger depot, and above that, the shared UP/CP turntable. Right of the UC crossing is Central Pacific's yard. Utah Central had its small enginehouse and passenger depot east of the UP/CP crossing. Narrow-gauge Utah Northern entered from lower right and terminated in its small yard adjacent to the UC passenger depot. (Union Pacific Museum Collection)

2. Utah Central Railroad

The construction of a connecting railroad line south from Ogden to Salt Lake City, and later into almost all parts of the state, exerted a much greater impact on the local populace and economy than did the joining of rails at Promontory. In early 1869, prior to the completion of the transcontinental railroad, leaders of the Mormon church began organizing a railroad to connect Salt Lake City with Ogden, and the soon-to-be-completed UP main line, with Brigham Young reportedly saying, "If the Union Pacific won't come to Salt Lake City, then Salt Lake City will go to the Union Pacific." The Utah Central Rail Road was organized on March 8, 1869, the same day that UP was completed into Ogden (which probably explains why Young was not in attendance at the Ogden ceremony), and just three weeks after the Utah Territorial Legislature passed the Railroad Incorporation Act, on February 19, 1869.

The completion of the Utah Central in 1870 was the beginning of a statewide rail network. In May 1871, Utah Southern Railroad began building south from Salt Lake City. During the following two years several railroads were proposed in the territory. A few were successful; most were not. Brigham Young promoted the completion of locally organized railroads more as a benefit to the communities they served than as profit-making enterprises; however he did not discourage members of the church from working for railroad builders as a source of cash to improve their farms and lifestyles. These "Mormon Roads," so named because they were organized and managed by local church leaders as well as local businessmen, radiated like spokes of a wheel from the population centers of Salt Lake City and Ogden. They included the already-noted Utah Central and Utah Southern, along with Utah Western, built west from Salt Lake City, and Utah Northern, which was built north from Brigham City, later connecting with Ogden. Others were projected east from both Salt Lake City and Ogden and from other points on the Utah Northern and the Utah Southern. Two present-day historians described the Mormon Roads well: Leonard Arrington said, "The

The Utah Central completed its bridge over the Weber River in October 1869. The wooden bridge shown here was replaced by a more substantial early iron design within a couple years. (Union Pacific Museum Collection, Negative 12-18)

11

Mormon railroads were not particularly profitable, but they were needed, and they served the economy, and they helped to assuage [reduce] the bitterness of the Mormons at the failure of the two transcontinental railroads to satisfy their construction contracts in cash." Mark Hemphill put it well when he said, "Mormon railroads would tie together the Mormon people, distribute the fruits of their fields, develop Utah's mineral bonanzas, and make the Mormon kingdom prosperous."

The story of Utah's pioneer local railroad, the Utah Central, begins with Brigham Young's unfulfilled desire to see the transcontinental railroad built through Salt Lake City. With the decision made in favor of Ogden, he immediately set about proposing a connecting road to Salt Lake City. The surveying of the Utah Central was started by Chief Engineer Jesse W. Fox, Sr., at Ogden on May 15, 1869. Two days later, on May 17, just a week after the Golden Spike ceremony at Promontory, Brigham Young held the groundbreaking for the Utah Central line at Ogden, near the Union Pacific depot at the west end of Fourth Street. With "no great display" and "no speech making," Young and his counselors in the church leadership broke ground, cutting the sod with a spade. The sod was "borne away in fragments as a memento of the event."

The rail and equipment to build and initially operate the Utah Central came from UP. With the transcontinental line completed, Young approached Union Pacific seeking payment due him, and the church, under the grading contracts he held with the company. Because of Union Pacific's difficulties in getting the government bonds for the completion of the transcontinental rail line, there were delays in payment for those and other grading contracts. On May 19, 1869, Brigham Young wrote to UP's Thomas Durant informing him that the grading was completed and that Young was due "some three-quarters of a Million Dollars." In September 1869, Brigham Young agreed to take rails, tools, and rolling stock from Union Pacific in partial settlement for the $1.14 million remaining on payment for the original $2.13 million contract for grading UP's line. The negotiations took place in Boston between Bishop John Sharp, along with Joseph Young, and the UP board of directors. The directors agreed to $940,138 and left $198,000 to

arbitration. On September 2, Bishop Sharp agreed to accept the rolling stock and track materials with an apparent value of approximately $600,000 as partial payment on the agreed $940,000 amount.

The Boston settlement for the grading contracts also gave Utah Central trackage rights over UP between Ogden and Echo Junction, for a period of five years, to get coal from mines near Coalville. Completion of the Utah Central to Salt Lake City allowed carloads of coal to be directly shipped into the city. The first two carloads, carrying coal from the Wasatch Mine of the Wasatch Coal Co. at Coalville and consigned to Frederick A. H. F. Mitchell, arrived in Salt Lake City on January 13, just three days after a January 10, 1870, celebration for the completion of the Utah Central. Unfortunately, research has not identified other documentation about Utah Central trains operating direct from Salt Lake City to Echo, by way of Ogden and Weber Canyon, and returning with carloads of coal from Coalville. The ready availability of Coalville coal would be important to Utah's early economy, especially considering the documented monopoly and stranglehold that UP was to gain on Utah's coal supply, beginning about 1874, at expiration of that five-year period. H. H. Bancroft, in his 1886 History of Utah, states that most of the supplies of coal needed for Salt Lake City and the northern settlements came from the Coalville mines.

Coal was a vital resource needed by Utah's growing population and economy, both as a source of home fuel and for the coal-fired power plants of mining, smelting, and manufacturing enterprises. Coal was so important that in 1854 the Territorial legislature offered a $1,000 reward to anyone who discovered a source of coal within 40 miles of Salt Lake City. In 1860 William Kimball and John Spriggs attempted to claim the prize for their Coalville mine, but were denied because the coal was found to be inferior, and a legislative committee found that the mine was more than 40 miles from Salt Lake.

In October 1869, just after the trackage rights agreement was signed allowing Utah Central to provide low-cost transportation for coal, local church leaders in Coalville, Echo, Ogden, and Salt Lake City organized the Coalville & Echo Railroad. Their goal was to build a rail line between the coal mines at Coalville and a connection with the Union Pacific main line, at Echo, 40 miles east of Ogden. It was the second of the Mormon roads to make use of the labor of local church members to construct the grade and lay the ties and rails, the first being the then-under-construction Utah Central. Progress was rapid, but soon stalled after grading was completed, with the company unable to finance the rails. Labor for grading was readily available, as was timber and labor for the laying of ties; but the iron rails required cash, something that the region simply did not have.

Work lay dormant for another year until investors became interested and organized the Summit County Railway. That company completed the tracks from Echo to Coalville (five miles) in 1874 as a three-foot narrow-gauge railroad, and reached Park City in 1880, converting the entire 28-mile line from narrow-gauge to 4 feet 8-1/2 inches standard-gauge at the same time. The same tracks later became Union Pacific's Park City Branch. UP abandoned the Park City Branch in

Utah Central Railway No. 6 shown in 1889, adjacent to the new Ogden Union Station. UC No. 6 was built in 1883 as Union Pacific's No. 65 and was sold to Utah Central for operation over the new Union Pacific-controlled line between Ogden and the Horn silver mine in central Utah. (Union Pacific Museum Collection, Negative 504387)

By the early 1870s, the city was growing rapidly, mostly due to the coming of the railroads. In this early view of the city from the West Ogden bluff, we can see Utah Central's early iron bridge over the Weber River, along with the adjacent twin wooden bridges for the Territorial Road to Salt Lake City. On the left, along the Central Pacific's tracks, are the stock yards and hide warehouse. Also visible is the large, fully enclosed Central Pacific water tower. In the center, visible between the railroad bridge and the road bridge, is the two-stall Utah Central enginehouse, with no apparent activity. On the right above the string of rail cars is the original Union Pacific passenger depot, soon to become the first Union Station. In the middle distance, just above the road bridges, is the freight transfer shed of Utah Central. This view predates the 1874 arrival of the narrow-gauge rails of the Utah Northern. *(William Henry Jackson, Utah State Historical Society)*

1987. The operation of the Park City Local, a mixed passenger and freight train, from Ogden to Park City and back was a daily event remembered by many persons with an interest in railroading in Ogden.

Grading for the Utah Central was already under way when on June 10 and 11, 1869, Brigham Young, along with the chief engineer and other officers of the railroad, made a trip north from Salt Lake City to Ogden, locating the proposed route along the way. The grade then under construction from Ogden ran west from the Weber River up to the bench of the West Ogden Sand Ridge, using an ascending grade not exceeding 0.75 percent (nine inches of rise in 100 feet of distance, or 40 feet rise in the distance of one mile). That original grade and trackage is still being used today, as Union Pacific's Evona Branch, which crosses the Weber River and parallels 24th Street through West Ogden.

The settlement of the grading contracts in September 1869 between Brigham Young and UP provided Utah Central with its much needed rail. With that critical component available, Young's son, John W. Young, organized track-laying crews, also from local church wards, and commenced putting down tracks at Ogden on September 22, 1869, at a point called "Weber Junction." The line west from the connection with Union Pacific to the crossing of the Weber River, basically paralleling today's 24th Street viaduct, was to play a significant role in the later separation of UP and Southern Pacific trackage in the Ogden yard; north of the line is SP and south of the line is UP. The track was laid across the Weber River by October 12, 1869, and by the end of the next day the tracks reached three miles west of the river crossing. Initial progress was rapid because the tracks were first laid on the west side of the river prior to the bridge being completed. The normal rate was about a half-mile per day. By the time the track-laying crews

reached Kaysville, 17 miles south of Ogden, on November 19th, they were building a mile of track per day. Ten days after reaching Kaysville, the Utah Central tracks reached Farmington. Operations began between Ogden and Farmington, 21 miles distant, on December 6th. Brigham Young halted construction at Farmington to wait for a additional rails to be delivered from Union Pacific. With the completion of the road to Kaysville, horse-drawn stages began operating between end of track and Salt Lake City, and as each community was reached, the stages shortened their route. The track-laying toward Salt Lake was resumed at Farmington and progressed on to Bountiful, another six miles. Bountiful was reached on December 22 and the road was completed to Salt Lake City (36 miles) during the first week of January 1870,

A day of celebration – January 10, 1870. The completion of the Utah Central showed that the people of northern Utah could get together and do what the two transcontinental roads would not – give the largest city between Denver and San Francisco the railroad service it deserved. (Charles William Carter, LDS Church Archives)

with a "last spike" ceremony being held on January 10. Passenger service between Ogden and Salt Lake City began on January 12th.

According to Seymour B. Young, Brigham Young's nephew and a contractor on the grading near Beck's Hot Springs north of Salt Lake City, the laying of Utah Central rails into Salt Lake City was completed at about noon on December 30, 1869. The grand celebration commemorating the event took place 10 days later, on January 10, 1870. For the celebration, a railroad flat car was decorated as a platform to hold dignitaries of the Utah Central (most of whom were also leaders in the LDS Church), Union Pacific, Central Pacific, the national press, and representatives of the U. S. Army stationed at Camp Floyd. Four brass bands were also in attendance, playing for the 15,000 citizens that participated. Just after 2 p.m., Brigham Young drove the last spike holding the last rail to the last tie. The last spike was fashioned of iron, and Young used an iron maul, both made specially for the occasion from native Utah iron. At last, because of a rail connection at Ogden, Salt Lake City had its connection to the East.

By mid-January 1870, 10 trains were operating through the Ogden terminal daily, including those of Union Pacific, Central Pacific, and Utah Central. To support these operations, both UP and Utah Central built and maintained facilities in Ogden. Utah Central completed a 14-foot by 60-foot enginehouse, along with a 700-foot-long, multi-span wooden bridge over the Weber River. UP completed a two-story, 20-foot by 40-foot express office; a 20-foot by 65-foot passenger house; a two-story 24-foot by 90-foot eating house with four rooms on the first floor and 12 rooms on the second floor; a two-story 20-foot by 30-foot baggage house; and a one-story 20-foot by 50-foot lodging house. Improvements for the UP mechanical department included a two-story, 20-foot by 35-foot car department; a 20-foot by 30-foot Master Mechanic's house, and a 40-foot by 157-foot enginehouse.

With the increasing exchange of traffic among the three roads, improvements continued in the Ogden terminal. In October 1873, the original single-stall Utah Central enginehouse, built in late 1869 at the west end of Fifth Street (now 25th Street), at Wall Avenue, was torn down and replaced by another located nearer the Weber River, and adjacent to the Utah Central tracks. UP built a two-stall enginehouse adjacent to its small turntable located in the area south of the Utah Central tracks, and between its main line and the Weber River. Although the original UP enginehouse, and later four-stall roundhouse, were abandoned by 1890, and the turntable "taken up," Utah Central's enginehouse remained in place until UP completed a new all-brick, 20-stall roundhouse in 1897 just south of the Utah Central line.

The September 1869 settlement for the Union Pacific grading contracts also provided the Utah Central with its first locomotive. Named "Blackhawk," Utah Central No. 1 was a 4-4-0 built by Hinkley & Williams as Union Pacific No. 15 in 1866, was sold to Utah Central on October 14, 1869. During January 1870 Utah Central No. 2 was delivered new, and on February 7, 1870 Utah Central received two additional new locomotives, Nos. 3 and 4, from McQueen & Co. of Schenectady, N. Y. The reported total cost of the two newest locomotives was $12,000.

Regular passenger service began with two trains running daily each way. A third ran on Wednesdays, Saturdays, and Sundays. The semi-annual conference of the LDS Church was an especially big source of revenue. On May 7, 1870, 11 carloads of conference-goers bound for Salt Lake City from Ogden required the muscle of two engines.

Utah Central was a money-maker right from the first. For March 1870, earnings were $6,518.89. A year later, the road made $18,740.96, and for the same month in 1872 the road had revenues of $26,832.21. In 1876 the annual earnings were $392,346.00, against expenses of $159,609, making costs only 40.6 percent of earnings, a percentage that today's railroads only dream about.

By the early 1870s Brigham Young, born in 1801, was ready for retirement. He began to lessen his involvement in local business and territorial affairs, reducing his titles and responsibilities to being president of the church, which itself was an all-consuming job. After Union Pacific failed to make good on its promises of settlement on the grading contracts of 1868 and 1869, Young began looking for other sources of cash with which to pay off his sub-contractors who had helped with grading. In December 1870, Young approached Central Pacific, offering to sell part or all of his holdings in Utah Central. CP was very interested due to its difficulties with UP. Almost immediately after the transcontinental line was completed, Union Pacific and Central Pacific had begun bickering over both major and minor issues, with CP regularly making noises about building a competing line through Utah to the East, parallel to Union Pacific's own. Young's offer fell right in with these plans. When UP officials heard of Young's proposed association with Central Pacific, they made an offer of their own. Throughout 1871, talks continued, with Young likely playing one side against the other, keeping in mind that his interest was to get cash to fulfill his obligations to his grading subcontractors. Eventually, Union Pacific prevailed. Contrary to his earlier strong desire to deny UP an interest in the Utah Central, Brigham Young in April 1872 sold 5,000 of his 7,600 shares (of 15,000 total) to Union Pacific.

Young still disliked dealing with the UP, but was resigned to the necessity of doing so. The Mormon church paid an average of $100,000 per year to UP in fares for its missionaries and immigrants alone. But because the original settlement of the grading contracts included a guarantee of half-fare tickets for church members, the railroad was less than cordial. In January 1876, Young complained, "they snap and snarl every time they have the significant pretext until I am tired." By the time of his death in August 1877, Young no longer had any financial interest in the Utah Central Railroad, but UP still owed him $130,000 on the grading contracts.

Union Pacific gained firm control of Utah Central in 1878 by combining the shares already owned by its officers and directors with those it had purchased from Young. UP consolidated its interests in Utah railroads in July 1881 when Utah Central Railroad merged with Utah Southern Railroad and Utah Southern Railroad Extension to form a new, Union Pacific-controlled carrier, Utah Central Railway. ☆

3. Utah Northern

With the 1870 completion of the Utah Central between Ogden and Salt Lake City, church and community leaders soon set their sights on expanding the territory's railroad network. In May 1871, work began on the Utah Southern south from Salt Lake City. As a locally-owned company, the road by February 1875 reached south of Salt Lake City 60 miles to Santaquin Summit (also known as York), six miles south of Payson. Later, as a Union Pacific-controlled enterprise in June 1880, Utah Southern, and its associated company, Utah Southern Railroad Extension, expanded south another 150 miles to the Horn Silver Mine, near Milford, in which several Union Pacific directors held a financial interest.

Brigham Young had also wanted a railroad to run north from Ogden as a companion to the Utah Southern's route south from Salt Lake City, seeing the need for a way to build the economies and provide transportation for the northern communities. In addition, there was a growing trade with Montana mining camps. The Montana miners were becoming regular customers both for Utah's farm products and for shipments of salt (which, of course, was in great abundance around Great Salt Lake) which they needed to refine silver ore. Also, there was the prospect of becoming a transfer point for Montana-bound freight, similar to what was being off-loaded from Central Pacific cars at Corinne. This freight was shipped to Corinne by railroad and transferred by the freight companies to their own heavy wagons for the 400-mile journey to the mining camps. Corinne was two days closer to Montana by wagon than was Ogden, and was at the southern end of a route up the Malad Valley into Idaho.

The Utah Northern Railway was organized on August 23, 1871, to build a three-foot, narrow-gauge route north from a terminal with Central Pacific, Union Pacific, and Utah Central at Ogden, to Soda Springs, Idaho Territory. Construction began just three days later when a ground-breaking ceremony was held adjacent to the CP line just west of the settlement of Three Mile Creek (today known as Perry) on August 26; present were Brigham Young and James Camell, president of the Utah Division of the Central Pacific. The same location, three miles south of Brigham City, was called "Utah Northern RR Junction" by Central Pacific, and "Brigham City Junction" by Utah Northern.

Work on the new line was only intermittent during the following winter and resumed in March of 1872. The first spike was driven on the 27th of that month and a connection was made with CP on the 29th. By mid-June 1872, rails had reached 23 miles to Hamptons, a new station in the foothills east of Hamptons Crossing, a toll bridge and stage station on the Bear River. The narrow-gauge line was completed to Logan on February 3, 1873. After reaching Logan, the company continued north, along with focusing its efforts to connect Brigham City with Ogden. The line

was completed to Ogden in February 1874. By early May 1874, Utah Northern was finished north to Franklin, just over the line into Idaho Territory. Regular passenger and freight service between Ogden and Franklin began on May 4, 1874, over a route of 75 miles of new construction.

With the Utah Northern line completed into Cache Valley, freight companies began moving their warehouses from Corinne, first to Logan, and later to Franklin, which was 50 miles, and at least two days, closer to Montana than Corinne. The new route also allowed wagons to avoid the heavy grade over Malad Hill to Downey, Idaho. The Gilmer and Salisbury Stage Line moved its passenger terminal to Franklin in May 1875, taking with it the U. S. Mail contract and the Wells Fargo & Co. express business that the stage line carried. The terminal at Franklin was indeed closer, but the road north turned out to be less usable to the freighters, and some moved back to Corinne. Within two years, Corinne was shipping more freight to Montana than it did in 1874. The greatest difficulty was Utah Northern's unprotected crossing of Collinston Divide between the Bear River Valley and Cache Valley. The original surveyors of Utah Northern had wanted to take the line through the protected Bear River Gorge, five miles further north. But the higher cost of heavy construction through the rocky passage forced the little road to choose the easier, less expensive route. During the following winters the road's owners came to regret the choice because of several snow blockades that closed it for weeks at a time.

As the freighters became disillusioned with the road north of Franklin and began returning to Corinne, the financial fortunes of the Utah Northern fell flat. Without Montana-bound freight, the railroad was left to "transporting carrots for the faithful." The declining business coming solely from the frugal Mormon agricultural communities in Cache Valley was so low that it recalled an axiom of agents of Wells Fargo & Co., "One Gentile makes as much business as a hundred Mormons."

Franklin remained as Utah Northern's northern terminal from May 1874 until the little railroad's bankruptcy and foreclosure sale on April 3, 1878. On that date the bankrupt Utah Northern Railroad was sold to the newly organized Utah & Northern Railway, a Union Pacific-controlled company. The old Utah Northern had completed 14.5 miles of grading northeast from Franklin toward Soda Springs, but when UP resumed construction on November 8, 1877, it built northwest through Downey, Virginia, and McCammon, Idaho, and abandoned the grade to Soda Springs. In late June 1878, construction reached Watson's Station (renamed Onieda), intersecting the Montana Trail. The freight companies then set up their terminals at the railroad end of track, completely cutting off Corinne from the Montana business. Three and a half years later, on December 15, 1881, the UP-controlled Utah

& Northern narrow-gauge railroad was completed to Butte, Mont., 397 miles north of Ogden.

Work on extending the Utah Northern south from Three Mile Creek (Perry) to Ogden was begun in November 1872, but the effort was stopped to allow completion of the line into Logan in Cache Valley. The work of grading the line south to Ogden resumed in September 1873, and the track-laying was started at Three Mile Creek on January 15, 1874. Track-laying north from Ogden was started at about the same time, and two weeks later, on February 4, Utah Northern's tracks were completed between Brigham City and Ogden when the two crews met somewhere near Willard. Regular scheduled service began the next day, February 5, 1874. The routes of the standard-gauge Central Pacific and the narrow-gauge Utah Northern were parallel along the seven miles of line between Three Mile Creek (Perry) and Hot Springs (Bonneville on CP). The original Utah Northern, and the later Utah & Northern, became part of the Oregon Short Line & Utah Northern in 1889, and the narrow-gauge route was converted to standard-gauge in 1890. The OSL&UN itself was reorganized as the Oregon Short Line Railroad in 1897 and later became part of the newly reorganized Union Pacific.

Utah Northern's Corinne Branch

In June 1873, during the summer following its completion to Logan, Utah Northern completed a branch from its line north of Brigham City, west to Corinne. The beginning of construction of the Utah Northern during late 1871 and early 1872 had made the Gentile (non-Mormon) residents and businessmen of Corinne sit up and take notice. After completion of the transcontinental line in 1869, they had hoped that Corinne would be designated as the junction point between Union Pacific and Central Pacific. They had UP's support, but CP wanted the junction nearer, or at, Ogden. Corinne had become the transfer point for freight bound for the Montana mines, earning its nickname of "Bullwagon Metropolis." By May 1870, the freight companies in Corinne had unloaded 180 rail cars and sent 1,088 tons of goods to Montana. During 1873, more than 5,000 tons of freight was on the road

to Montana, with the wagons returning loaded with 500 tons of rich ore for the smelters.

To influence the decision in favor of Corinne as the final junction for the Pacific railroad, much the same way that the connection with Utah Central seemed to be helping Ogden, townspeople in April 1872 organized their own Utah, Idaho & Montana Railroad, but failed to raise enough cash to begin construction. Then, during the autumn of 1872, they approached Utah Northern management seeking construction of a branch line from Brigham City to Corinne. This was a year and a half before Utah Northern completed its line south to Ogden, so the railroad saw a chance to take the Montana-bound freight away from the wagon-freight companies, at least as far as Logan. The Corinne boosters were possibly hoping that Utah Northern, by building the branch to Corinne, would then not see the need to build to Ogden. Utah Northern agreed to construct a four-mile branch and operate trains connecting with Central Pacific trains at Corinne, at least until it could extend its line to Ogden. Construction began in April 1873 with the grading starting at Corinne Junction, about four miles north of Brigham City, along with construction of a new bridge, north of Corinne, over the Bear River. The bridge was completed on June 9, 1873, and regular service began on June 11.

The opening of the Corinne Branch did not, however, deter Utah Northern from continuing south to Ogden, which it reached in February 1874. The interchange point between Utah Northern and Central Pacific was then moved to Ogden, eliminating the need for the Corinne Branch. Service to Corinne formally ended on January 1, 1876. The branch was abandoned and the rails removed, with the remaining connection to Utah Northern's main line becoming Baker Siding. A portion of the grade was later renovated by a Utah Northern successor, Oregon Short Line, in 1909 when the Ogden Portland Cement Co. (Opco) paid for a spur to be built to its new cement plant, which was processing raw cement from the adjacent alkali flats. In May 1918, the 1.1-mile Opco Spur was extended north to become the 4.9-mile Urban Branch, serving a sugar-beet-growing region east of the Bear River. The branch line that started out as the narrow-gauge Utah Northern's Corinne Branch in 1873 ended its days as a standard-gauge line in May 1948 when the Urban Branch was abandoned. Its starting point, Baker Siding, just north of the small community of Calls Fort, was abandoned in 1964. The much-graffitied skeletal remains of the Ogden Portland Cement Co. plant still stand, adjacent to Interstate Highway 15. ✰

After being assigned to the Ogden-to-Brigham City local, UP McKeen car M-20 sits stored at Ogden on September 7, 1936, awaiting another assignment. McKeen cars were built by UP at its Omaha, Neb., shops from 1905 to 1908, when the McKeen Motor Car Co. was organized to manage the growing market for self-propelled cars and matching unpowered trailers. By 1920, the new Electro-Motive electric transmission cars were outselling McKeen's mechanical transmission cars, and the company was dissolved. M-20, shown here, was completed in 1908 and retired by UP in 1944. (Otto C. Perry, Western History Department, Denver Public Library, Negative OP-19470)

4. Oregon Short Line & Utah Northern

The Oregon Short Line & Utah Northern Railway was organized on July 27, 1889, by merging the Utah & Northern Railway, the Utah Central Railway, the Utah & Nevada Railway, the Salt Lake & Western Railway, and the Ogden & Syracuse Railway (all in Utah), the Idaho Central Railway (in Idaho), and the Oregon Short Line Railway (in Idaho, eastern Oregon, and southwestern Wyoming), and the unbuilt Nevada Pacific Railway in Nevada. The Oregon Short Line & Utah Northern was organized in part to provide financing for both a new standard-gauge line between Ogden and McCammon, in southeastern Idaho, and the extension of the former Utah Southern Railroad Extension line south from Milford to mines at Pioche, Nev.

The predecessor Oregon Short Line Railway was incorporated in Wyoming on April 14, 1881 by Union Pacific to build a line by the shortest route – "The Short Line" – from Wyoming to Oregon, hence its name, Oregon Short Line. Construction began in May at Granger, Wyo., at a connection with the Union Pacific main line, 148 miles east of Ogden. The tracks were completed to Montpelier, Idaho, 115 miles, on August 5, 1882, and to Pocatello, 215 miles, during the fall of the same year. The last 12 miles of track between McCammon and Pocatello, Idaho, was used jointly with the Utah & Northern narrow-gauge line. The OSL shared the U&N grade by laying a third rail, set to standard-gauge, outside of Utah and Northern's three-foot-gauge rails. OSL trains began operating between Granger, Wyoming, and Huntington, in eastern Oregon, in February 1884, and the first through train from Omaha to the Pacific Northwest reached Portland in January 1885. The completion of the Oregon Short Line between Wyoming and Pocatello had an immediate effect on the Montana-bound traffic that was being shipped north from Ogden by way of the narrow-gauge Utah & Northern. Pocatello was 135 miles closer to Montana than was Ogden, and much Montana-bound freight immediately went to Pocatello instead of Ogden.

With growing traffic on the new line between Omaha and Portland, and with the increasing traffic moving north from Pocatello to the Montana mines, the narrow-gauge Utah & Northern north of Pocatello was hard pressed to keep up, due to the delay and cost caused by the change of track gauge at Pocatello. In the early years, the freight had to be transloaded from narrow-gauge cars to standard-gauge cars. Later, standard-gauge cars were lifted and narrow-gauge wheel assemblies substituted for the trip to Montana. Still, it was a cumbersome arrangement at best. Preparation for converting the track to standard-gauge began with engineering studies as early as 1885. Union Pacific officials found that the original Utah Northern line between the Great Salt Lake Basin and the 1875 end-of-track at Franklin, Idaho, had been engineered at less than Union Pacific standards, and would require much

more work than simply changing the distance between the rails on the existing grade. On the positive side, the 250-plus miles of line from Franklin through Pocatello to Butte had been built by UP's own forces and would not have to be reconstructed.

By mid-1887, the Utah & Northern was ready to convert its line between Pocatello and Butte to standard-gauge, which took place, amazingly, on a single day. To minimize the disruption in service, men, tools, and materials were distributed along the line over the preceding months, and the changeover was done on Monday, July 25, 1887. The preparation included new bridges, new longer ties, and many general improvements of the grade itself. The line south from McCammon to Ogden, 111 miles long, took another three years to convert because it required more than 50 miles of new right-of-way construction, including a new line through the Bear River Gorge. It was completed in the first week of October 1890, after the Oregon Short Line & Utah Northern had already been organized. The new standard-gauge line between Ogden and McCammon included just over 48 miles of newly constructed and relocated main line between Dewey, Utah, and Oxford, Idaho, 21 miles north of the Utah-Idaho line.

The construction of the new standard-gauge line also included an 8.58-mile Cache Valley connection between the former Utah & Northern narrow-gauge line at Mendon and a station on the new line to be called Cache Junction. Operation over this connection began on October 24, 1890. The conversion to standard-gauge of the original 1873 Utah Northern line across the Cache Valley, between Mendon, Logan, and Preston, was completed on October 26, 1890. The entire line between Cache Junction and Preston then became the Cache Valley Branch, which is still being used today by Union Pacific.

The remaining 15-mile section of the old narrow-gauge main line north from Preston to the connection with the new line at Oxford, Idaho, was abandoned upon completion of the standard-gauge line. Also abandoned was 12 miles of the original narrow-gauge line between Dewey and Mendon, by way of Collinston Summit. This original route over Collinston Divide was used 25 years later by the Ogden, Logan & Idaho Railway to build an interurban electric line between Ogden and Logan in 1915.

Within two years, during 1892, Oregon Short Line & Utah Northern completed the 1.09-mile Five Points Branch in Ogden. Built to serve the agricultural area directly north of the city, the branch left the main line north of Ogden at Five Points Junction, paralleling what is now Second Street. At that point, freight was interchanged with the Ogden & Hot Springs Railroad for movement to and from the agricultural area around North Ogden, north along Washington Street (now Washington Boulevard).

Along with all of Union Pacific's other subsidiary and feeder companies, the Oregon Short Line & Utah

Northern Railway was forced into bankruptcy with its parent company in October 1893, and was reorganized as the Oregon Short Line Railroad in February 1897, a new company separate from UP but still controlled by the same individuals, who were bondholders of both companies. The old Union Pacific Railway was sold to the newly organized Union Pacific Railroad in November 1897. By 1900, Wall Street financier Edward H. Harriman had gained control of the new Union Pacific, and set about gathering the former feeder lines back into UP's protective arms. On January 10, 1899, the new UP increased its stock by $27 million and traded that new block of shares to the owners of the Oregon Short Line, in return for full control and ownership of OSL. ☆

In this view from 1946, a matched pair of Union Pacific's famous Big Boy 4-8-8-4 locomotives await its next assignment, taking eastbound freight up the Wasatch grade in Weber and Echo canyons into western Wyoming. Visible above the two locomotives is the 350-ton coaling tower completed in late 1927. (Emil Albrecht, James W. Watson Collection)

4. Union Pacific in this Century

With control of UP and its two most important subsidiaries, Oregon Short Line Railroad, and Oregon Railway & Navigation Co., firmly in hand by 1900, E. H. Harriman immediately set about making much-needed improvements. The newly reorganized Union Pacific soon began making numerous improvements on the 70 miles of main line in Weber and Echo canyons, east of Ogden. In 1904, 40 miles of line between Ogden and Echo was improved and relocated. The changes included laying more than five miles of new track and alignment, which reduced the total length by a half-mile. A second track was completed between Riverdale and Gateway (also known as Devil's Gate), and between Emory and the top of the grade at Wahsatch in 1916-1917. The remainder of the Wasatch grade east from Ogden acquired a second track in 1921 and 1926.

The economy of the West in general, and California in particular, was booming in the decade between 1900 and 1910. The amount of rail traffic moving through Ogden and Salt Lake City was growing rapidly, especially with the completion of the San Pedro, Los Angeles & Salt Lake Railroad between its namesake cities in 1905. This, along with the general

increase in business following Harriman's improvements, soon made a severe bottleneck of the single-track route between Ogden and Salt Lake City, and UP made plans to convert the line to double track. However, that would have to wait for other improvements that would prepare the way. To make an easier entrance into Ogden from the west, a new six-mile cutoff was surveyed that would put the connection to and from Salt Lake City directly at the south end of the yard at 30th Street, completely bypassing the congestion of Ogden, rather than along the original Utah Central line through West Ogden.

By the turn of the century, construction techniques had improved and plans were made to simply cut through the West Ogden sand ridge and enter the city at a point about a mile south of the original Utah Central line. Oregon Short Line completed the "Sand Ridge Cutoff" between Roy and Ogden in 1906. The new line left the original Utah Central 1869 main line at Roy, cut through the sand ridge, crossed the Weber River on a new bridge, and connected at the western end of a new OUR&D wye track at 30th Street, at a new point called Bridge Junction. The construction of the cutoff was completed on December 10, 1906. The

Union Pacific's first Challenger locomotives came to the railroad in August 1936, preceding the Big Boys by five years (the Big Boy was essentially a stretched Challenger). These 4-6-6-4 locomotives (105 were built between 1936 and late 1944) were designed for the difficult climb up the Wahsatch grade east out of Ogden. The design was so successful that they soon saw service over almost every main line on Union Pacific, from Omaha to California and the Pacific Northwest. Here oil-burning Challenger number 3701 (built as 3931 in August 1944 and converted to burn oil in 1952) sits under the coal chute on October 12, 1958, awaiting its next run east. (Emil Albrecht, James W. Watson Collection)

opposite page, **This northward-looking aerial view of the Ogden yard in February 1950 shows many of the landmarks of the city's railroads. Four years later, during 1954-1955, Ogden's railroad yard was at its peak in both mileage and operation. By that time, the expanded Riverdale yard (not visible here) was just coming on line, and the SP roundhouse was yet to be torn down.** *(Union Pacific Museum Collection, Negative 55-50)*

The completion of the Sand Ridge Cutoff in 1906 made Union Pacific's entrance into Ogden from the west much less complicated. In this view we can see the depth of the cut through the sand ridge, along with the bridges at Bridge Junction. There are actually four bridges, the three visible and a fourth bridge for the Shasta Track just to the left of the other three. The name Bridge Junction comes from the junction between the Oregon Short Line-owned cutoff and the OUR&D 30th Street Wye, completed at the same time. (Emil Albrecht, James W. Watson Collection)

Union Pacific began the dieselization of its freight operations in 1947, with the delivery of five A-B-B-A sets of General Motors Electro-Motive Division Model F3 locomotives. On May 20, 1949, Emil Albrecht captured this two-year-old set as it arrived in Ogden, coasting under the Bamberger Railroad overhead viaduct. Also visible is a train in the seven-year-old East Yard, later known as Riverdale Yard. (Emil Albrecht, James W. Watson Collection)

original Utah Central line remained in place as a secondary main line until the second track between Salt Lake City and Ogden was completed in 1912. At that time, the original Utah Central line became UP's Evona Branch, named for a now-abandoned small community near today's Farmer's Co-op grain elevator.

The Ogden-Salt Lake City double-track project began in 1910, and included major line changes that were completed in May 1911. The longest line change was between Layton and Clearfield. Utah Central's original 1869 main line had been located adjacent to Territorial Road No. 1, later to become U. S. Highway 91. The business sections of both Layton and Clearfield developed along the same route, giving each town a mainline railroad right down its main street. The line change moved the line about a quarter mile west to its present location. A short section of the original track was left in place at the south end of Layton's Main Street, until at least 1930, to allow access to shippers, including Layton Milling Co. and the Layton plant of

the Woods Cross Canning Co. Another modification, called the Shepherd Lane Line Change, was completed in August 1911 bringing an easier curve and improved grades to the stretch between Farmington and Kaysville. There was also a minor line change at Roy.

Union Pacific in Utah was in fact, at least until 1987, the combined operations of three distinct companies, two of which were subsidiaries: Oregon Short Line Railroad; San Pedro, Los Angeles & Salt Lake Railroad; and the parent company, Union Pacific Railroad. In a note from present-day history, on December 30 and 31, 1987, Oregon Short Line Railroad, Los Angeles & Salt Lake Railroad, and the Oregon-Washington Railway & Navigation Co. vanished as separate corporations when they were officially merged with UP.

Oregon Short Line and its predecessors built all Union Pacific lines in Utah, except the original 1869 main line east from Ogden to Wyoming. San Pedro, Los Angeles & Salt Lake Railroad (its name was shortened to just Los Angeles & Salt Lake Railroad in 1916) completed its 782-mile line between Salt Lake, Las Vegas, and Los Angeles in 1905, but didn't actually build any trackage in Utah. Instead, it purchased its line between Salt Lake City and the Utah/ Nevada line in southeastern Utah from Oregon Short Line in 1903, as part of a complicated land ownership and right-of-way settlement.

Union Pacific Railroad rails from the East ended at Ogden, at Mile Post 992.55 (992.55 miles west of Omaha), adjacent to Ogden Union Station. Oregon Short Line trackage ran from Salt Lake City through Ogden to southern Idaho, with Ogden Union Station being Mile Post 0 for distances measured both north and south. Sandy, Utah, south of Salt Lake City, where historic ownership between OSL and LA&SL split as part of the 1903 sale, was Mile Post 49.98 from Ogden and Mile Post P-786.35 from Los Angeles. (During the mid 1970s, the distance from Los Angeles was changed from Sandy to Ogden, ending at the west end of the 30th Street Wye, at Mile Post 818.57.) OSL tracks continued north from Ogden to Pocatello, which was Mile Post 135, and on to Butte, Montana, at Mile Post 397 (397 miles north of Ogden).

The three companies, UP, OSL, and LA&SL, were kept separate for a variety of financial reasons, and to satisfy labor agreements. Union Pacific formally leased the lines and consolidated operations in 1936. Financial arrangements included certain portions of trackage and property being used as collateral for bonds, and labor agreements were kept separate for similar reasons, the three companies still being distinct corporations. Until the late 1970s, as the bonds were paid off, and as labor agreements were renegotiated, operations of OSL were kept separate from those of Union Pacific, especially at Ogden. UP crews terminated at Ogden, their trains being turned over either to Southern Pacific crews for their continued trip west, or to OSL crews who ran them to Salt Lake City, where LA&SL crews took the trains on south to Los Angeles. All switching in Ogden was done by the jointly owned Ogden Union Railway & Depot Co., although portions of OUR&D's switching operations were contracted to either Union Pacific or Southern Pacific. Most trains through Ogden were UP System trains that originated in the East and operated over Union Pacific, OSL, and LA&SL with effective indifference, changing crews as division and ownership boundaries were crossed. Trains that originated or terminated on LA&SL or OSL were different. OSL did not serve Ogden. It only ran its trains through Ogden from Salt Lake City to Idaho, with some minor set-outs at Ogden for interchange with Union Pacific. Technically, OSL did not own either tracks or land in Ogden, but operated its trains by trackage agreements with both Union Pacific and OUR&D.

As OSL's Salt Lake City-to-Idaho and Montana business grew throughout the first decades of the 1900s, the operation of its freights through the Ogden yards continued to be a concern to both OSL and OUR&D in its terminal operations. OSL trains were being regularly delayed, sometimes for hours, by either Union Pacific or Southern Pacific trains, or passenger train movements, or by a variety of switching and transfer moves. As early as 1922, proposals were made to build a cutoff that would get OSL trains through Ogden without delay. In 1923, proposed budget items included, along with improved mechanical facilities for Union Pacific, an OSL freight bypass through Ogden. The mechanical facilities were forced to wait for another year, as was the OSL bypass, officially known as the "OSL Run Around Track." Work on the bypass finally began in September 1927, and it was completed in April 1928 along with several other improvements to Ogden yard during the 1920s, which included a new roundhouse, a new Pacific Fruit Express ice plant and icing platforms, extension of the 24th Street Viaduct, and the new Union Station. In some early engineering drawings, the OSL freight bypass was shown as the "Belt Track," and by 1953 it was shown as the "Shasta Track" (for reasons as yet undiscovered), and the later name stuck.

The Shasta track connected with the double-track OSL main line to Salt Lake City west of the Weber River bridge, at Bridge Junction, crossed the river on its own bridge and ran along the east bank of the

Bridge Junction was the connection between Ogden Union Railway & Depot Co. and Union Pacific's Oregon Short Line from Salt Lake City. The junction came into being with the completion of the Sand Ridge Cut Off in 1906, and was double-tracked in 1912. In 1928 the Shasta Track (far left in this view), with its two adjacent home signals, was added as a run-around track for OSL trains between Salt Lake City and Idaho. Here we see Union Pacific U30C number 2903 at East Bridge Junction (Control Point 817, situated 817 miles from Los Angeles) in August 1982, leading a special military train bound from Kansas for training exercises in southern California. (D. B. Harrop)

The north connection of the Shasta Track to OSL's own trackage required Idaho-bound trains to weave across the north end of Southern Pacific's Ogden yard. Here, northbound (railroad westbound), UP GP30 861 and its 105-loaded cars of coal off the Utah Railway at Provo looks more like a snake than a 7,500-ton train of this vital fuel bound for Pocatello. In this view, with the 20th Street viaduct in the background, the OSL passenger main is at the far left, the OSL freight lead occupied here by 861 and a DD35 and a borrowed Chicago & North Western SD40 (typical motive power for the "Short Line"), then the double track SP main, then two SP switch leads. June 29, 1978. (D. B. Harrop)

Weber to a connection with OUR&D tracks at about 25th Street, just north of the Pacific Fruit Express ice plant. The route beyond was mostly by trackage rights agreements with OUR&D and Southern Pacific, allowing OSL trains to move in a series of crossovers from the Shasta track on the west side of Ogden yard to the east side at 18th Street, north of SP's crossing of the Ogden River, where it separated at a point called Union Pacific Junction and ran north along its already established route completed in 1890. The new bypass allowed the 10 daily OSL trains to avoid the congestion of the 30th Street wye, UP-SP interchange trains, and the multiple passenger trains operating in and out of Union Station. With the traffic-pattern changes in operations in the late 1970s, along with the 1982 merger between Union Pacific, Missouri Pacific, and Western Pacific, the need for a bypass for Idaho-bound trains went away, and while the Shasta track remains today, it is little used except for the occasional storage of cars.

Other improvements continued throughout the 1920s. The state highway department, in 1924, completed a concrete overhead viaduct carrying Riverdale Road over the UP tracks. First proposed in May 1919, with costs being equally shared by UP and the state, in April 1920 the federal government was asked to assist in the construction funding, under the provisions of the Transportation Act of 1920. In return for its funding participation, the federal government requested a 20-foot roadway, instead of an 18-foot roadway, and a five-foot sidewalk, instead of a four-foot sidewalk. These changes in the design delayed

completion until 1924. In addition to the Riverdale bridge, in 1931, the original wooden bridge carrying U. S. Alternate Highway 91 over the UP tracks at 31st Street was replaced by a modern concrete viaduct.

Another improvement came in March 1929, when Union Pacific completed a new Terminal Railway Post Office, which was leased to the Post Office Department. The original railway post office was renovated as a crew locker room for OUR&D crews.

In May 1942, Oregon Short Line retired and removed the western 1.15-mile portion of the Evona Branch, between a connection with the OSL main line at Roy and a crossing with the Roy-Hot Springs Road (U.S. Highway 91). The Evona Branch was the remaining portion of the original 1869 Utah Central between Ogden and Salt Lake City. The portion of the branch to be abandoned had been used only to store cars since 1912, when OSL completed a second track on the new Sand Ridge Cutoff main line. In July 1930, the state had designated the Roy-Hot Springs Road as U. S. Highway 91 by making it an "improved gravel highway," including building a new concrete bridge over the double-track OSL main line. Abandonment for the portion of the Evona Branch west of the Highway 91 crossing came in 1942 because the state now wanted to pave the entire length of Highway 91 between Roy and Hot Springs, and Union Pacific did not want to pay for grade-crossing improvements for the little-used branch. In October 1945, OSL retired and removed an additional mile of the Evona Branch between its new western end at the Roy-Hot Springs highway, and the jointly-owned (with D&RGW), spur to the Ogden sugar factory, at Evona Branch mile post 1.59. The remaining portion of the branch is still in service today. The steel bridge for the Evona Branch over the Weber River, near the west end of today's 24th Street Viaduct, is the oldest metal bridge (highway or railroad) in the state, being a Peagram truss design, built in 1889. Traffic today on the pioneering Evona Branch (also known as the Evona Industrial Spur) is made up of cars bound for customers in the Ogden Industrial Park, an occasional carload of sugar from the Amalgamated Sugar Co. plant, and a regular large quantity of grain and grain products cars to and from the Cargill, Inc. flour and grain mill in West Ogden.

The continued rising volume of traffic through the Ogden yard, along with its strategic place in Union Pacific's operations, qualified it as one of earliest locations at which diesel switcher locomotives were placed in service. Omaha, Neb., and Los Angeles, Calif., were the first of UP's yards to receive diesel switchers in 1940, but Ogden received its first diesel switcher soon after. Ogden's East (Riverdale) Yard has a slight 0.3 percent (four inches rise in 100 feet of distance) grade down to 30th Street, and the rest is level, at least to the Ogden River. This means that switchers need a bit more power to work both ends of Riverdale Yard. In late 1951, Union Pacific purchased six 1,600-horsepower Baldwin heavy switchers, known as model AS-616. Two were to be assigned at each of the retarder hump yards in Pocatello, Idaho, and North Platte, Neb., two were assigned to local service in Kansas (soon reassigned to heavy switching in North Platte), and the other two, numbers 1264 and 1265, were specifically purchased for and leased to OUR&D for the heavy "flat" switching at Ogden. Crews immediately labeled

The Baldwin-Lima-Hamilton Corp. (Baldwin Locomotive Works until 1950) built 168 examples of its 1,600-horsepower AS-616 model road switchers between 1950 and 1954, of which Union Pacific purchased only six. Southern Pacific purchased 56 units, using them as road switchers, the assignment intended by Baldwin. But UP needed heavy switchers for its new hump yards in Pocatello and North Platte, and for heavy switching at Ogden. Two of UP's six units were immediately assigned to Ogden upon their delivery in late 1951, and both units (numbers 1264 and 1265) remained at Ogden throughout their 17-year careers. A regular assignment called for them to pull entire trains between the two OUR&D yards, the main yard between 20th Street and 29th Street, and Riverdale Yard between 31st Street and Riverdale Road, passing the large Sperry mill at 30th Street, shown here as UP 1264 heads toward Riverdale with a cut of interchange traffic between SP and UP.

(Emil Albrecht, James W. Watson Collection)

the two units as "Mike" and "Ike." They remained at Ogden throughout their careers, until they were retired in 1968. OUR&D also leased Southern Pacific locomotives. From 1943 to 1946, five SP 0-6-0 steam switchers were leased. These were replaced in 1946-47 by four Alco model S-2 diesel switchers.

A passenger balloon track was completed adjacent to the 30th Street wye during the mid-1940s to allow Idaho-bound trains access to the UP main line into Union Station. In the space inside the balloon track, Union Pacific, in June 1961, constructed a facility to unload automobiles from rail cars. Using an apparatus called a "Buck Unloader," it had a capacity to unload 200 automobiles per day for distribution throughout northern Utah. During mid-1965, the major rail traffic customers included four packing plants, three grain mills, and the continuing traffic of the Ogden Union Stockyards, which handled $40 million in livestock during 1964, mostly in lambs.

As with many other railroads in the late 1960s, Union Pacific and Southern Pacific began operating more "run-through" trains assembled in predetermined blocks for particular destinations, and doing away with random switching operations at various yards along the line. With the opening of UP's giant hump yard in North Platte in 1968, all of the railroad's operations changed. All eastbound trains were preblocked for movement to North Platte, avoiding switching at points such as Nampa and Pocatello in Idaho; Yermo, Calif.; Las Vegas, Nev.; and Salt Lake City and Ogden. More and more trains in the late 1960s and throughout the 1970s simply moved through Ogden with only a change in crews, and without any switching. To support the run-through concept, in December 1971 a new track was added to the Ogden yard, south (railroad direction east) from the 30th Street wye, and along the west side of Riverdale Yard. It avoided the congestion of trains from Salt Lake City and California having to wend their way across the Riverdale lead tracks to the main line on the east side, dodging switching operations and trains bound for points on Southern Pacific. (The same concept had worked very well for Oregon Short Line trains bound for Idaho in the mid-1920s when the Shasta track was built along the west side of the yard north from the 30th Street wye.) The run-through track was part of a general modernization of Riverdale Yard, including a locomotive service track at the south end of the yard. With a new service track at Riverdale, the service track at the roundhouse near 29th Street was closed, and a highway truck was equipped to bring fuel, water, and other supplies to the locomotives, including the numerous switchers that still worked in Ogden.

When Riverdale Yard was increased to its present size in 1954, a new yard tower was needed. A water tower was already standing at the north end, so the tank was removed and a small shanty was lifted up to sit atop the support structure. This unique structure became a landmark among railroad enthusiasts nationwide. With the modernization of Riverdale yard in the mid-1970s, computers were added along with other improvements. Rather than spend money to upgrade the unique little shanty, UP in July 1976 replaced it with a $250,000 all-metal tower that served both as a yardmaster's office and as a communication building. Another improvement, made in 1977, was con-

During both the steam era and the diesel era, Ogden Union Railway & Depot Co. leased switching locomotives from its two parent companies. Here we see UP 1093, an EMD NW2, and SP 1365, an Alco S-2, work in front of the Sperry mill at 30th Street. (Emil Albrecht, James W. Watson Collection)

struction of a different connection to the 6.8-mile Hill Field Branch, which had been built in 1908 by the Salt Lake & Ogden Railway, a predecessor to the electrified Bamberger Railroad. Union Pacific purchased the branch, which serves Hill Air Force Base, in 1959, when Bamberger went out of business. Originally, access for a UP train was over the former Bamberger/UP interchange on the east side of the main line, then by a saw-back move to enter the branch, and cross above the UP main line on the former Bamberger bridge. In 1977, after UP removed the bridges and embankments (completed in 1914) that raised the former Bamberger line up and over the UP, the Hill Field Branch connected directly with the west side of the yard.

Union Pacific's Little Mountain Branch

During the mid-1960s, laboratory studies showed that it was commercially feasible to extract minerals, in addition to salt, from Great Salt Lake. In May 1967, Great Salt Lake Minerals and Chemicals Corp. began building a large plant for commercial extraction of potassium sulfate, sodium sulfate, and magnesium chloride, along with common salt. The plant included 17,000 acres of evaporation ponds just north of Little Mountain, west of Ogden on the lake's eastern shore. In February 1969, Union Pacific secured Interstate Commerce Commission approval to construct its Little Mountain Branch. The line was to extend 13.27 miles southwesterly from Hot Springs to mineral industry trackage on the east shore of Great Salt Lake, where Great Salt Lake Minerals and Chemicals was developing its extensive facility. Union Pacific's application was protested by both Southern Pacific and the Denver & Rio Grande Western Railroad, arguing that the new trackage would duplicate SP's already existing 1.7-mile spur, and that shippers had not shown that they required duplicate service from two railroads. The two roads argued that SP, as the existing carrier, was entitled to an opportunity to serve the shippers prior to Union Pacific being granted entry into the area. SP had constructed its 1.7-mile spur northward from its main line to transport construction materials to the site, intending further extension into the area to connect with industry trackage as the area developed and industrial plants were completed. The ICC found that the Little Mountain industrial area was not exclusive SP territory, and that the area was as yet undeveloped and not generating any substantial traffic. Great Salt Lake Minerals, the largest potential shipper, testified that it required single-line service access to Union Pacific, because its markets were all located within Union Pacific territory in the Pacific Northwest, southern California, and in Utah, Idaho, Colorado, Nevada, and Wyoming. Other shippers in the area wanting competitive Union Pacific service included Prior Chemical Co., Boise Cascade Corp., Potlatch Forests, Inc., and Amalgamated Sugar Co. Construction was completed by the end of 1969.

Union Pacific Laundry

The successful operation of passenger trains on Union Pacific always took a lot of attention to detail and much planning. Handling thousands of passengers every day during the peak World War II years required a large number of employees just to support the trains themselves. It took teamwork to keep the trains running, especially the road's premier Streamliner fleet - teamwork among the dispatchers, locomotive engineers, train conductors, car attendants, porters, and dining car waiters and cooks. The locomotives had to work. The car heating and air conditioning had to work. The dispatchers had to get the trains over the road on time, every time. And everyone had to work together to see that passengers were comfortable. What passenger ever considered what was needed to get him or her over the road to a destination. There always seemed to be plenty of food in the dining car, a pillow for your head in the coach seat, and sheets for your bed in the sleeping compartment or Pullman bed, along with clean towels in the rest rooms. Clean towels, sheets, and pillows, and good food was the responsibility of Union Pacific's Dining Car and Hotel Department, or DC&H. The department also took care of the uniforms of train personnel, and the drapes on the car windows.

The Dining Car and Hotel Department operated large commissaries to store and distribute food and supplies to all of UP's passenger trains. Large DC&H commissary operations were located at Omaha, Denver, Los Angeles, Portland, and at Ogden. The DC&H laundry at Ogden was the only laundry operated by the railroad, and did all washing for the entire system, taking care of 940,000 (in 1945) pieces of linen and cotton items, including 40,000 tablecloths and 285,000 napkins, as well as thousands of aprons, coats, pillow slips, sheets, and dish towels. In 1945, the DC&H laundry monthly cleaned soiled linen of 125 dining and club cars, and 14 hotels, restaurants, and crew clubs operated by Union Pacific, together with several business cars and the widely known Sun Valley Resort for skiers. The laundry operated 24 hours a day, seven days a week. At that 1945 peak, laundry arrived from all of the other DC&H points, plus Kansas City, washing 60,000 to 70,000 pieces every 24 hours. On average, every laundry item on the railroad was cleaned and ironed twice a month. The laundry employed more than 200 people, most of whom were women. A large sewing operation both repaired and manufactured needed items. The sewing room employed 20 women, who at times hemmed 6,000 towels per day.

The original laundry was completed in 1906, located in the old Commissary Building just south of the depot. It was styled after the then-adjacent Union Depot, built in 1889, and remained after the new depot was completed in 1924. The passenger business grew in the post-World War II years, and soon the railroad found itself sending a large amount of its laundry out to several commercial laundries in Ogden and other locations along the system. To expand its capabilities, in 1951 the railroad completed a new laundry facility in Ogden, which still stands today, just south of the Union Station parking lot. The 100-foot by 180-foot building was completed in July 1951 as a large and modern facility that could process up to 110,000 pieces during an eight-hour shift.

Every hour of the average eight-hour shift, an average of 3,300 pounds of dry laundry (about 13,333 pieces) would be unloaded at the south side dock, and within an hour and a half, it would be available at the other side of the building, washed, dried, ironed, folded, counted and tied in bundles ready for delivery to commissaries all over the system. Equipped with eight washers and three dryers, the laundry also included four flatwork ironers, 42 individual pressers, six folders, and numerous other machines needed to handle the volume of work. The facility needed large quantities of steam, which came from seven Vapor-Clarkson steam generators, identical to those used to produce steam heat on the railroad's diesel passenger locomotives. This unusual arrangement allowed the laundry to operate at peak times with all the steam it needed, but at slower times, some of the steam generators could be turned off to conserve fuel.

As the number of passenger trains began to diminish in the mid-1960s, the amount of laundry sent to Ogden also fell. Soon, the cost of keeping the laundry in operation, and shipping the soiled and clean laundry all over the railroad, exceeded the cost of simply sending the railroad's laundry out to commercial laundries located in cities with large passenger terminals. As the work began slipping away to commercial businesses in other cities, the employees were laid off. In January 1970, Union Pacific announced that the Ogden laundry would be closed.

The Ogden Commissary was completed in 1906 to house the Union Pacific Ogden laundry operation. Its architecture matched that of the adjacent 1889-built original Union Station, but outlasted that building by 27 years, until 1950, when the commissary was torn down and replaced by a new Union Pacific laundry. (Union Pacific Museum Collection, Negative 504447)

In its original configuration, the stalls of UP's 1927-built roundhouse were all of equal length. This view shows the back of the structure from its east side. (Union Pacific Museum Collection, Negative 504032)

Union Pacific Mechanical Facilities

As the new Union Pacific continued to make improvements after its reorganization in 1897, traffic continued to grow and new locomotives were purchased to move it. Between 1911 and 1921, UP purchased 362 Mikado-type 2-8-2 locomotives and, between 1917 and 1925, 144 TTT-class 2-10-2 locomotives. These two types were the state of the art in locomotive design at the time, and many operated into and through Ogden. The June 28, 1918 issue of the trade publication *Railway Age* stated that of the 27 2-10-2 locomotives purchased by UP during 1917, 10 were placed in service on the 75.8 miles of grade between Ogden and Evanston, Wyo., and that these locomotives were powerful enough to eliminate helpers on the same grade. Conquering the Wasatch grade east of Ogden was always a consideration with mainline steam locomotives purchased by Union Pacific, along with every turbine locomotive, and many of the later diesel locomotives. Between 1922 and 1925, Union Pacific placed in service 60 thoroughly modern 7000-class 4-8-2 Mountain-type locomotives. These locomotives were designed and used, as their name implies, on UP's mountainous routes to pull its fastest and most important passenger trains. The 7000s were UP's mainline passenger motive power for another 15 years, until the arrival of the first examples of the 800-class 4-8-4s in mid-1937. The arrival of modern locomotives in the 1920s required UP to construct correspondingly modern facilities to care for them, but some of the facilities at Ogden had been built during the railroad's earliest days in the city.

Union Pacific had built an enginehouse in Ogden in 1869 immediately after the driving of the Golden Spike, but the road's main shops were at Evanston, 100 miles east. The Ogden enginehouse was a single-stall building, 40 feet by 157 feet, located between the main line and the Weber River, sharing a common turntable with Central Pacific's own enginehouse. Locomotives continued to increase in size and capacity, and the turntable and small enginehouse soon became inadequate. In October 1870, the single-stall building was replaced by a four-stall roundhouse. By 1885, CP had completed its own turntable and roundhouse adjacent to its own yard, and by 1890, the original UP enginehouse had been abandoned and the turntable taken up. In 1897, a new 20-stall roundhouse was completed just north of the original enginehouse and turntable. This new roundhouse was all-brick, and its stalls were 77 feet long. According to UP's 1897 annual report, other improvements in Ogden at the same time included a new 60-foot iron turntable, a 40-pocket coal chute (measuring 30 feet by 120 feet), a new oil house, sand house, and storehouse, a brick hospital, track scales, yard office, water tanks and water columns, and additions to the stockyards. The 60-foot iron turntable was replaced in 1900 by a longer, 66-foot steel model from Lassig Bridge and Iron.

A grand late-summer Sunday afternoon in Ogden. Visible in this view taken from the West Ogden bluff is the 1897-built Union Pacific brick roundhouse. The roundhouse here is surrounded by railroad cars, showing that this photograph was taken after UP had transferred its locomotive facilities to Southern Pacific's shops, a move completed in 1914. (Utah State Historical Society)

Edward H. Harriman was in control of Union Pacific by 1900, and in 1901 he gained control of the Southern Pacific as well. One of the most enduring impacts from Harriman's control of both UP and SP was the engineering designs and improvements made under what was called "Common Standard," a concept meant to reduce costs by buying and maintaining standard designs common to all companies controlled by Harriman. Although Harriman died in 1909, and Union Pacific was forced to sell its interest in Southern Pacific in 1912, the two companies continued to cooperate under the Common Standard concept for many years after. Even today, many of both Union Pacific's and Southern Pacific's engineering designs have their roots in the Common Standard era. In an early example from those Common Standard days, Union Pacific and Southern Pacific in 1914 combined their mechanical facilities in Ogden into a joint facility to serve the needs of both companies. In November 1914, Union Pacific vacated its 1897-built, 20-stall roundhouse and moved all of the machinery to a newly expanded Southern Pacific shop. SP had completed its new mechanical facilities in 1906 (while Harriman was still alive and controlling the SP) in the form of a new 33-stall roundhouse with 88-foot-long stalls. Two years later, in 1908, Southern Pacific completed the adjacent machine shops, and added a transfer table. As part of the improvements in 1914 for a joint shops complex, SP added an all-steel 100-foot Pony truss turntable, and completed a large Blacksmith and Tin Shop north of the transfer table, making the facility the most modern in the West, and capable of handling both its own and Union Pacific's repairs. The old UP roundhouse became the railroad's Ogden passenger coach repair shop.

One block south of the old UP roundhouse stood the 1897-built former UP ice house, leased to Pacific Fruit Express in 1906. When the ice house burned in 1919, Pacific Fruit Express set out with immediate plans to replace it. Planning and engineering activity took a year, and studies showed that the best location for a new PFE facility was right where the old one had stood, but with longer platforms and easier access for through trains. This last consideration meant that the old UP roundhouse was in the way. Demolition began and was completed in September 1921, along with the removal of the 66-foot turntable, the 40-pocket coal chute, and other shops and buildings.

By the early 1920s, the expansion of traffic through Ogden, and the use of new, modern locomotives, made Union Pacific acutely aware that it no longer had its own locomotive repair facilities in Ogden. Since 1914, UP had been sharing Southern Pacific's facilities, and those joint facilities were be-

coming overcrowded. SP's roundhouse stalls were too short, and too few in number, with the result that many UP locomotives were forced to be serviced outdoors. Many proposals were made to improve this condition, including new facilities at a new location. Two locations were considered. The first was south of the 30th Street wye (in the area later occupied by the passenger balloon track), locating the roundhouse and other structures (including a transfer table and rectangular large shop buildings) in the area bounded by the wye on the north, the Weber River on the west, the elevated Bamberger line on the south, and the main line on the east. This site may have been ruled out due to its lack of room for expansion. The second site was on the north side of the same 30th Street wye, bounded only by the Weber River and the proposed OSL freight bypass track on the west and the wye on the south. A 1923 map illustrating these proposed sites shows essentially the same configuration as what became the final roundhouse and car-repair track design, with only minor variations being made later for easier access.

When SP learned that UP was considering moving out, it proposed another joint facility, as the SP terminal was also inadequate to handle its own fleet of larger and more modern locomotives. A committee was formed and a study was made. SP wanted to simply add on to its present site, and keep UP as a tenant. But UP's heart wasn't in the committee effort, and the road declined SP's offer, mostly because Union Pacific felt it was being taken advantage of in the current situation. In 1923, UP President, Carl Gray, stated in a memo that new, solely-Union Pacific

mechanical facilities would generate almost $192,000 in annual savings. Gray was especially upset that SP wanted UP to build the roundhouse and other improvements at UP expense, but locate it on SP property, and let SP direct its operations. Southern Pacific tried a different proposal, with "better" arrangements, but it was too late. Nothing motivates better than a bad offer mixed with significant savings on the bottom line, and UP decided it needed its own engine terminal in Ogden. UP had just opened new facilities at Evanston and Green River, Wyo., providing excellent examples of significant savings offered by modern facilities. A solely-UP location would cost Union Pacific just as much as a new joint facility, but would be at a better location for access by the road's own locomotives.

With the decision made, UP purchased property in 1923. Located west of the main line at 28th Street, this land was occupied by several private dwellings. Union Pacific had been fielding complaints from the residents about the need for a viaduct on 28th Street to allow better and safer access, because "the [grade] crossing was almost continually used by trains and switching moves" (remember that congestion here was the reason for the proposed OSL bypass in that same year). Purchase of this property, for a mere $30,000, allowed Union Pacific to move out the residents, quiet the complaints, and obtain land for its new facilities, all at the same time. UP spent additional money in 1924 and 1925 to improve and prepare the site, and in 1926 budgeted a final amount to build the buildings and install machinery. On July 1, 1927, the new 20-stall

Union Pacific's new roundhouse, service tracks, and RIP (repair-in place) tracks are shown in a view taken from atop the new coal chute, itself completed in late 1927, about six months after the roundhouse was formally opened in July 1927. Note that here, the RIP tracks were single-ended, with no access from the far end. UP was concerned that if access had originally been provided from both ends, rather from just the OSL end near Bridge Junction, Southern Pacific, through the jointly owned depot company, might object and call for an increase in switching fees for the depot company to provide access to the solely-UP RIP tracks. In 1931 that situation was remedied, and access was provided from both ends. (Union Pacific Museum Collection, Negative 504450)

27

brick roundhouse and RIP (Repair-In-Place) tracks were opened for business, at a total reported cost of $712,000. Facilities included a 40-foot by 82-foot brick machine shop attached to the roundhouse, a 100-foot steel turntable, two concrete cinder pits, an electric Whiting traveling cinder pit crane, and a new power plant. By the end of 1927, a 350-ton conveyor-type steel coaling station was completed at the site. With all structures and machinery fully operational and ready for full use, the facility was officially completed on March 1, 1929. The cost of the roundhouse alone was put at $573,000. By the end of 1928, Union Pacific figured it had already saved $149,000 over having SP maintain its locomotives at the former joint shop. In 1931, additional tracks were added that allowed the RIP tracks to be switched not only from the west side, as originally built, but also from the east side.

By the mid-1930s UP was looking for improved locomotive designs that would get more traffic over the road faster. In late 1936, the road found the answer in its Challenger design, an articulated locomotive with a 4-6-6-4 wheel arrangement. These locomotives were longer then conventional engines and consequently needed longer shop facilities to handle them. To do so, UP in 1941 replaced the 100-foot turntable with 135-foot model. In December 1942, nine stalls of the roundhouse were extended to accommodate the 4-6-6-4 Challengers and the first 20 4-8-8-4 Big Boy locomotives that were delivered that same year. Stalls 15 and 16 were extended 153 feet, and stalls 12, 13, and 14 were extended 233 feet to provide room for a new machine shop. The original machine shop had been located at the end of stalls 17 to 20, and rails were laid into the old machinery space to extend these stalls for the

*left, **Inside the Union Pacific roundhouse, the scene was usually clouded by both steam and smoke. In this view, Challenger 3963 and Big Boy 4016 sit quietly while the shop men do what is needed to keep the two locomotives in top running order.** (Railway Age, Ogden Union Station Collection)*

*below, **By the mid-1950s, railroading in Ogden had changed. On both Union Pacific and neighbor Southern Pacific, the use of steam locomotives had fallen off sharply, with diesel locomotives being the motive power of choice. Steam was kept around in very limited numbers, mostly to fill in for the regularly assigned diesel units. In 1952, a coal miners' strike forced UP to convert eight Challenger steam locomotives to burn oil, joining several others already converted. These oil-burners were usually used on the western end of the railroad (west of Green River), including the Oregon Short Line between Ogden and Pocatello. Here, on May 20, 1956, waiting for its next assignment, is Challenger 3706, and it is apparently the only steam locomotive at the roundhouse. The overhead structure situated between the 3706 and the roundhouse is a gantry crane installed by UP to dispose of ashes from coal-fired steam locomotives, dropped into pits between the rails during regular servicing and moved by the gantry crane to adjacent open-top rail cars, just visible behind 3706's tender. The placement of the ash-service cars indicates that in 1956, Ogden was still the home of big coal-fired UP steam.** (Emil Albrecht, James W. Watson Collection)*

longer locomotives. The original two-track drop pit was also increased to be a three-track facility.

In 1953-54, Riverdale Yard (completed in 1942) was expanded to accommodate the growth in traffic. Included in the construction was a new car repair facility. Completed in December 1955, the four new RIP tracks included a 50-ton traveling crane, 1,300 feet of concrete runway between tracks, and space to work on 70 cars at any one time. The old, nine-track car repair shop north of the roundhouse at 29th Street was retired in April 1959.

The presence of railroads and railroading in Ogden was always an important element in the local economy. During the labor debate in the early 1960s over reducing crew sizes of the local switching locomotives by elimination of the fireman position, Ogden's residents were reminded in the media of the benefits of railroaders to the local economy. Edward Peters, manager of the Weber County Industrial Bureau, figured that for every 100 railroad jobs lost in Ogden, the local economy lost $600,000 in yearly earnings.

With the arrival of large numbers of diesel locomotives in the early 1950s, and the end of the use of steam locomotives later in that decade, UP made modest improvements to the Ogden roundhouse to better serve the new motive power. These improvements included facilities to fuel UP's growing fleet of diesel locomotives, and its unique gas-turbine locomotives. The scope of these improvements was limited because Ogden was only 36 miles away from Salt Lake City, with its large diesel shop, completed in 1955. The large coal dock was removed in the early 1960s, after steam locomotives were no longer coming into Ogden. In 1969, most of the roundhouse work force was either laid off or transferred to the Salt Lake shops. The roundhouse, used only to house and service the local switcher fleet, was finally demolished in 1974.

Union Pacific Today

The summers of 1983 and 1984 saw much flooding in the areas around the shores of Great Salt Lake. Among the many railroad lines affected was the single track Denver & Rio Grande Western line between Salt Lake City and Ogden, especially the portion west of Centerville and Farmington. A quick fix allowed D&RGW and connecting Southern Pacific trains to detour over the adjacent double-tracked Union Pacific line. The temporary fix soon became a long term solution. In the meantime, UP was finding it difficult to justify the expense of keeping up its Salt Lake City-to-Provo line for the once-daily train it was seeing. Thus, in October 1985, the two companies swapped trackage rights, allowing Rio Grande and SP trains to use Union Pacific's tracks between Ogden and Salt Lake City, and UP trains to use D&RGW's tracks between Salt Lake City and Provo. This change brought Rio Grande and SP trains into Ogden over UP's tracks, entering the yard at Bridge Junction at the west end of the 30th Street wye. Since D&RGW trains interchanged only with Southern Pacific, they either terminated in the SP yard or continued on as Southern Pacific trains, without even entering D&RGW's own Ogden yard.

Changes will continue, especially with the merger of Union Pacific and Southern Pacific that went into effect on September 11, 1996. Ogden is now a one-railroad town. All Union Pacific and former Southern Pacific operations in Ogden are expected to be consolidated in Riverdale Yard, leaving only a double-track main line in place of the old main yard between 30th Street and 20th Street. The general plans are that trains bound to and from northern California will be operated direct through Ogden, and west over the former SP Great Salt Lake causeway, and trains bound to and from southern California will pass through Ogden to Salt Lake City, then south through Utah and Las Vegas. ☆

Union Pacific dieselized the west end of its railroad from 1947 to 1952 with a large fleet of 237 cab units from General Motors' Electro-Motive Division, and in 1947 and 1948 with 88 cab units from American Locomotive Company. Both types of units regularly ran into Ogden, from both Idaho and from California. Here, EMD F3 1403 and three stablemates await their next assignment under Union Pacific's large coal chute at Ogden. (Emil Albrecht, James W. Watson Collection)

What started out as a single-story depot at Ogden soon became a more substantial two-story depot in late 1869. Soon, separate baggage and hotel facilities were added. Other buildings sprang up as the railroads needed more office and maintenance space. By the mid-1880s, the local press was calling for a replacement for the "group of shacks and shanties," as shown in this view from the late 1870s. *(Ogden Union Station Collection)*

Changing trains at Ogden. Here Central Pacific's California Limited *exchanges passengers with Union Pacific's version of the same train. On the left are two of Central Pacific's best locomotives, numbers 988 and 815, with the 815 having just brought CP's most important train into Ogden from the west. Passengers then transferred to UP's cars to continue their journey eastward, in this case behind UP locomotive 14 (center). On the right is Central Pacific's Ogden switcher, number 1203, and on the far right is narrow-gauge Utah Northern number 2. Note the early versions of pilot snowplows on the CP locomotives, and the nearby early Union Pacific cabooses with eight-sided cupolas. (A side note for locomotive fans: Union Pacific number 14 was later sold to Brigham Young's Utah Southern, making a date for this photo a problem. By all currently available information, the sale of UP 14 to the Utah Southern took place in 1871, but the existence of Utah Northern number 2 in this photo makes its date after 1874, when the UN completed its tracks into Ogden. The source photo is dated 1884, which is possible, if (contrary to existing records) there was a second Union Pacific number 14.) (Union Pacific Museum Collection, Negative 504455)*

6. Ogden Union Railway & Depot Company

When Union Pacific first came to Ogden in early 1869, the apparent need for a junction point of UP and Central Pacific pushed Mormon leader Brigham Young and other church leaders to work with owners to acquire land "for the purpose of locating a railroad town and depot." Some sold their plots for $50, while others donated their land. This was the initial depot grounds used by the Utah Central after its completion in 1870, and formed a triangle with its long side laid along the west side of Wall Avenue. The common point of the other two sides of the triangle was near the Utah Central crossing of the Pacific roads. The completion of Utah Northern in February 1874 brought that narrow-gauge line down Wall Avenue to Third Street (today 23rd Street), then angling slightly south-south-west to a connection with Utah Central, but still east of the Union Pacific-Central Pacific crossings of the Utah Central. This connection was all within the initial triangle of land owned by the Utah Central in Ogden. Being a narrow-gauge line, Utah Northern had its own passenger depot and stub-ended freight yard, adjacent to and north of the Utah Central yard.

Regular passenger trains between Omaha and Sacramento began running within a week of the driving of the Golden Spike at Promontory. The passenger station facilities at Ogden at the time consisted mainly of a group of shacks, as the town was not originally intended to be the junction. The first real passenger depot was a two-story wooden frame structure, completed in November 1869.

By 1874, the two Pacific roads still hadn't decided on a site for their common junction. As an inducement to speed their decision, and to make it in favor of Ogden, Brigham Young in May 1874 arranged for 131 acres of privately owned land just west of the city to be made available for use as the terminal yards. Young arranged with the owners to sell their land to him, and still more was donated. In October 1874, Ogden City

Council appropriated $5,000 (presumably to pay Young for the land), "for the purpose of securing the location of the Junction of the U.P., C.P., U.C. and U.N. Railroads in Ogden City." The space was located directly west of the city, between the city and the Weber River, in the vicinity of Fourth and Fifth streets, now 24th and 25th streets. The area included space for facilities serving UP and CP, the Utah Central branch line to Salt Lake City, and the Utah Northern line to Cache Valley. Until 1878, when a common depot was put into use, each company maintained its own depot facilities.

As passenger traffic continued to grow throughout the 1870s, the carriers could see that all would benefit from the use of a common depot. On September 20, 1878 the trains of UP, CP, and Utah Central, along with those of the newly reorganized narrow-gauge Utah & Northern, began using a "Union" depot in Ogden, that station being the original red Union Pacific 1869-built two-story wooden structure. In addition to providing a ticket office, the depot held waiting rooms, a baggage office, and less-than-car-load-freight facilities. Next to the depot stood the Union Depot Hotel.

By 1878, passenger traffic on the transcontinental line had grown to three trains a day in each direction, with four trains a day in each direction on the Utah Central and a single train arriving and departing on the narrow-gauge Utah & Northern. The transcontinental trains consisted of an express train, an accommodation train, and an emigrant train. Utah Central's service consisted of two passenger trains and two mixed trains, which were made up of both passenger and freight cars.

Almost immediately, and continuing into the mid-1880s, the local press was filled with complaints about the dark and gloomy depot, with its quarter-mile of wooden sidewalks across swampy mud flats at Wall Avenue and 25th Street that served as the embarrassing entrance to Ogden. The complaints included calls

In 1889, Ogden finally got the Union Station it deserved. Streetcar service was operated on the Ogden City Railway from the depot to downtown Ogden, evidenced here by a single mule-powered car awaiting its next trip up 25th Street. (C. R. Savage, Utah State Historical Society)

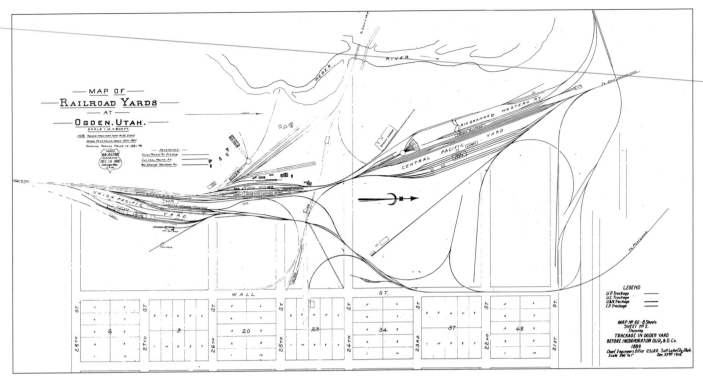

MAP OF
RAILROAD YARDS
AT
OGDEN, UTAH.

By 1885, Ogden yard had grown, and included the narrow-gauge Denver & Rio Grande, connecting with the narrow-gauge Utah & Northern, and a larger Central Pacific yard. Also by this time, Central Pacific had finished its own turntable and roundhouse, adjacent to its own yard. This map also shows the D&RG/CP interchange tracks. (Union Pacific Museum Collection)

for the carriers to erect permanent buildings and workshops, and to "go to work like substantial corporations, instead of dickering around in shanties and balloon tinderboxes, like some two-and-a-half dollar concerns." Between 1870 and 1890, the city's population quadrupled, from 3,127 to 12,889. In 1890, Union Pacific inaugurated the *Overland Limited*, a luxury train that passed through Ogden on its 71-hour journey between Omaha and San Francisco. Ogden was growing, both as a passenger destination and as a center for industry. The young city needed a new depot, and Ogden Union Railway & Depot Co., a company whose purpose was to meet that need, was organized on September 17, 1888.

The tracks of Ogden Union Railway & Depot Co. were specified to run "from a point on the Union Pacific Railway about 1/2 mile south of the point where said line crosses 8th Street in the City of Ogden, then north to a point on the Central Pacific Railroad about 1/4 mile north of where said line crosses 1st Street." This general area from the 20th Street crossing on the north to the 29th Street crossing on the south (with East Yard added in 1942) was the home of OUR&D operations from the time of its organization until the late 1960s when its two owners, Southern Pacific and Union Pacific, took over its freight operations. As with any terminal company, OUR&D was organized to allow the member railroads to share facilities, mostly to avoid conflicts of operation and to ensure that each road had an equal say in the operations.

While the timing of the formation of a depot company was a reaction to the complaints of Ogden's citizens to the lack of service by UP and SP, the depot company, operating as a terminal railroad, would oversee the operations of UP and SP, along with Utah Central, Utah & Northern (soon to be combined as the Oregon Short Line & Utah Northern), and Ogden's newest railroad, Denver & Rio Grande Western. But first the depot needed attention. During the 1880s, Union Pacific's president, Charles F.

Adams, had commissioned noted architect Henry Van Brundt and his Van Brundt & Howe firm in Kansas City, Mo., to design new stations for UP at Omaha, Cheyenne, and Portland. In September 1886, he added Ogden to the list after it became apparent that it, too, needed a new building.

Van Brundt published his preliminary sketches of the new Ogden depot in *American Architect and Building News* in November 1886. They showed that the design was Romanesque in style, a treatment that was being promoted by another noted American architect, H. H. Richardson. The final design contained many of the preliminary features, but other details were altered to make the building more functional. Both the north and south wings were built with two floors. In the center was a three-floor building with a clock tower, and the roof was finished with dormers replacing the suggested Romanesque steeple and spirals. Included in the design were 33 hotel rooms in the south wing. In the center upper floor were railroad offices, including the superintendent's office, with the lower floor taken up by ticket offices and waiting rooms. In the north wing was the baggage handling facilities and an emigrant waiting room. In early September 1886, Adams commissioned Francis M. Sharp of Kansas City to be the building contractor. Construction commenced immediately, and by late December the sandstone foundation was laid.

Mayor David Eccles declared a city-wide holiday for the laying of the corner stone. He invited businessmen to close their establishments and urged citizens to "engage in the ceremonies." Reporting on the 5,000 to 6,000 persons that attended, the *Ogden Standard* commented that "the old shanties called the depot will not be used much longer."

Work halted, however, during 1887 as Union Pacific's attention turned to defending itself before the Pacific Railway Commission, formed by Congress to fully investigate the affairs of the government bond-aided railways, and their questionable methods of repaying the government for obligations coming due during the late 1890s. To separate the mainline roads from any improvements they wanted to make, and to aid in the financing of the depot, and other improvements at Ogden, UP and CP organized the Ogden Union Railway & Depot Co., as noted, in September 1888. Work resumed and the depot was completed in July 1889, with July 31 being set aside as the day of grand celebration.

The station was open to the public all day. The celebration was capped off that evening with a round of speeches and a dance. At 1 a.m., a special train returned Salt Lake City guests to their homes, while the Ogden guests danced until 2 a.m. One speaker remarked that "after long years of anxious waiting, we have at last secured the great prize, and the people of Ogden are happy." In addition to the new depot, OUR&D built a freight house, and in 1889, Union Pacific completed a large addition to its ice house.

Growth continued and Ogden became one of the largest railroad centers in the West. By the turn of the century, the city was the home of numerous canneries, wholesale houses, clothing mills and factories, foundries and machine shops, brick yards, and other factories of all kinds. As a railroad center, Ogden was the home of UP's Wyoming Division, SP's Salt Lake Division, the Salt Lake & Ogden Railway (later called the Bamberger), and the Ogden & Northwestern Railroad, later to become the Utah Idaho Central. New mechanical facilities (roundhouses and car and locomotive shops) were completed for UP in 1897, and for SP in 1906. The Southern Pacific shops acted as its General Eastern Shops, and employed more than 500 men in its "three immense buildings of white stone and brick." Both Union Pacific and the Denver & Rio Grande also maintained their shops in Ogden, employing 125 men between them. In 1910, a new OUR&D freight house replaced the one built in 1889. Located just north of Union Station on Wall Avenue, it was 700 feet long and could handle 100 cars on its seven tracks. [The OUR&D freight house was closed and demolished in 1972.]

By the turn of the century, Ogden was a busy and growing city, and its Union Depot was a center of activity and a gathering place. This view was made on the occasion of the opening of Southern Pacific's Lucin Cutoff in 1904. (J. E. Stimson, Wyoming State Museum)

The November 1906 Official Guide of the Railways provides an excellent look at passenger railroading in Ogden. In 1906 there were six Rio Grande Western trains operating through Ogden. Included were trains that connected with one of Oregon Short Line's trains to Seattle. Union Pacific ran six through trains, four of which connected directly with Southern Pacific trains. UP also ran a local between Ogden and Echo. SP's trains connected with UP at Ogden, except for a mixed train that operated between Ogden and Kelton on the old Promontory line.

At the time, Oregon Short Line did not name its passenger trains, using only train numbers. During 1906, it ran four through trains (two in each direction) between Salt Lake City and Seattle, with connections at Pocatello for Butte, Mont. OSL also operated a Salt Lake City-to-Cache Junction local.

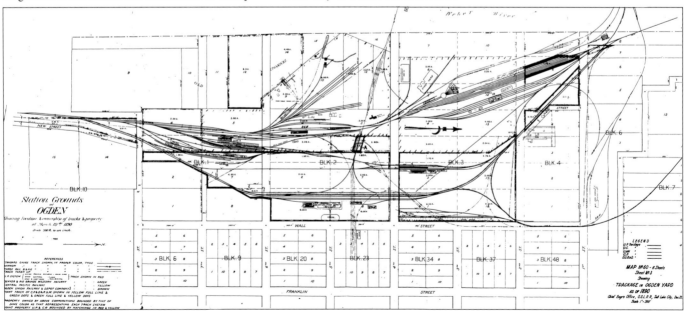

With the completion of the passenger depot of Ogden Union Railway & Depot Co. in 1889, Ogden yard was changed to accommodate the larger passenger facility. This map shows the newly completed standard-gauge tracks of the newly organized Oregon Short Line & Utah Northern, entering the city from lower right. The narrow-gauge tracks of the Rio Grande Western remained, and are shown here including the crossing with Central Pacific at upper right. (Union Pacific Museum Collection)

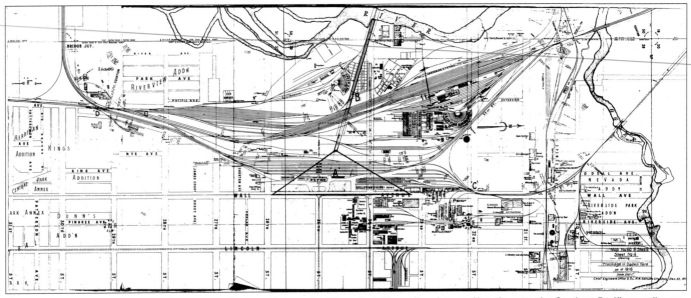

Shown in this map of Ogden yard in 1916 are several features that remained throughout the yard's existence. Note the extensive Southern Pacific roundhouse (completed in 1906 and 1908), along with UP's 1897-built roundhouse, and the D&RGW roundhouse adjacent to the D&RGW/SP 90-degree crossing. Immediately north of the UP roundhouse are the large stockyards just prior to their being moved across the river west to their 1917 location. As shown here, there were no tracks, other than UP's double-track main line, south (railroad direction east) of the 30th Street wye tracks. The area shown as 'A' is the original Utah Central station grounds. The area shown as 'B' is the alignment of the original Utah Central track, which remained as the demarcation between UP's portion of OUR&D trackage, and SP's portion. At bottom center is the interurban terminal. (Union Pacific Museum Collection)

In 1915, the Chamber of Commerce was promoting the city as a warehousing center, a canning center, a packing house center, and a food manufacturing center, in addition to being a railway center. During the early part of the 1900s, the depot handled 76 passenger trains a day. By the 1920s, Ogden was experiencing explosive growth in railroad traffic. The number of freight and passenger trains grew almost daily, with 1921 being the peak year for passenger train revenues on Union Pacific.

The growing congestion called for more and better facilities. In 1917, the Ogden Union Stockyards were completed, making the city the largest center west of Denver for handling livestock in railroad cars. A freight bypass for Oregon Short Line trains was completed, as were mechanical facilities (roundhouse and car shops) to maintain Union Pacific locomotives and cars. Pacific Fruit Express rose from the ashes of an icehouse destroyed by fire in 1919 to complete (in 1921) an up-to-date concrete ice manufacturing plant, with ex-

panded facilities for the icing of entire trains of refrigerator cars. Tracks were added to the OUR&D yards to accommodate the increased traffic, and to make room for the new PFE facilities. This forced the reconstruction in 1927 of the steel 24th Street Viaduct (completed in 1909) to extend it directly to the West Ogden Bluff.

In the midst of all this growth in the mid-1920s came a huge setback. On February 13, 1923, one of the hotel rooms in Union Station caught fire, and the blaze spread all too quickly. By 2:30 a.m., when the fire department brought it under control, the center part of the building and all its equipment were a total loss, but no injuries occurred. The north wing and south wing were still intact, but all that remained of the center were the stone exterior walls. The loss of the large Victorian depot was not mourned. It was 34 years old and had served its days. The day after the fire, the *Ogden Standard Examiner* reported that "the squatty, poorly lighted, ill-vented, unattractive old depot will now be replaced," adding that the building had recently become "dilapidated, ill-ventilated, unsightly, overcrowded and unsanitary." Yet, imagine the community's consternation when the railroad companies announced that the structure would be repaired rather than replaced. After much pleading by community leaders, the railroads relented, and by April 1924 the depot grounds were cleared.

Hired to design the new depot were John and Donald Parkinson, principals in a Los Angeles architectural firm that had also designed UP Mission-style depots at Caliente, Nev., in 1921, and Kelso, Calif., and Milford, Utah, in 1923. The same firm also furnished the designs for Los Angeles Union Passenger Terminal, Los Angeles City Hall, and Los Angeles Memorial Coliseum.

A fire started on the third floor of the center portion of Ogden Union Station on February 13, 1923, and spread quickly. When the fire was finally put out, only the brick and sandstone exterior walls of the center portion of the 34-year-old structure remained standing. The only fatality came later when a stone fell from the clock tower and struck a clerk while he sat in his temporary office. (Ogden Union Station Collection)

On November 22, 1924, the station was declared complete, and a dedication ceremony was held. The new depot stood on the foundation of the depot that burned. Ogden historian Richard C. Roberts described the new depot this way:

"Its architectural design is Italian Renaissance of the style which flourished in the fifteenth century in Europe. The building is 374 feet long and an average of 88 feet wide, with a waiting room of 60 feet by 112 feet, and a ceiling height of 56 feet. The ceiling and roof are supported by six huge wooden trusses which are made from Oregon or Douglas Fir. The trusses were highly ornamented in brilliant colors' and attractive designs,' (which have since been painted over). The roofing is of a Cordova Spanish tile. The brick is a pink buff brick produced in Ogden and faced with Boise sandstone. The two main entrances on the east of the building are carved Boise sandstone. The designs in the sandstone are of fruits,' featuring mostly clusters of grapes. Over each entrance door is a carved buffalo.

"Inside, the building has the large waiting room in the center. On the north end of the building on the ground floor is a smoking room for men, and a ladies rest parlor. Farther along are the baggage and mail rooms. There was also a small emergency hospital' located in the north wing. The south wing of the ground floor housed the Western Union and the station master's offices.

"On the east of the waiting rooms was the ticket office which was separated from the waiting room by a long counter reaching across the arcade openings.' On the west side of the waiting room was the Union News Company stands and the parcel checking area. At each end of the waiting room were built two artistic drinking fountains with colored tile designs. The floor of the waiting room is laid in six inch alternating red and grey tile to match the wall plastering done in old ivory with buff tiled wainscoting.

"On the second floor were the division offices of the Southern Pacific, the Superintendent of the Ogden Union Railway & Depot Company, the Union Pacific Telegraph Department and the Claims Agent. The building was steam heated by a boiler plant built about 600 feet west of the structure with the steam carried to the station through an underground pipeline. The total cost of the structure was $400,000." [The power plant was built in 1913.]

When completed, the depot directly replaced the old one in both size and function. To solve an earlier problem of limited access to the multiple depot tracks, sometime before 1920, a passenger subway (underground walkway) was completed between the waiting room and stairways up to the depot tracks. In March 1927, the subway was extended to serve the outside tracks, allowing passengers to walk directly from the waiting rooms to the platform of their choice, without regard to whether tracks above were occupied by waiting trains.

With the completion of the passenger subway, officials considered adding umbrella sheds to protect passengers from the elements. As with many things at the jointly owned Ogden Union Station, minor disagreements surfaced over the design of these new sheds. Union Pacific wanted sheds that were 19 feet wide, similar to those just installed at Salt Lake City. Southern Pacific wanted sheds that were 23 feet wide, similar to those installed at Sacramento. A decision was made in November 1927 to use the Sacramento design, and the sheds were completed between April and September 1928. In all, there were 5,600 linear feet of sheds protecting the four tracks. [The sheds were torn down during April 1969.]

Other improvements came to Ogden during the mid- and late-1920s. As noted earlier, UP built a new roundhouse and shops, and PFE built a new ice plant and icing platforms. The extension of the 24th Street viaduct to reach the West Ogden Bluff, cleared the way for more expansion in the railroad yard below.

In 1930, there were 119 freight trains operated daily through Ogden yard. During the previous year, just over 1.4 million cars moved through the yard, which was said to have the capacity a 12,000 cars. During 1929, the stockyards handled more than 2.1 million head of livestock, including cattle, hogs, sheep, horses, and mules. The stockyards accepted 13,298 carloads of livestock, and shipped 13,531 carloads. At

In 1924 a new depot rose from the ashes of the burned-out Union Station, literally. The new structure was built on the original foundation stones, making the replacement exactly the same dimensions as the original 1889 depot. The fine Italian Renaissance architecture, with the dramatic Spanish tile roof, is shown in this view taken on March 19, 1926. (Utah State Historical Society)

During the 1920s, Ogden's new Union Station was the focus of much activity, but only at train time. The depot area was a much quieter place between train arrivals, as seen in this view from the 24th Street viaduct. (Union Pacific Museum Collection, Negative H9-36)

The Northern-type locomotive was Union Pacific's premier steam power for its passenger trains. Several were painted in a striking two-tone gray scheme that matched that used on UP's extra-fare passenger runs. Here, UP 825 is getting ready to back down to the depot to take Train 24, the daily San Francisco Challenger, *east to Omaha and its eventual destination of Chicago. The train arrived daily at Ogden over Southern Pacific. (Emil Albrecht, James W. Watson Collection)*

the PFE icing plant (which could produce 400 tons of ice a day, and store 2,000 tons), 82,302 cars were iced at the two icing platforms. These platforms could re-ice 272 cars at one time, and have all 272 cars completely re-iced in just one hour. Also during 1930, more than 750 carloads of wheat were inspected each month at Ogden, placing it second only to Portland, Ore., in amount of wheat shipped by rail; this was in the days before covered hoppers, and grain was shipped in 40-foot boxcars. By 1946, 140 trains were moving through Ogden every day, counting both eastbound and westbound movements.

Union Pacific's Streamliners

The economic depression of the 1930s had deeply affected America's railroads. Businesses stopped shipping goods because no one was buying. Passenger traffic plummeted, especially railroad travel by businessmen, the bread and butter of intercity passenger service. Between 1920 and 1932, the number of passenger train-miles nationally fell 65 percent, from 47 billion to 16 billion. Reflecting the availability of cheap automobiles and government-funded public highways, registrations of private automobiles leaped from 8 million in 1920 to 24 million in 1930. To lure business and pleasure travelers back to the rails, and

away from new commercial airline companies, and buses and automobiles, Union Pacific bought a fleet of soon-to-be-famous Streamliner passenger trains. These new distillate- and diesel-powered trains offered air conditioning, reduced noise, bright decor, modern furnishings, and a better ride than that of conventional steam-powered trains.

The first Streamliner was M-10000, nicknamed "Little Zip," which came through Ogden only during its nationwide tour in March 1934. It later entered revenue service as the *City of Salina*. Union Pacific's second Streamliner, M-10001 (later the *City of Portland*) ran through Ogden while on its historic and record-making cross-country dash from Los Angeles to New York City in October 1934. The first Streamliner to enter regularly scheduled service through Ogden was the *City of Los Angeles*, M-10002, in May 1936. This was Union Pacific's third Streamliner, and like the others, it was designed to operate as a single train set, each car being permanently connected to the next. The *City of Los Angeles* was an 11-car, 714-foot-long articulated train with two locomotives instead of the single locomotive that had been used on the previous two. The extra power was needed get the long train over some of UP's steepest grades, including the Wasatch grade up Weber Canyon east of Ogden, and Cima Hill and Cajon Pass in California.

Entering service between Chicago and Los Angeles as Union Pacific Trains *103* (westbound) and *104* (eastbound), Streamliner M-10002 "sailed," rather than departed, five times per month. The schedule brought the westbound train to Ogden on the 1st, 7th, 13th, 19th, and 25th of each month, and the eastbound train on the 4th, 10th, 16th, 22nd, and 28th. This was a premium train with Pullman service and other extra-fare amenities. The next Streamliner to serve Ogden was the *City of San Francisco*, which entered service just a month after the *City of Los Angeles*, also as an extra-fare train. It, too, ran on a schedule of five round trips per month, between Chicago and San Francisco, as Union Pacific Trains *101* (westbound) and *102* (eastbound). The *City of San Francisco* arrived in Ogden westbound on the 6th, 12th, 18th, 24th, and 30th of each month. The opposite eastbound runs were in Ogden on the 3rd, 9th, 15th, 21st, and 27th.

Over the next five years, between 1936 and 1941, the railroad responded as public acceptance of the Streamliners increased. More powerful locomotives were introduced, and larger additional cars were built. Added equipment allowed an increase in frequency from every sixth day to every third day. Because most passengers chose sleeping accommodations over regular-fare coach service, more sleeper and Pullman cars were added. As the trains got heavier and the cars became larger, the concept of permanently connected cars and locomotives fell by the wayside. The more powerful locomotives were separate from each other, and from the now-separated larger cars. All equipment used standard railroad couplers. The *City of San Francisco* and the *City of Los Angeles* each grew to 14 cars and three locomotive units.

Other trains operating through Ogden to San Francisco during these glory days of American rail passenger service included the *Forty-Niner*, the *San Francisco Overland Limited*, *The Challenger*, and the *Pacific Limited*. The *Forty-Niner* is remembered for its specially streamlined steam locomotives, the only two to be so modified by Union Pacific: P-13-class 4-6-2 Pacific-type number 2906, and MT-1-class 4-8-2 Mountain-type number 7002. While the Streamliners were the glamour trains, many other regular trains continued to offer both Pullman service and more economical coach service, using regular, heavyweight (as opposed to the Streamliners' lightweight) cars, behind steam locomotives. A 1937 UP Utah Division timetable shows four daily passenger trains operating north from Ogden, arriving and leaving Ogden Union Station. One daily train was Train *559-560*, a local between Ogden and Brigham City, using a self-propelled motor car.

World War II brought tremendous increases in traffic to America's railroads. Passenger train-mileage alone rose sharply to a peak in 1944 of 95 billion, a six-fold increase from the bleak days of 1932's 16 billion miles. With Union Station being on the main east-west route, more and more freight and passenger trains arrived, straining the terminal and its yards to their very limit. More freight capacity came with construction of the new East (later Riverdale) Yard in mid-1942. After America entered the war in late 1941, people began traveling at a furious pace. Men and women entering military service were moved to military bases all over the nation. Executives and other business travelers took to the rails to oversee the greatly increased production of the country's factories. Wives, children, parents, and sweethearts traveled to visit with a member of the military, if only for a brief moment before that soldier went overseas. Soldiers and sailors traveled cross-country in countless troop trains, moving from inland training bases to coastal ports to be shipped out. After fighting broke out, entire trains of wounded soldiers returned home and were moved to hospitals all across the nation. It was a hectic time on the railroads, but they were up to the challenge. In Ogden, OUR&D increased the number of passenger tracks to 17, to accommodate the sharp increase in train travel. Union Station always seemed to be full of people hurrying to catch a train, at all times of the day and night. There was a train to Salt Lake City every hour, with a round-trip fare of just $1.10. At the peak of war traffic in 1944, 60 to 70 passenger trains in each direction passed through Ogden every day. It was good economic times for Ogden's railroaders, but they were not happy times. Almost every family, railroaders included, had someone in uniform, or knew a close friend or neighbor who was awaiting the return of a soldier.

When the war ended, the number of passenger trains through Ogden fell back to a more reasonable number, but still more than before the war, and the

The number of trains arriving in Ogden, and the variety of their destinations, required shuffling of their cars at the depot. UP 0-6-0 steam switcher number 4740 switches a Southern Pacific Railway Post Office car on the depot's north end in this view taken from the 24th Street viaduct. (Emil Albrecht, James W. Watson Collection)

Union Pacific's City of San Francisco *was the first streamlined passenger train to operate regularly through Ogden. The early version was powered by Pullman-built (with EMC Winton engines) Model E2 locomotives. From the very first, the train was jointly operated, and owned, by UP, Southern Pacific, and Chicago & North Western. Train 102, the eastbound train, arrives from the SP and enters Ogden, bound for Chicago, in this view taken about 1940, just before the E2s were replaced by more powerful Model E6 locomotives. (Raymond P. Gledhill, Ogden Union Station Collection)*

While Union Pacific usually assigned some of its small 0-6-0 steam switchers to the OUR&D lease, SP regularly assigned much larger power to its portion of the joint operation. Here, on September 6, 1937, SP 4-8-0 2922 works as the Ogden Union Station depot switcher. (William A. Gibson, Sr., William A. Gibson Jr. Collection)

quality and scheduled frequency of regular service improved. All three mainline railroads – UP, SP, and Rio Grande – continued to expand their passenger-car fleets with lightweight, modern cars. The coming of the diesel locomotive made for cleaner trains, and railroads took the opportunity to make their trains brighter and more visible. UP bought more locomotives and more cars, allowing the railroad to run Streamliner trains daily instead of every three days. By purchasing still more locomotives and cars, Union Pacific replaced most of the 20- to 30-year-old heavyweight fleet and all but the most modern steam locomotives. Between 1946 and 1965, Union Pacific purchased 291 sleeping cars, 196 coaches, and 112 diner and lounge cars, along with 16 Domeliner coaches, 16 Domeliner lounge cars, and 11 unique-to-UP Domeliner diners. To promote the expanded services, Union Pacific in 1952 began painting all passenger equipment in its Streamliner yellow and gray colors. Up until that time, only the Streamliners had been yellow, and the older, heavyweight cars were either dark green or two-tone gray, depending on the service to which they were assigned. When Union Pacific began buying diesel road freight locomotives in quantity in 1946 and 1947, they were delivered in

Streamliner colors to call attention to the railroad and its expanded, daily service. By 1948, the Streamliner colors were associated with Union Pacific, and vice versa. The railroad's switchers, including those working in Ogden, were repainted from all-black to the Streamliner colors. Cabooses also were repainted, from dark reddish-brown to yellow. Railroading in Ogden was becoming much more colorful.

Denver & Rio Grande Western never approached UP or SP in numbers of trains or passenger market share at Ogden, but soon it withdrew from the city entirely. On November 25, 1953 the company received permission from the Utah State Public Service Commission to discontinue its daily Salt Lake City to Ogden passenger train, train numbers *8* and *9*. The commission said that there was sufficient other train and bus service to handle demand, and the train was terminated on Christmas Day 1953.

The peak year for post-war rail travel turned out to be 1952. By that time, many more families could afford cars and they drove them over a rapidly expanding network of publicly funded highways, traveling at their own convenience and on their own schedule. Business travel was growing with the economy, but it was going by air, not by train. And in 1956, the Interstate highway system was signed into law, making personal and business travel by car even easier, more convenient, and cheaper.

Union Pacific's *City* Streamliners were combined in September 1960. The *City of San Francisco* and *City of Los Angeles* ran as one train from Chicago to Ogden, where they were split. The *City of San Francisco* headed due west over Southern Pacific to Oakland, Calif. The *City of Los Angeles* continued on UP tracks south to Salt Lake City and on to Las Vegas and Los Angeles.

For many years, UP also operated seasonal trains to national parks. In 1908, UP opened a branch to serve Yellowstone National Park, created in 1872 and nestled in the northwest corner of Wyoming, and nearby Grand Teton National Park after its creation in 1929. In the 1920s, the railroad helped develop the national

*The **City of San Francisco** was only the second Streamliner passenger train to operate regularly through Ogden, where Union Pacific handed the train off to Southern Pacific to continue its journey to its namesake city. The train's original locomotives operated at the head of the train from its inaugural run in June 1936 until their replacement by more modern locomotives beginning in 1940. Train **101**, the westbound **City of San Francisco**, is shown here near South Ogden under the control of Electro-Motive model E6 locomotives: number 993 (built in 1946), number 988B (built in 1941), amd number 987 (built in 1940) trailing. (Emil Albrecht, James W. Watson Collection)*

parks in southern Utah, building another branch to reach Bryce Canyon and Zion Canyon national parks and forming a subsidiary, Utah Parks Co., to build and operate the park lodges. UP offered summer train service to its Utah national park destinations, and Yellowstone National Park, running the *Yellowstone Special* with coaches and sleepers from Salt Lake City through Ogden to West Yellowstone, Mont., as part of its regular trains. At times the service was via the *Butte Special* and at times the *Portland Rose*, and later, the *City of Portland*. The 1960 season was the last for direct service to Yellowstone, via West Yellowstone, and 1965 was the last year for any national parks service, which offered connecting bus service to Yellowstone through a branch line to Victor, Idaho.

Beginning in January 1967, Railway Post Office cars were discontinued between Ogden and Los Angeles, bringing to an end service that began with the San Pedro, Los Angeles & Salt Lake Railway in 1905, and which continued with the diesel Stream-liner *City of Los Angeles* in 1936. Southern Pacific ended its Ogden-to-Oakland RPO service ten months later, in October 1967.

On November 16, 1967, SP reduced the number of its passenger trains that used Ogden Union Station from nine to seven when it eliminated its fast mail trains between Ogden and Oakland. UP was operating four trains through the station at the time. SP's action was precipitated by the U. S. Post Office terminating its Railway Post Office service.

Union Pacific's passenger revenue fell by two-thirds between 1955 and 1970. Many changes were made in passenger-train operations, including creation of the unofficially named "City of Everywhere," when UP combined all of its cross-country Streamliner trains into one train between Cheyenne and Green River, Wyo.

Since the mid-1940s, there had been a balloon track south and east of Bridge Junction and the 30th

For its normal operations, Ogden Union Railway & Depot Co. leased switching locomotives from its parent companies, Union Pacific and Southern Pacific. Research shows that the SP locomotives, like Alco S-2 shown here, generally stayed in the depot area or were used in the northern portion of the Main Yard, while UP-owned locomotives stayed in the southern part of the yard. UP switchers were almost exclusively used in East, or Riverdale Yard. In this view, taken in April 1949, SP 1364 waits for its next assignment as depot passenger switcher. Built in 1944, this switcher was renumbered to SP 1715 in 1969. It likely spent its entire career working in the Ogden yard. (Emil Albrecht, James W. Watson Collection)

Street wye. This track allowed the Idaho- and Montana-bound passenger trains (especially Trains *35-36, The Butte Special*) to enter the UP main line and OUR&D trackage south (railroad direction east) of the crossovers between 29th Street and Patterson Avenue, along the east side of the 30th Street wye. This permitted passenger trains to cross over to the Union Station lead tracks adjacent to the Sperry Flour Milling Co. grain elevators and enter depot trackage directly, instead of having to be pulled into the station by a series of time-consuming and expensive OUR&D

The westbound City of Los Angeles (Train 103) enters Ogden after passing beneath the Bamberger bridge in the distance. Leading the train is Union Pacific's GM-EMD E6A number 954A, built in 1940 as number 7-M-2A. This unit was retired in 1956 as number 993. This train will continue into Ogden Union Station. Upon departure it will be pulled back by an OUR&D switcher to approximately its current location and will depart bound for Salt Lake City, Las Vegas, and Los Angeles via the 30th Street wye under its own power. In the immediate foreground is the connection for the passenger balloon track, which allowed OSL trains to enter Union Station via the same direct route as UP trains. (Emil Albrecht, James W. Watson Collection)

When the National Railroad Passenger Corp., better known as Amtrak, took over the operations of most passenger trains in America in May 1971, the operation included the new San Francisco Zephyr, westbound Train 5 and eastbound Train 6. These trains operated between Chicago and Oakland, and arrived at Ogden where Union Pacific gave the train over to Southern Pacific for a trip across Great Salt Lake. During the 1970s and 1980s Union Pacific was in the habit of adding an additional locomotive to the Amtrak trains operating across Wyoming to ensure that they were able to maintain their schedules. By 1980, the date of this photo, UP owned only eight of its famous passenger locomotives (of an original fleet of 149 units). Here is Model E9 number 954 at the headend of number 6, awaiting its eastbound departure from Ogden. (D. B. Harrop)

switch maneuvers. Freight trains also used the balloon track to put them onto the UP main line along the east side of the yard, making the use of the Shasta track unnecessary, with its serpentine route of crossovers to get across the SP tracks at the north end. The balloon track was removed in 1970 to make way for a new UP freight by-pass.

Many passenger trains using Ogden Union Station required the use of a switcher locomotive, leased from either UP or SP, but usually from UP, and operated by OUR&D crews. Most passenger traffic was bound for Salt Lake City and points south and west. As westbound trains passed Riverdale Yard, they headed directly into the station under their own power. Upon arrival at the station, an OUR&D switcher coupled onto the rear of the train. At departure, the switcher pulled the train south past the Bamberger overhead viaduct and uncoupled; the train would then proceed under its own power around the south leg of the 30th Street wye toward Salt Lake.

Eastbound trains required an opposite move; the train proceeded around the south leg of the wye to the UP main adjacent to Riverdale Yard. An OUR&D switcher then coupled onto the rear and pulled it back to Union Station. After its station work was completed, the train departed east, leaving under its own power. The exception to this was the *City of San Francisco* and other trains handed over to Southern Pacific. They usually required a change of locomotives, from UP to SP, or vice versa, but they all operated directly through Union Station trackage without the use of OUR&D switchers.

At times, this changing of motive power made for interesting variations. From their inception in the mid- and late-1930s, the *City* Streamliner fleet was jointly owned and operated by Union Pacific, Southern Pacific, and Chicago & North Western Railway. The locomotives and cars were jointly owned until 1948, when that arrangement was dissolved and the equipment was split up among the three railroads. After this, C&NW locomotives regularly appeared in Ogden, usually in consist with UP locomotives. SP usually put its own locomotives on the trains for their trips farther west, and the UP power was serviced and held at Ogden for the next eastbound trip. During late 1954

and early 1955, Union Pacific became displeased with the performance of C&NW on its part of the operation. On short notice, UP dumped C&NW and on October 30, 1955, a new joint operation went into effect with the Milwaukee Road – Chicago, Milwaukee, St. Paul & Pacific Railroad – to operate all Streamliner trains between Omaha and Chicago. These were the *City of San Francisco* (Trains *101-102*), the *City of Los Angeles* (Trains *103-104*), the *City of Portland* (Trains *105-106*), and the *City of Denver* (Trains *111-112*). Milwaukee Road purchased six sets of EMD E9 passenger locomotives in February 1956 to operate its portion of the joint service. They were painted in UP's yellow and gray Streamliner scheme, and the new partnership regularly brought these and other Milwaukee Road locomotives to Ogden.

After the 1948 split, Southern Pacific briefly continued to use the former jointly owned locomotives to pull the *City of San Francisco* between Ogden and Oakland, immediately repainting them from their original Union Pacific yellow and gray scheme to SP's striking red and orange "Daylight" scheme. By 1950 the three units, an E2A (nicknamed "Queen Mary") and two E7Bs, were reassigned to other SP trains in Southern California, being replaced in Overland Route service by passenger units newly delivered from American Locomotive Co. These 2,000 horsepower Alco units (known as models PA and PB) were purchased especially for the Overland Route Streamliner service and were also painted in the Daylight scheme. In 1959, they were repainted to the a "Lark" gray and scarlet scheme adopted by SP, and they were a daily sight on the Ogden service tracks until they were replaced by EMD 3,600-horsepower SDP45 units in July 1967.

Until early 1968, UP operated two local, mixed trains. One, the Malad Mixed, left Ogden at 5:30 a.m. for its nine-hour journey north up the OSL main line as far as Brigham City, then northwest via Malad Branch trackage to its southern Idaho destination (73 miles distant), and return. The Park City Mixed also took all day to travel its route up Weber Canyon to its destination at the end of the Park City Branch, 68 miles from Ogden. The Malad Mixed ended its days in April 1968.

As part of the service to its patrons, Ogden Union Station furnished both curbside and trackside help to the traveling public. These employees, here as elsewhere, were popularly known as "Red Caps," for the headgear they wore as part of their uniforms. The decline of passenger service also led to fewer station employees, and the last Red Cap was laid off in April 1969.

Beginning in March 1970, the Interstate Commerce Commission approved several changes in western passenger train operations that affected service at Ogden Union Station. ICC allowed the discontinuance of Western Pacific's Salt Lake City-to-Oakland portion of the *California Zephyr*, a Chicago-to-Oakland train with stainless steel dome cars that began running in 1949 as a joint operation of the Burlington, Denver & Rio Grande Western, and WP, in direct competition to the combined C&NW, UP, and SP *City of San Francisco*. Although its endpoints were the same as those of the *City of San Francisco*, its route was via Denver and Salt Lake City rather than Cheyenne and Ogden. The federal agency required that Rio Grande continue the operation of its Denver-Salt Lake City portion of the *California Zephyr*, forcing D&RGW to

run what then became the *Rio Grande Zephyr* through the Rockies three days a week. To provide a connection for *Rio Grande Zephyr* passengers headed to and from northern California, the road operated a stub train of a single locomotive (usually SP FP7 6447) and a single coach between Ogden and Salt Lake City, connecting with Southern Pacific's portion of the *City of San Francisco* which was cut back to a three-times-a-week schedule at the same time.

This situation remained until May 1, 1971 when the federally-supported National Railroad Passenger Corp., or Amtrak, began operations, taking over intercity rail passenger service from most of the nation's freight railroads. Passenger trains through Ogden then took the form of the reorganized *San Francisco Zephyr*, which operated from Chicago to Denver over Burlington Northern, then over UP from Denver to Ogden, and over SP from Ogden to Oakland, with a bus connection to San Francisco.

Both UP and SP were major sources of equipment for Amtrak's initial operations. UP was always well known for the quality of its passenger-train operations, and the condition of its passenger fleet. The railroad couldn't fight the tide of passengers leaving to travel over publicly funded highways, but Union Pacific kept the cars in good shape right up to the end. UP's rolling stock was in such excellent condition that Amtrak purchased 124 cars (64 coaches and 60 sleepers) to begin its operations. Also in excellent condition was UP's fleet of passenger diesels. Twenty-nine of these model E8 and E9 locomotives were also sold to Amtrak. The first Amtrak trains through Ogden used those former Union Pacific E8 and E9 locomotives. Then in 1973 Amtrak began to put in service its specially designed six-axle, 500-class SDP40F locomotives. In 1976 those six-axle

units were replaced by the more versatile four-axle, 100- and 200-class F40PH locomotives.

Amtrak operations in Ogden remained stable between 1971 and 1983. For some time before 1983, Amtrak had been wanting to shift its Chicago to Oakland train away from UP's Wyoming main line to Rio Grande's more scenic Colorado line between Denver and Salt Lake City, and was negotiating with the two railroads to make it happen. Nature stepped in and forced a quicker start of the new service. In April 1983, a mudslide at Thistle, Utah, on D&RGW's line through Spanish Fork Canyon, southeast of Provo, closed that line. All Rio Grande trains detoured between Salt Lake City and Denver by way of Ogden and the UP main line across Wyoming, including the non-Amtrak *Rio Grande Zephyr*. For 10 days, D&RGW continued to detour its *Rio Grande Zephyr* through Wyoming. On April 25, 1983, Amtrak formally changed the routing of Train 5-6, its Chicago-to-Oakland train, to run through Colorado rather than Wyoming, christening the new operation as the *California Zephyr*. The train operated through Wyoming, and through Ogden, until July 16, 1983, when the Amtrak *California Zephyr* went east from Salt Lake City over the D&RGW and through the new Thistle tunnel for the first time. The tunnel was completed, and the first Rio Grande train ran through it, on July 4.

On October 30, 1983, the last eastbound Amtrak *California Zephyr* left Ogden Union Station after having come east on SP's Great Salt Lake causeway, ending almost 115 years of continuous passenger service between Ogden and Oakland-San Francisco. After leaving Ogden, the train proceeded south to Salt Lake City and then headed east across Colorado instead of east through Wyoming. The next day, the

By the time Amtrak trains had reached the south end of the Ogden yards, at Riverdale Road, they were usually operating at mainline speed. Eastbound Amtrak Train 6 is shown here at Riverdale during spring of 1981. Also visible in this view looking north is the entire south (railroad east) end of Riverdale Yard, including the engine servicing facility and, at far left, the runaround track completed in late 1971. (D. B. Harrop)

eastbound train ran into Salt Lake City over Union Pacific's tracks (formerly Western Pacific) along the south shore of the lake, bypassing the causeway and Ogden completely. From then on the only regularly scheduled Amtrak train through Ogden was the *Pioneer*, Amtrak trains 25 and 26, which from 1983 to 1991 ran from Seattle to Portland, across Oregon and Idaho, to Salt Lake City, where it connected with the *California Zephyr* to Chicago. At this time, and throughout the 1980s, a typical consist of the *California Zephyr* east from Salt Lake City was two F40 locomotives, eight cars from Oakland, two cars from a connection with the *Desert Wind* from Los Angeles, and two more cars from the *Pioneer* connection, by way of Ogden.

Union Station was reinstated as a full-agency Amtrak station in March 1991. This was the first time an agent was on duty there since January 1985, when the facility was closed due to Ogden's close proximity (36 miles) to Salt Lake City. This took place in preparation for the rerouting of the *Pioneer* from Ogden, east up Weber canyon and across Wyoming to Cheyenne and Denver, there to meet and combine with the *California Zephyr* as had been done previously in Salt Lake City. The rerouting of the *Pioneer* through Wyoming took effect in June 1991, and remained in effect into early 1997. In a round of budget cuts, Amtrak had planned to drop the *Pioneer*, along with the *Desert Wind*, in the fall of 1996. Last-minute Congressional action kept the train running – and kept Ogden from becoming a freight-only town – for six months, after which the future of these and other threatened Amtrak routes was indefinite.

OUR&D's Riverdale Yard

As America recovered from the depression of the 1930s, and with a war coming in Europe, traffic on America's railroads was booming. Much industrial effort was going into the economy of the West, and Ogden was on the route for trains to and from the West Coast. The number of trains was growing steadily, and the yard was feeling the pinch. It needed more room. During the fall 1941 peak, as many as six trains were held on the main line at any one time awaiting space in Ogden yard. Additional space came to the south (east in railroad terms). To build its new "East Yard," Ogden Union Railway & Depot Co. in 1942 purchased

Prior to the completion of East Yard in 1942, the main yard in Ogden was regularly congested with empty Pacific Fruit Express refrigerator cars awaiting their next load of California perishables. In this view taken about 1940, at least seven tracks are filled with empty PFE cars. (Emil Albrecht, James W. Watson Collection)

305 acres of land, situated between the Union Pacific main line on the east, the Weber River on the west, the embankment for the Bamberger over-crossing on the north, and the Riverdale Road bridge on the south. The "East Yard" name came from the fact that it was located (railroad) east of the Bamberger Railroad crossing at 33rd Street. The new yard would consist of four 125-car tracks and a new switch lead. One of the projected uses for the new yard was to store westbound empty Pacific Fruit Express refrigerator cars, which were taking up valuable space in the then-current Ogden yard. Empty PFE cars were also taking up valuable space in numerous sidings along the UP main line across Wyoming, and as far east as the Omaha/Council Bluffs terminal. In addition to OUR&D holding tracks for westbound PFE cars, Pacific Fruit Express itself leased space for two additional 125-car tracks, located nearer the Weber River, to serve as clean-out tracks for its fleet of refrigerator cars. East Yard was completed and placed in operation in June 1942. The resulting expansion of switching operations required UP to add a second and third diesel General Motors Electro-Motive Division (GM-EMD, or just EMD) NW2 model switcher to the single unit that was already working in Ogden.

Until East Yard, situated between 33rd and 50th streets, was completed in 1942, all trains were operating in and out of the original OUR&D "West Yard" between 21st and 29th streets. In addition to the seasonal storage of empty PFE cars, East Yard handled all Southern Pacific eastbound traffic, along with all Union Pacific traffic bound for Salt Lake City and Los Angeles. It also handled the seasonal eastbound PFE shipments. West Yard handled all westbound traffic for SP, all westbound Union Pacific (OSL) traffic for Idaho and the Northwest, and all local industrial traffic. Construction of East Yard eased the congestion somewhat, but within 10 years, more space was needed again.

Rail traffic growth continued through the post-World War II years, again squeezing the yard facilities. The amount of perishable traffic from California's agricultural industry produced a peak in PFE traffic in 1953, with almost 500,000 cars being loaded. An average of 7,000 to 8,000 cars of perishable traffic per day were moved by way of the Overland Route from California through the "Ogden Gateway," with a winter season peak of more than 9,000 cars. To handle this surge, UP and SP announced in July 1953 that the jointly owned Ogden Union Railway & Depot Co. would expand its Ogden East Yard.

This expansion would permit better handling of all eastbound traffic. The original, main yard (briefly known as West Yard) would then be dedicated to the better handling of all westbound traffic. Included in the East Yard (by then known as Riverdale Yard) expansion was almost 22 miles of new yard tracks, a new overhead viaduct for Ogden's 31st Street, two new yard offices, a diesel fueling facility, two new control towers, floodlights for both yards, a new 150-ton track scale, a pneumatic tube message system, and radio and paging communications. Also included was a second steel overhead bridge for the Bamberger Railroad, whose original steel bridge had stood since 1914. At the same time, UP would build a new four-track car repair area, with shop, office, locker room, and storehouse.

Riverdale Yard, as it appeared during the mid-1970s. At the bottom of the photo is the Bamberger bridge, completed in 1914, along with an adjacent second bridge completed in 1954. By this time, the former interurban trackage was being operated by UP as its six-mile Hill Field Branch, between Ogden and Hill Air Force Base. At the top is the Riverdale Road bridge, completed in 1924. These two bridges limited the size of Riverdale Yard. The portion of the yard at left was completed in 1942 as Ogden Union Railway & Depot Company's East Yard, and the portion along the photo center, including the car repair tracks, was completed in 1954 under the name of Speedway Yard. Along the right edge of the yard is the 1971-built runaround track. Also visible just above the Bamberger bridge and running completely across the photo is the original crossing of 33rd Street. (Union Pacific Museum Collection, Negative 874-2-7)

Also included was a new island-type icing platform for Pacific Fruit Express that would allow the company to mechanize part of its operation at Ogden, along with expanding its facilities to allow the re-icing of two full-length, unbroken 110-car trains at once. This platform would replace the 1927-built 70-car platform in the main yard. PFE would retain the older 66-car icing platform, also located in the main yard. To mechanize the icing operations, the new platform at Riverdale would be equipped with three Preco mechanical icing machines and a 500-ton ice manufacturing and storage facility, and an ice conveyor system connecting the storage facility with the icing platform.

The new "Speedway Yard" opened on September 1, 1954. The new name was only briefly promoted (railroaders then, as now, knew it as Riverdale Yard), but its intention was to highlight the fact that the yard would enable both Union Pacific and Southern Pacific to move trains through the Ogden Gateway with greater efficiency and speed. To build Speedway Yard and complete other local improvements, UP, SP, and their subsidiary OUR&D, spent $4 million in 1953-54. Union Pacific spent $78,000 for additional tracks and track cleaning in 1957. An additional $123,000 was expended in 1959 for UP to expand its car repair facilities. Between 1957 and 1962, OUR&D spent $400,000 for improvements, including water treatment facilities, mail handling equipment, and train crew facilities, along with other building and trackage changes.

On a typical day in October 1955, either a passenger train or a freight train arrived or departed Ogden every 11 minutes. An average of 20 passenger trains and 7,000 to 8,000 freight cars moved through the city daily.

During the early 1960s, the State of Utah changed its tax code, increasing the tax liability of OUR&D's two owners. This, together with the impending settlement of the Ogden Gateway case (a rate and traffic-division dispute that will be covered in detail later) negated many of the advantages of maintaining a separate terminal company. The two railroads agreed that OUR&D had served its purpose, so in 1965 they applied to the ICC for the "curtailment" of its operations. In October 1967, the ICC approved the request, which allowed D&RGW and SP to start a direct interchange, bypassing the switching of their interchanging trains by OUR&D crews. The order also allowed UP and SP to perform all of their own freight switching, with OUR&D continuing to operate the passenger depot and to handle passenger-train switching. In March 1968, OUR&D was reorganized, affecting 1,050 workers. Union Pacific hired 550 workers to support its former-OUR&D operations, Southern Pacific hired 150 workers, and the remaining 350 stayed with OUR&D to support the passenger-train operations.

Ogden Union Railway & Depot Co. was always an important employer in the area. In 1939, the company employed 950 workers, with a combined payroll of $1,528,309. By 1950, the annual payroll for its 1,450 workers was $4.7 million.

The December 1982 merger in which Union Pacific took over Missouri Pacific and Western Pacific radically changed railroading in Ogden. Until the merger, UP and SP cooperated closely in their Overland Route operations. Many trains were handed off between the two railroads at Ogden, with SP locomotives operating as far east as UP's North Platte yard in Nebraska, and UP locomotives operating deep in SP's California territory. When Union Pacific acquired the Western Pacific Railroad main line from Salt Lake City to Oakland, Calif., in 1982, it then had its own direct route to northern California and no longer needed an interchange with SP. After the UP-WP merger, Union Pacific and Southern Pacific met several times in an attempt to come to terms with operation of Ogden Union Railway & Depot Co. Finally, an agreement was made, with a color-coded map showing specific track ownership as a visual aid. Reflecting the 1968 reorganization and subsequent operational changes, all of Riverdale Yard and all trackage south of 29th Street became solely Union Pacific property. SP took over much of the former UP trackage in the old main yard, including the area directly west of the passenger depot tracks. Several tracks adjacent to the old PFE facility stayed with UP. The remaining property around and under Union Station itself, and the former site of the freight house, remained as a joint OUR&D holding. ☆

In 1954, UP completed a new four-track car repair facility as part of the expansion of Riverdale Yard. The new facility was equipped with the most modern features, including a work area fully paved with concrete, and a 50-ton traveling crane (from which this photograph, looking north, was taken), and plenty of space for material storage, with room for future expansion. (Union Pacific Museum Collection, Negative 43382)

The 1954 completion of a new icing dock for Pacific Fruit Express at Riverdale Yard included three Preco automatic icing machines. These machines traveled the length of the ice dock on rails mounted to the outside edges of the dock. The Precos were able to swivel from one side to the other, allowing the re-icing of cars on either of the two 110-car tracks. (Union Pacific Museum Collection, Negative 38105)

7. Central Pacific and Southern Pacific

Union Pacific's connecting partner in the historic 1869 completion of the transcontinental railroad was Central Pacific. Until September 1996, it was Southern Pacific that operated into Ogden from California, across the Great Salt Lake and Nevada. The narrative of how one became the other begins with the organization of the Central Pacific Railroad by the "Big Four," a group of Sacramento, Calif., businessmen headed by Collis P. Huntington, in 1863 to construct the western portion of the Pacific Railroad. After the Golden Spike was driven, Central Pacific aimed its sights on completing feeder lines in Oregon and northern California that would furnish, or "feed," traffic to the new transcontinental rail line. One of these was the Southern Pacific Railroad, started by other individuals in 1865 as a line from San Francisco to San Diego. Its construction stalled until Huntington became financially interested in mid-1868, and he gained control in September 1869.

By the end of 1882, with the completion of its line into Oregon, CP operated 1,330 miles of railroad in Utah, Nevada, Oregon, and in northern California. By the late 1870s, its sister company, Southern Pacific,

had built and operated a railroad throughout central and southern California, and had reached Tucson, Arizona Territory, in mid-March 1880, and Texas in 1883. A new holding corporation, the Southern Pacific Co., was organized in 1884 to manage all of Huntington's railroad interests, including Southern Pacific Railroad, Central Pacific, and several other leased railroads. CP was leased to the Southern Pacific Co. on April 1, 1885, giving the SP complete control of Huntington's Central Pacific lines in California and Oregon, together with the Overland Route, between Sacramento and Ogden (the original Central Pacific), and the Sunset Route, between southern California and New Orleans (the original Southern Pacific).

In the years following completion of the transcontinental railroad, both Union Pacific and Southern Pacific sought ways to circumvent and delay making payments on their respective government bonds coming due in 1899, 30 years after completion of the transcontinental railroad in 1869. As set down in the original 1862 Pacific Railway Act, these payments were to be based on the net earnings of each road. UP delayed its payments by questioning the

The crew of Southern Pacific switcher 1192 takes a break to pose for an unknown photographer in this view taken in 1903. The practice of Ogden Union Railway & Depot Co. leasing both UP and SP locomotives for operation by OUR&D's own crews began immediately upon its organization in 1888, and continued until 1968. (Ogden Union Station Collection)

definition of "net earnings." The company also used other delaying tactics, trying to keep its various improvements, including its development of badly needed feeder lines, such as Oregon Short Line, Utah Central, and many others, separate from the business of the original transcontinental trunk line. As already noted, the creation of Ogden Union Railway & Depot Co. in 1888 was one of these tactics. Central Pacific's owners chose to avoid the question of net earnings by acquiring control of the SP, and transferring much of Central Pacific's business to the southern route, completed in 1883, draining traffic away from the Ogden interchange.

The 1885 lease of Central Pacific by Southern Pacific brought SP to the forefront of railroad operations in Ogden. Throughout the 1880s and 1890s, SP's profits were slowly losing ground in keeping up with expenses, in part due to terms of the Central Pacific lease. This, together with government debt coming due from 1896 to 1899, led SP and CP, along with committees of their shareholders and bondholders, to enter into negotiations with the federal government that resulted in a reorganization of the CP in 1899.

The Central Pacific Railroad was reorganized as the Central Pacific Railway on August 1, 1899. A direct benefit of this reorganization was that, over the next 10 years, CP's debt of $58 million to the federal government for bonds of the original transcontinental rail line was repaid in full, with interest. SP owned and controlled the new Central Pacific by lease and full ownership of its capital stock. Southern Pacific Co. then operated 8,200 miles of railroad, from Portland, Oregon, south and southeast through southern California and Arizona, across Texas to New Orleans, along with its Overland Route across Nevada and Utah, to a connection with Union Pacific at Ogden. Central Pacific remained a separate corporate entity, as owner of the route into Ogden, fully controlled by SP, until it was formally merged into the parent company 60 years later – on June 30, 1959.

The patriarch of Southern Pacific, Collis P. Huntington, died on August 13, 1900. Huntington's

The original Central Pacific freight house in Ogden was located south of the UP passenger depot. This view, looking north, shows the freight house, with the passenger depot just to the left in the background.
(Utah State Historical Society)

rival, Edward H. Harriman, was taking the newly reorganized Union Pacific Railroad into its industry-leading position by throwing large amounts of money at numerous improvements. Harriman had tried unsuccessfully to talk the aging Huntington out of his SP holdings, but Huntington would have nothing to do with Harriman. Upon Huntington's death, Harriman saw his chance and took it, buying Huntington's 46 percent of SP, and voted himself a seat on SP's board of directors. Harriman's move immediately shut out D&RGW, along with other interlopers into Utah, including the Burlington through its Colorado Midland subsidiary. Harriman said at the time that UP had to control the larger Southern Pacific "to maintain and protect the position of the [Union Pacific] system and to safeguard its future against combinations of other lines . . ." He later said, "We have bought not only a railroad, but an empire."

This gave Harriman control of both SP (the largest railroad in the nation), and UP (the most profitable road), providing a one-company connection between the Missouri River and the Pacific Coast via the Overland Route, along with SP's Sunset Route from Oakland to New Orleans. Harriman also controlled rail access to most of the ports along the Pacific Coast, from Portland on the north, to Long Beach on the south, along with the Gulf port of Galveston, Texas. All of this unfolded against the backdrop of president Teddy Roosevelt's campaign of "trust busters," in which he sought to break up corporate cartels such as Rockefeller's Standard Oil petroleum trust, James J. Hill's Northern Securities railroad trust, and Henry Havemayer's American Sugar cane sugar and beet sugar trust. Harriman's purchase of SP attracted the attention of the trust busters, and soon he found himself fighting the U. S. government over his growing collection of railroads, which included Illinois Central, Alton & Southern, and Erie. Although Harriman fought the federal lawyers until his death in 1909, the government eventually won its case.

The case of the *United States vs. Union Pacific* (226 US 61), decided in 1912, was the government's successful action to force UP to divest itself of SP. That 1912 decision by the Supreme Court also dealt with SP's lease and control of Central Pacific. In February 1914, the government sued to break that control, in *United States vs. Southern Pacific* (259 US 214), with the case being decided, again by the Supreme Court, against SP in 1922, forcing the road to terminate control of Central Pacific and separate the properties.

In the meantime, the Transportation Act of 1920 changed the Interstate Commerce Act of 1887 to allow the Interstate Commerce Commission jurisdiction over the issue of one railroad controlling another, if the public interest was maintained. The ICC found that the 1920 act constituted a "radical change in the legislative policy of Congress, in respect of the application of the Sherman [anti-trust] law to the railroads of the country." The timing of the 1922 Supreme court decision, coming after the 1920 Transportation Act, gave SP the opportunity to re-present its case for control of Central Pacific, this time to the ICC.

SP's major argument before the ICC was that it and Central Pacific were dependent on each other, and that an independent CP would have difficulty meeting its financial obligations. Union Pacific filed a brief with the ICC supporting SP's continued control of the Central Pacific, saying that if CP failed after being broken away from SP control, UP would lose its connection for westbound traffic at Ogden. Next came the question of the percentage of traffic that SP was diverting to its Sunset Route through southern California, and across Arizona, New Mexico, and Texas, and away from the short haul along the Overland Route across Nevada to UP at Ogden. Evidence showed that due to the competitive position of its southern route, SP was giving itself the long-haul, and attendant higher profits.

In return for supporting Southern Pacific's control of Central Pacific, UP in 1923 won an agreement with SP to send traffic via the Overland Route through Ogden. This pact became known as the "Santa Margarita Agreement." It stated that all eastbound traffic originating north of Santa Margarita, at the south end of California's Salinas Valley, would travel by way of Ogden. With the agreement in place, SP was forced to furnish a dependable amount of rail traffic to Union Pacific at the Ogden Gateway, with a small bit going to D&RGW to satisfy the ICC government regulators. The ICC decided in Southern Pacific's favor in 1923, giving it control of CP but insisting that Southern Pacific solicit traffic for the Overland Route, via Ogden, for interchange with Union Pacific there.

In using such specific language, the ICC unwittingly shut Rio Grande out of sharing any meaningful amount of SP traffic at Ogden. This decision effectively forced D&RGW to depend even more on its connection with Western Pacific at Salt Lake City.

D&RGW endured the imbalance until the post-World War II boom, pleading its case before the ICC in a bid for a share of the postwar prosperity. In 1953, D&RGW was granted limited joint rates with Union Pacific through Ogden. UP contested the decision, claiming that it was entitled to all of SP's traffic at Ogden as a provision of both the Pacific Railway Act of 1864 and the 1923 ICC decision. In a series of legal maneuvers that continued in the courts from the mid-1950s through to the late-1960s, Union Pacific attempted to avoid being forced to share its Ogden traffic with upstart D&RGW. When SP trains began running directly into Rio Grande's Roper Yard in Salt Lake City in 1970, it was a direct result of a final settlement of what has been called the Ogden Gateway case.

The Lucin Cutoff

After Central Pacific was reorganized in 1899, it was able to concentrate on improving its railroad. Surveys were run in an effort to find ways bypass or ease the many difficult curves and severe grades across Nevada and western Utah. Over the next 10 years, 221 miles of the 443 miles of line across Nevada were relocated to better alignments. One of the first improvements was a plan to eliminate the operational bottleneck over Promontory summit in northern Utah, with its just over 700 feet of climb above the level of the lake. This would be accomplished by building the Lucin Cutoff, a new east-west water level route between the Utah/Nevada state line and Ogden, directly across Great Salt Lake.

Planners had envisioned a direct route across the lake as early as the first surveys for the transcontinental railroad. In June 1868, a party of Central Pacific

Southern Pacific 4-8-2 engine 3683 waits at Patterson Avenue for clearance to return to the SP yard. September 21, 1946. (Emil Albrecht, James W. Watson Collection)

surveyors took depth soundings of the lake and found that at its deepest it was not 11 feet, as previously estimated, but 38 feet deep. UP's Chief Engineer G. M. Dodge's original survey had UP building its line west from Ogden, across the Bear River arm of the lake to Promontory Point, then north along the western slope of the Promontory Mountains to the north end of the lake, then west to Nevada. Construction technology did not yet exist to build the route across the lake. The direct route had to wait for another 30 years and the construction of the Lucin Cutoff, which would slice 43 miles off the trip between Ogden and Nevada. Later, after operations had begun, Southern Pacific found that the cutoff saved an average of 24 hours of transit time. Also, the cutoff would eliminate as many as three helper locomotives on every train on the 2.2 percent climb up to Promontory summit, compared to the almost level cutoff route. At the time of the construction of the cutoff, the Promontory line was handling six million tons of railroad traffic per year – ten trains per day, each made up of 33 50-ton cars.

Planning for the 103-mile Lucin Cutoff, with its 12 miles of wood trestle and 11 miles of earth fill causeway, began in November 1899 and got under way the next month when engineers started taking depth soundings. In June 1900 a separate corporation, the Ogden & Lucin Railroad, was organized to construct the cutoff. Construction was delayed after Huntington's death in 1900, but resumed with Harriman's ownership and control of Southern Pacific. When the railroad announced its intention to replace the original Promontory route, Salt Lake City boosters called for the new route to come to their city instead of Ogden. As with the original transcontinental line, Salt Lake lost out, this time to simple distance. A route through Salt Lake City would be 67 miles longer than a line directly across the lake to Ogden. Contracts for construction were awarded in late February 1902 (which included a grand celebration in Ogden). Work began in March 1902, and the first pile was driven on August 2.

The problems were immense. Using state-of-the-art construction techniques, workers dumped enor-

After the completion of East Yard in 1942, Southern Pacific eastbound trains arrived directly at the new yard. Here, an A-B-B-A set of Southern Pacific Electro-Motive F7s backs down through the crossovers at Patterson Avenue between the East Yard and the Main Yard on its way to the SP service track. The photo was taken from the Bamberger Railroad bridge on June 4, 1960. (Emil Albrecht, James W. Watson Collection)

mous amounts of rock fill into the lake (70,000 carloads at Rambo alone), with the bottom of the lake seeming to open up and swallow whatever was offered. At times, the fill would appear to be stable, only to sink below the water's surface later. One of the construction engineers lamented, "We know what it ought to do, what we don't know is why it doesn't do it." The original plan called for an earth fill over the entire distance, but the engineers finally gave up and completed the most troublesome portion as a wooden trestle instead.

SP drove the last pile in the trestle on October 26, 1903, and the last rail was laid on November 13, 1903. The total cost was said to be $4.5 million. Freight trains began using the cutoff on March 8, 1904, but because parts of the fill were still settling in places, passenger trains continued to use the longer Promontory line until September 18, 1904. The Lucin Cutoff was officially opened on January 1, 1905.

In building the Lucin trestle, Southern Pacific operated of a sternwheeler named "The Promontory," along with a fleet of seven barges. The design of the trestle included a deck of planks three inches thick, topped by a layer of asphalt, then a foot or more of rock ballast, and finally the ties and rail. At the center of the trestle was a telegraph station named Midlake, with a store, telegraph office, living quarters for the operator and section crews, and later, even a small garden plot. Planned during the construction of the original trestle, Midlake was first known as Camp 20. Fire protection for the 11.67-mile-long trestle consisted "of a bucket hung here and there and a fire extinguisher every half mile." Between 1920 and 1927, the trestle was strengthened with additional decking, stringers, and struts. The added strength was needed to handle the heavier trains that were coming into use with the advent of steel cars, heavier shipments, and more powerful locomotives.

Telegraph stations on the Lucin Cutoff were situated at (from west to east) Lakeside, Midlake, and Promontory Point. When double track west of Ogden was extended west over the earth fill between Little Mountain and Promontory Point to the east end of the trestle in 1929, a new station called Bridge replaced the telegraph stations at Promontory Point and Midlake, which were both closed. The buildings at Midlake,

where there was also a passing siding, remained in place as section men's quarters. The telegraph office at Midlake was reopened in 1941 to help with wartime traffic, but all telegraph stations on the cutoff were closed with the completion of Centralized Traffic Control in 1945. The station buildings and living quarters at Midlake, which rested on a wide spot in the trestle 40 feet wide and 240 feet long, were dismantled in August 1945.

Southern Pacific's Promontory Branch

Over the 30 years following the building of the Lucin Cutoff, the original Central Pacific line into Ogden by way of Promontory Summit got little more than routine maintenance. In April 1933, Southern Pacific applied to the ICC for permission to abandon operation of the western 55-mile portion of the Promontory Branch, between Kelton and Lucin. At that time, two principle areas of settlement existed in the vicinity of that part of the branch; Rosette had 15 families and Park Valley had 45 families, and neither was situated directly on the rail line. Traffic for the once-a-week local train consisted mostly of seasonal livestock shipments, particularly the movement of 125,000 sheep to their winter ranges, and 10,000 head of cattle, along with in-shipment of hay and grain to supplement the sparse desert grazing. Other traffic came from a deposit of infusorial earth, a product used in filtering water. During 1932, four carloads of this highly specialized commodity were shipped from Peplin, a station just west of Kelton.

Only 5,161 tons (about 100 carloads) of rail traffic originated on the western part of the branch between 1928 and 1932, compared to the several hundred carloads that were moving over the Lucin Cutoff every day. Most of the traffic on the Promontory Branch, about 83 percent, was in the form of wheat shipped from Lampo, east of Promontory Station on the eastern part of the branch. At one time, Lampo was one of the largest originating points for wheat in Utah. Much of the wheat on the eastern portion of the Promontory Branch was purchased by Sperry Mills and shipped either to its mill and silos in Ogden for storage and partial milling, or to the company's extensive milling operation at South Vallejo, Calif. Hilton Flour Mills in Ogden was also a customer for the area's wheat.

The abandonment proceedings for the west end of the branch lasted until June 1934, at which time the ICC denied the application, because SP lawyers revealed that the railroad was planning neither to dismantle the line, nor to halt maintenance that would keep it in operating condition. They merely wanted to withdraw the line from participation in interstate commerce. Southern Pacific was hesitant to abandon and dismantle the entire Promontory Branch due to possible problems that might arise from its status as collateral for the 1899 mortgage for the reorganization of Central Pacific. An SP attorney at the ICC hearings stated that "We feel that this mortgage is a possible barrier to the abandonment of that line by the Central Pacific Railway Co." ICC denied the application because the inconvenience to the shippers along the line outweighed the small potential savings for the railroad.

The case was reopened in December 1934 at the request of SP, which argued that the population along the line consisted only of a section gang and two persons on one ranch and three part-time residents on another ranch. Parties protesting the abandonment, namely Box Elder County and the Utah State Economic Development Board, stated that railroad service was needed due to a severe drought in the region, citing the fact that 269 tons (about five carloads, or 50,000 gallons) of water had been shipped in during 1934 alone. They added that in 1928, 435 tons of water had been shipped in for the livestock along the line. In 1933 and 1934, only 576 tons of "freight-all-kinds" had originated on the line, about one carload every two weeks. The application for reconsideration was denied again on March 17, 1936, because the railroad still could not show that the benefits from abandonment would outweigh the inconvenience to livestock shippers on the line. Service between 1937 and 1940 consisted of various combinations of mixed trains (freight and passenger) and on-call freight service.

From December 1937 to June 1938, a mixed train ran between Ogden and Lucin on Wednesdays, and another mixed train ran between Ogden and Kelton on Mondays and Fridays. From June 1938 to June 1939, the only service was the mixed train between Ogden and Lucin. From June 1939 to March 1940, the mixed train operated between Ogden and Kelton, only on Wednesdays, with on-call service at other times, including after the mixed train was dropped in March 1940. After 1940, the on-call, freight-only service ran only on Wednesdays. During its final years, a few passenger specials were run - for example, rabbit hunter excursions in 1937 (238 passengers) and again in 1939 (346 passengers). Also, the Civilian Conservation Corps had operated special trains between Ogden and Kelton in July and December 1938 (both totaling 306 passengers), and again in January 1939 (137 passengers).

The livestock industry provided the only business on the west end of the line, between Kelton and Lucin. Between Kelton and Corinne there was grain farming, livestock, sugar beets, and asphalt mining. The grain was loaded at Kosmo, Promontory, and Lampo. Livestock was shipped in and out at Lampo, Balfour, and Conner. Sugar beets were shipped from Dathol (Corinne Junction) and Stokes. The asphalt, in the form of eight carloads during 1941 and 1942, came from subsurface deposits developed by the Rosette Asphalt Co., 13 miles from the branch rails at Rozel.

The grades and curves on the Promontory Branch were difficult at best. Between Lucin and Kelton, the line climbed over the flanks of Terrace Mountain and Peplin Mountain, where there was an eastbound 1.59 percent grade, meaning 1.59 feet of rise in 100 feet of distance, and a 1.61 percent westbound grade. The climb up and over the Promontory Mountains required a grade of 1.62 percent grade up the west side, and a grueling 2.21 percent up the east side. Because of its close proximity to the northern reaches of Great Salt Lake, the rest of the route averaged grades of 0.1 and 0.2 percent, with very little of it actually being level. The curves were numerous and sharp. More than 31 miles of track lay on curves less than 6 degrees (3 degrees is a sharp curve on a main line, with 6 degrees being very sharp) and another two miles of curves greater than 6 degrees, with a short stretch of 10 degree curvature. All trains were restricted to 15 mph.

Freight traffic on the line was predominantly outbound, with 676, 879, 691, 572, and 660 carloads

for each of the years from 1937 to 1941, respectively. Inbound traffic for the same years were 23, 26, 23, 10, and 15 carloads, respectively. Total carloads for the five-year period were 12 cars of asphalt, 121 cars of sheep, 165 cars of cattle, 820 cars of wheat, and 2,325 cars of sugar beets (all originating from Dathol, Stokes, and Rochefort on the east end of the branch). The carloads of sugar beets were interchanged with UP at Corinne, and were shipped to the Utah-Idaho Sugar refinery at Garland. Sheep and cattle were all loaded at Kelton, with carloads diminishing after 1937, when stockmen began using Bear River City on UP's Bear River Branch as their main loading point.

Southern Pacific's Promontory Local out of Ogden traveled over Union Pacific (OSL) from Ogden to Corinne. In 1903, UP had completed its Malad Branch north from Corinne. Construction of this line included the four-mile "Brigham City Cut-off," a connection between the UP's Ogden-to-Pocatello line at Brigham City and a connection with Central Pacific's Promontory Branch at a new station called Corinne Junction, 1-1/2 miles east of Corinne. The agreement that allowed UP to use the 1-1/2 miles of Central Pacific tracks from Corinne Junction to Corinne also allowed SP trains to use Union Pacific's line between Ogden and the new Corinne Junction, thus saving SP the cost of maintaining the old Central Pacific line between Ogden and Corinne Junction. A side note from the Promontory Branch abandonment hearings in 1935 was SP's revelation that over the prior 30 years, about 10 miles of tracks between Corrine Junction and Bonneville (Hot Springs), eight miles north of Ogden, had been "removed by persons unknown to the railway company." With trackage rights over UP having been in effect since 1903, the original Central Pacific line (purchased from UP in November 1869), had lain dormant and unused.

In a reflection of the line's status, SP applied for, and received on August 26, 1929, authority to close the agency station at Cecil Junction, a point less than a mile north of its Ogden yard, where the Lucin Cutoff joined the original CP line to Promontory in 1904.

Operations on the Promontory "Old Line" continued to exhibit the difficulties that forced the construction of the Lucin Cutoff 40 years earlier. A former locomotive fireman, David Mann wrote in 1969 about his experiences on the line. The regular train, he said, consisted of a locomotive, as many as six freight cars, and a single passenger car. According to Mann, six freight cars were the limit, due to the steepness of the climb over the Promontory summit.

With the federal ICC denial of abandonment in 1936, SP tried a different tack. In February 1937, the railroad applied to the Public Service Commission of Utah for permission to abandon its mixed (combined freight and passenger) trains over the line. These mixed trains included a once-weekly train over the entire branch, from Ogden to Lucin on Mondays, returning to Ogden the next day. Also included was another mixed train between Corinne and Kelton three days a week, on Mondays, Thursdays and Saturdays. SP stated that in 1935 and 1936, no passengers rode between Kelton and Lucin, and the company collected only $12.89 per trip in freight revenue, against costs of $56 per trip. On March 31, 1937, the Utah commission allowed SP to discontinue all trains, both freight and passenger, on the western 20 miles of the branch between Lucin and Watercress. The commission also allowed for "on-call" freight service over the 34 miles of branch between Kelton and Watercress, while still requiring regular, scheduled service to continue on the 92 miles between Ogden and Kelton.

The end of the Promontory Branch came five years later, in 1942. It took the form of a letter, dated April 22, 1942, from the War Department office in Sacramento, Calif., to SP officials, seeking help in procuring secondhand railroad rail and assistance in fabricating railroad switches for numerous National Defense projects then under way. The military specifically asked about the 114 miles of "very rarely used" 62-pound rail laid on the Promontory Branch. In a letter dated April 27, the Navy Department assured Southern Pacific that it would receive "prices not exceeding the ceiling quotations for relay rails and scrap." Later communications requisitioned a total of 120 miles of rail, approximately 15,000 tons, with which to lay track in the new Naval Ammunition Depot at Hawthorne, Nev. The requisition was based on a newly enacted law dated October 16, 1941. It is unclear, considering the March 9, 1942, date of its application for abandonment to the ICC, whether SP volunteered the rail, or whether the Navy asked for the rail earlier in other communications. In either case, a public hearing was held on May 1, 1942. The abandonment was opposed by Box Elder County, by the Public Service Commission of Utah, and by several other interests. But it was all for naught. SP insisted that the Navy needed the rail, and the matter was therefore settled. The railroad also stated that further operation of the line would require extensive rebuilding to bring it up to current safety standards, citing that the branch had only dirt ballast and many narrow rock cuts.

On June 11, 1942, the ICC approved the abandonment, and Southern Pacific set about immediately removing the rail. Some of the rail was actually used at the Navy facility at Hawthorne, but most was used right in Utah on the many defense projects under way, including Hill Field, Clearfield Navy Supply Depot, Tooele Army Depot, and Utah General Depot. In a ceremony arranged by the Ogden *Standard-Examiner* newspaper, with Utah Gov. Herbert Maw and officials of UP and SP

in attendance, on September 8, 1942, a ceremonial last spike on the branch was removed at Promontory, where the first Golden Spike was put into its laurel tie in 1869. All that remained then was the 1-1/2 miles of line between Corinne and Corinne Junction (Dathol).

SP sold several buildings at Corinne in 1942, including the depot and the agent's dwelling. The agent's dwelling was sold in November, and the 30-foot by 80-foot passenger and freight depot, built in 1870, was sold in December 1942, and removed from railroad property.

On March 16, 1945, Union Pacific, in the name of its subsidiary Oregon Short Line, leased (with right to purchase) all of the trackage, facilities, and right-of-way of the 1-1/2 mile remnant. OSL purchased the property, buildings and tracks on October 16, 1947, including 1.83 miles of branch line and another 1.4 miles of spurs and sidings. SP had already removed their remaining tracks between Corinne Junction and Ogden in 1942, except for a 962-foot stub at Corinne Junction, which it had sold to Utah Idaho Sugar Co. for use as a beet loading station. OSL bought the spur from the sugar company on April 21, 1950.

On February 13, 1951, Southern Pacific sold a 16.5-foot right-of-way along the 34 miles of the original Central Pacific main line from Ogden to Corinne Junction to the Salt Lake Pipeline Co., for use as a natural gas pipeline route to southern Idaho. Pieces and parts of the abandoned original transcontinental roadbed, the unused remnants of the rail line that tied America together in 1869, are visible today along the west side of Interstate Highway 15. Pipeline markers show its location, with many farmers using the alignment for their roads, and its flat spaces to stack their bales of hay.

The Salt Lake Causeway

The Lucin Cutoff, with its combination of trestle and rock fill causeways, served Southern Pacific well and long for more than 50 years. By the early 1950s, the wooden decking of the trestle was in need of repair, and maintenance costs were rising. Trains were becoming heavier and heavier, and the trestle needed to be strengthened. In addition, the threat of fire damage from both accidental causes and vandalism was be-

Southern Pacific eastbound trains arrived in Ogden and operated directly into East (Riverdale) Yard, where the motive power was removed and the train's cars reshuffled for a trip over Union Pacific rails to their final destinations. Southern Pacific Electro-Motive F7s 6236 and 6404 lead an eastbound freight past the Sperry mill at 30th Street on October 21, 1955. In just three years, SP 6404 would be destroyed in a wreck in Nevada. SP 6236, with its shiny new paint job and perfectly smooth nose, appears to have been recently shopped.
(Emil Albrecht, James W. Watson Collection)

coming a concern. A standing slow order of 15 mph was imposed for all trains because the trestle tended to move and sway as a train traversed it. Plans were made to improve the Great Salt Lake crossing by replacing the trestle with a new causeway that would replace the original wooden trestle between Promontory Point, and Lakeside, on the west shore.

Several alternatives were examined, including varying combinations of rebuilding and new construction. The minimum effort would have been to re-deck the existing trestle and look at complete replacement in 25 years. Other alternatives included combinations of additional earth fill and new trestle, either wooden or concrete. The final selection was to replace the wooden trestle completely and construct a 13-mile rock fill causeway, with work starting right away.

Preliminary planning started as early as 1950, and engineering work started in 1953 with a study of the lake bottom and its ability to support the proposed causeway. Work began in June 1955 when Southern Pacific construction crews started dumping fill material to improve the existing partial fills at each end of the new causeway. On February 20, 1956, SP signed a $45 million contract with Morrison-Knudsen Co. of Boise, Idaho, to construct the 12.7 mile New Fill. SP spent an additional $4 million for track and signaling improvements. Morrison-Knudsen's work began in March 1956. The construction methods called for approximately 20 to 30 feet of lake bottom mud to be dredged out, producing a trench varying from 175 feet wide, for the hard salt-crust sub-layer, to 480 feet wide for the hard clay sub-layer. The trench was then filled with material taken from a large quarry on the west side of Promontory Point, called Little Valley, where an extensive worker's village was established. The 43.7 million cubic yards of fill material was transported by means of a fleet of tugs and barges that kept moving day and night (the typical 100-ton hopper car on today's railroads holds approximately 134 cubic yards). Due to varying lake depths and a maximum lake depth of 38 feet, the fill would be between 85 and 102 feet high, with plans for the finished track to be 17 feet above lake level. The actual finished height was 12 feet above the water. Morrison-Knudsen mobilized an army of 670 men, six shovels, 30 dump trucks, eight tugboats, eight barges, and two dredges to move the fill and quarry-rock material.

During construction of the fill, the potential problems of the wooden trestle became apparent when, in May 1956, a fire caused by discarded oil-soaked packing from an overheated car axle bearing burned 645 feet of the trestle. The railroad and Morrison-Knudsen cooperated to rebuild the trestle and get it back in service within just one week by placing special trusses atop the unburned portions of the wooden piles that lay below the water's surface. After the causeway was completed, Southern Pacific's own crews laid the track and installed the Centralized Traffic Control signaling, which was controlled by dispatchers in Ogden.

The Salt Lake causeway was completed on July 9, 1959, when Morrison-Knudsen formally turned the then-trackless causeway over to SP for actual track-laying, which was completed over the following 30 days. Regular passenger service started on August 19. The new causeway includes the 7.3-mile Bagley Fill

between Little Mountain, on the lake's eastern shore, and Promontory Point, at the south end of the Promontory Mountains. From Promontory Point, the causeway is made up of the 2.5-mile Saline Fill on the east end and the 5.1-mile Rambo Fill at the west end, connecting to the western shore at Lakeside. Between is the 12.7-mile New Fill, which jogged north of the original trestle by 1,500 feet to allow maneuvering of construction equipment and to avoid any delays in train operation during its construction. The three smaller fills - Bagley, Saline, and Rambo – were part of the construction of the original 1904 Lucin Cutoff and were improved at the same time as the construction of longer New Fill. When completed, the New Fill held only a single track, with a passing siding at its center, instead of the full length of double track on the trestle.

The Salt Lake causeway is the focus of Southern Pacific's operations in Utah. Since its completion in 1959, through to today's modern operations, the railroad has kept a close watch on the causeway's condition, adding rock fill on a regular basis to keep the track in good maintenance. But the wet winters of 1983 and 1984 and the subsequent high waters of following years tested the railroad's maintenance forces to their limits. One of their tricks included filling retired boxcars, hopper cars, and gondola cars with rock and lowering them in the water on the north side of the causeway to act as a buffer to the destructive wave action. During the worst storms out of the north, waves could rise as high as 15 feet. Throughout 1983 and 1984, SP spent $25 million to raise the level of the causeway five feet. To do this, the railroad operated three or four work trains, 12 hours a day, six days a week, for more than a year, moving vast quantities of rock and fill material. These trains operated from both the Lakeside Quarry on the west shore, and the Saline Quarry, at Promontory Point.

When the Salt Lake causeway was completed 25 years before, it cut off the flow of water to north arm of Great Salt Lake. Since there are no inlets of fresh water to the north arm, it soon stood 37 inches lower than the rest of the lake. To equalize the north and south arms of the lake, Southern Pacific, under contract to the State of Utah, cut a 300-foot opening in the causeway in August 1984. A bridge was installed and trains continued to operate over the causeway. In the following two-week period, the difference in lake level between the two sections was reduced to 23 inches.

During the summer of 1986, the lake rose to its modern record of 4,212 feet (above sea level). The high water level, along with the wave action of the heavy salt water during storms, literally beat the causeway down to and below the level of the lake's waters. The railroad's maintenance crews did their best, adding rock and fill material to stabilize the causeway and keep the track above water level.

The lake remained at or near its record level for another two years, with the railroad maintenance forces just barely keeping the track above water, at times losing the battle. Between 1983 and 1986, SP spent $85 million on keeping its 60 miles of rail line between Little Mountain and Hogup (14 miles west of Lakeside) above water. In April 1986, the causeway was closed on two occasions, for four days between April 2 and April 5, and again for three days between April 12 and April 15. The route was closed again in May, between the 3rd and the 5th, and again between the 21st and the 24th. At times when a train was caught out on the causeway during a storm, with waves as high as six feet and winds blowing at 70 mph or more, it appeared that the train was actually a boat in a storm-tossed sea, with waves crashing against the locomotives and cars.

Finally in June 1986, a series of storms destroyed the causeway, and Southern Pacific began operating all of its trains over Union Pacific's former Western Pacific southern route (UP had merged WP in 1982). With the closure of the Salt Lake causeway, all SP mechanical and clerical personnel in Ogden were laid off, pending a return to normal operations. To some, it looked like the end of railroad operations across Great Salt Lake. Train crews were taxied down to Salt Lake City and westbound SP trains began departing out of D&RGW's Roper Yard there. After a frantic 78 days of reconstruction, the causeway was reopened for very limited operation on August 23. After the causeway reopened, SP continued to operate its more important trains over UP's tracks along the southern edge of the lake, running from two to four trains per day.

When natural emergencies strike, railroads have agreements for short-term use of each others' tracks for periods of 30 or fewer days, with reasonable use-rates for longer periods of less than 90 day's duration. In the case of SP trains operating over Union Pacific, the period of 30 days passed all too quickly, and the longer 90-day period was soon past also. After 90 days, UP raised the rate from $9 per train-mile to $63 per train-mile. SP objected to the higher rate and took the argument to court, saying that the rebuilt causeway could not withstand a return to its previous number of trains, and that since the emergency continued, the lower rate should prevail. With the argument unsettled, in February 1987, Union Pacific informed SP that it was terminating the detour contract. A new detour agreement was negotiated, allowing Southern Pacific to continue UP tracks. SP would continue to close the causeway whenever wind storms would cause wave action to threaten the causeway.

Throughout the remainder of 1986 and early 1987, SP continued to operate over the causeway only at night. SP was using the daylight hours to work on raising the causeway above the lake level, by operating work trains six days per week, and during these periods, Southern Pacific trains running in daylight used the UP route. During the summer of 1987, Great Salt Lake became less of a problem for both SP and UP, which had been having its own problems with the former Western Pacific route along the lake's south shore. The lake level peaked again at 4,212 feet that year. In June, Southern Pacific's trains detoured for a single day after a storm washed out short lengths of track at nine locations. By July 1987, the lake level dropped five inches lower than its previous level the summer before, due in part to three new pumps located at Lakeside, installed and paid for by the State of Utah. Subsequent years brought a still lower lake level, and an end to the contentious and costly detours.

Southern Pacific Mechanical Facilities

After the transcontinental line was completed in 1869, Central Pacific built a large yard and locomotive and car shops at Terrace, Utah, 70 miles west of Promontory and 123 miles west of Ogden. The shops at Terrace, which were designated as the main eastern shops for Central Pacific's Salt Lake Division (Sparks, Nev., to Ogden), consisted of a five-stall car and machine shop, along with a wooden framed roundhouse. The roundhouse originally had 10 60-foot stalls (as shown in an 1869 inventory of buildings on the Salt Lake Division), but is shown in a map dating from the 1880s as having 15 stalls. An 1878 photo shows a unique fully enclosed water tank adjacent to the machine shop.

A map of Ogden dated 1874 shows the first Central Pacific shop in the new junction city as a single-stall enginehouse sharing a common turntable with Union Pacific. This turntable was located on the UP side, south of the Utah Central crossing, between the Weber River and the joint passenger station. The CP enginehouse was unique in that it held a large water tank inside the structure. The existence of the large yard and mechanical facilities at Terrace, 123 miles to the west, explains these minimal facilities in Ogden. The 1874 map was prepared to show the railroads' facilities just prior to Ogden being designated as the junction city through the efforts of Brigham Young and the City of Ogden. As the city's importance grew with its status as the actual junction between the two Overland Route railroads, so too did the need for better Central Pacific engine facilities. Sometime before 1882, and before its 1885 lease to Southern Pacific, CP increased the size of its yard and built a seven-stall roundhouse and turntable adjacent to the west side of its freight yard, all of which was north of the Utah Central crossing.

As already noted, Ogden Union Railway & Depot Co. was organized in 1888 as a joint company to own and operate the Ogden terminal and yards. With the creation of OUR&D, Julius Krutschnitt, assistant manager of Southern Pacific, announced that the eastern shops of SP's Salt Lake Division would be moved from Terrace to Ogden. The Ogden Chamber of Commerce cooperated with this move by furnishing 300,000 bricks to erect the shop buildings. The roundhouse and shops were completed in late 1890.

By 1902, 10 trains per day (each with an average of 33 cars) were running on SP's line across northern Utah and through Nevada, reflecting E. H. Harriman's efforts to increase the capacity of the Overland Route

One of the more unusual steam locomotives on the Southern Pacific roster was this shop switcher assigned to the SP roundhouse in Ogden, shown here about 1938. (Emil Albrecht, James W. Watson Collection)

after his purchase of SP in 1900, and illustrating the need for the Lucin Cutoff, completed in 1904 (by 1917, the number had risen to 12 trains per day). More SP trains in Ogden meant more SP locomotives in Ogden, and those locomotives needed a better home for their maintenance. In 1906, the shops built in 1890 were replaced by a modern 33-stall brick roundhouse, with stalls that were 88 feet long. The adjacent Machine Shop (the large building that still stands today) was also completed in 1906. In 1908, a transfer table was completed immediately north of the Machine Shop, and a coal chute with six 100-ton coal pockets was added. After completion of these facilities, the local press commented that the shops were among the area's most important industries, with almost 800 employees.

In 1914 and 1915, UP and SP agreed to set up joint mechanical facilities. The Blacksmith and Tin Shop (also known as the Tin and Tank Shop) was completed in 1915, just north of the 1908-built transfer table, at the same time that the 100-foot pony truss turntable was installed. The next changes in SP's locomotive facilities were prompted by dieselization, which began with the operation of the *City of San Francisco* in 1936. Special inspection pits for the passenger power and new diesel switchers were completed in 1950. Until that time, the diesels were serviced in converted space in the Machine Shop and in the roundhouse. Four roundhouse stalls were retired in 1950 and 1951. The entire roundhouse was retired in October 1954 and torn down. Part of the transfer table pit was removed in 1957 and replaced with diesel inspection pits at the west end. An addition was built on the south side of the Machine Shop in 1954, and a drop pit was added on the east side in 1961. In a reflection of the October 1988 merger with D&RGW, and Rio Grande's now-available Roper Yard and service tracks in Salt Lake City, all of the remaining SP locomotive and car repair facilities were officially retired on December 31, 1988, in what was noted in company records as the "Big Bang."

Southern Pacific in Ogden, 1960 to 1996

The completion of the Salt Lake Causeway in 1959 was a major step for the modernization of Southern Pacific in Utah. But as with any railroad, many small improvements were completed between major projects. Small changes made by SP in Utah and Ogden helped it to move trains better and faster. Southern Pacific opened a new Centralized Traffic Control center in Roseville, Calif., and in mid-December 1963, SP announced that in February 1964 it would move the 15 train dispatchers for the Salt Lake Division from Ogden to Roseville.

Between the mid-1920s and the late-1960s, SP was involved in what has been commonly termed the Ogden Gateway case, a series of legal decisions affecting the flow of freight traffic among railroads at Ogden. (The case is covered in more detail in the Rio Grande section of this book.) After the case was settled in 1968, SP operations in Ogden became more balanced. The Gateway case, together with the almost complete dissolution of Ogden Union Railway & Depot Co. in 1968 (jointly owned with Union Pacific since 1888) led SP to interchange more trains with Denver & Rio Grande Western. The settlement of the case also led to Southern Pacific operating complete trains, including SP locomotives, south over Rio Grande tracks to D&RGW's Roper Yard in Salt Lake City. To accept the new traffic, in late 1968, Rio Grande added four new tracks along the west side of its Salt Lake City yard. But the majority of SP traffic at Ogden still came from Union Pacific.

On December 22, 1982, the merger of the Union Pacific, Western Pacific, and Missouri Pacific railroads became final, and it brought wrenching changes for rail operations in Ogden. No longer would there be a dependable number of UP trains handed over daily to Southern Pacific. Prior to the merger, UP regularly gave SP 12 (and as many as 20) trains per day. With the merger, most of those UP trains now were channeled to the former Western Pacific, SP's competitor across Nevada to northern California since its completion in 1909. Southern Pacific's only traffic was reduced to two or three trains per day from UP and two trains per day from D&RGW, plus a daily Amtrak train each way. UP's diversion of freight touched off a fierce competition from the combined services of SP and Rio Grande. UP and SP still connected at Ogden, but most eastbound SP trains ran right through

Southern Pacific's mechanical facilities grew over a period of several years. The roundhouse, just visible at the upper center of this photo taken about 1940, was completed in 1906, replacing the roundhouse at Terrace, 123 miles west of Ogden on the Promontory line. The Machine Shop, at right, was completed in 1914 when SP and UP began using the same facilities in Ogden to repair their locomotives. The Tin and Tank Shop, located between the other two large buildings, was completed in 1906. The transfer table between the Machine Shop and the Tin and Tank Shop was completed in 1908. (Emil Albrecht, James W. Watson Collection)

Southern Pacific's roundhouse was still intact in this February 1950 aerial view looking south. At top center is UP's roundhouse, and at photo center is D&RGW's small roundhouse. Close examination of the photo shows what appear to be the tenders of four Southern Pacific steam locomotives inside the SP roundhouse, along with three sets of Electro-Motive F-7 diesels, and a single set of Daylight-painted Alco passenger units. Note the extensive number of train sheds at Union Station at the far left of the photo, and the long Pacific Fruit Express ice docks at the upper center. (Union Pacific Museum Collection, Negative 55-47)

Ogden, then south over D&RGW tracks to Salt Lake City. In February 1983, SP and Rio Grande announced a joint traffic agreement, and by 1984 the cooperation was becoming successful in marketing their shorter route (by 178 miles) between Ogden and Oakland, Calif., especially after SP spent millions of dollars to improve its route across Nevada, allowing for much higher train speeds. The improvements included tens of thousands of new ties, high-quality crushed granite ballast, and miles upon miles of new continuous welded rail. The most important trains, such as the hot *CHOAT* (Chicago-Oakland Trailers) now rolled smoothly across Nevada at 70 mph.

Southern Pacific trains from the D&RGW connection in Salt Lake City began entering Ogden over UP tracks in late 1983, after portions of Rio Grande's line near Centerville and Farmington in south Davis County were flooded by the rising Great Salt Lake. The change in operations became permanent in October 1985 with the signing of a mutual trackage rights agreement, which also allowed UP trains to use Rio Grande tracks between Salt Lake City and Provo.

Merger of Southern Pacific and Rio Grande

In a defensive reaction to the 1982 merger of Union Pacific and Western Pacific, Southern Pacific and Atchison, Topeka & Santa Fe announced the next year that they would combine to form a new railroad to be called Southern Pacific Santa Fe Railway, controlled by a newly merged parent company, Santa Fe Southern Pacific Corp. (which later became Santa Fe Pacific Industries). The formal application for the merger was filed on March 23, 1984. In July 1986, the ICC turned down the proposed merger, and the subsequent appeal in June 1987, ordering the already-merged parent corporation to sell one of its railroads, with a plan to do so due within 90 days. During the interim of the merger appeal of 1986-1987, both Rio Grande and Kansas City Southern separately announced their interest in purchasing Southern Pacific if the appeal failed. After the appeal was rejected, and to satisfy the ICC's 90-day mandate, D&RGW's parent company, Rio Grande Industries, announced on September 25 its intention to purchase the Southern Pacific railroad (formal name: Southern Pacific Transportation Co.) from Santa Fe Southern Pacific Corp. All the details were worked out and the sale was made final on December 28, 1987. At the time of Rio Grande Industries' offer to buy the Southern Pacific, SP employed only 80 people in the Ogden area, compared to 2,000 during the peak of its operations in there during the years following World War II.

On August 9, 1988, the Interstate Commerce Commission approved Rio Grande Industries' purchase of the Southern Pacific Transportation Co., at a cost reported to be $1.8 billion. The agreement became effective on October 13, 1988, when Rio Grande Industries took full ownership of SP. After the merger, the SP facilities in Ogden were closed and most operations were moved to the former D&RGW's Roper Yard in Salt Lake City.

The two railroads' operating departments were combined on May 1, 1989, with the former routes being separated into three regions. Ogden was included in a new Central Region for the lines between Kansas City and California, which included all of the former Rio Grande lines and the former SP's Salt Lake and Modoc divisions. On October 9, 1989, the portion of the former Rio Grande from Ogden to Helper,

Utah, including Salt Lake City, became part of the new Salt Lake Division, a component of the Central Region. This new division, with offices in Salt Lake City, included Southern Pacific's route from Ogden west across Great Salt Lake to Carlin, Nev. This brought to a close 101 years of a Southern Pacific offices in Ogden, beginning in 1888 when the offices of the original Salt Lake Division were moved there in conjunction with the organization of Ogden Union Railway & Depot Co.

Over the next seven years after the 1988 merger, the combined Southern Pacific and Rio Grande railroads, now operating as the new Southern Pacific Lines, competed fiercely with Union Pacific for transcontinental traffic, and was successful at increasing its traffic along both the combined Rio Grande/SP Central Corridor and the former SP-only Sunset Route. In 1995 Burlington Northern, Inc. and Atchison, Topeka & Santa Fe Railway merged to form the Burlington Northern Santa Fe Railroad. In late 1995, reacting to the BNSF merger, Union Pacific and Southern Pacific announced that they would merge to protect their competitive positions. The UP/SP merger was approved and became final on September 11, 1996. ☆

It took another 2-1/2 years following the 1988 merger of SP and D&RGW for the railroad to display its new image. Southern Pacific Lines' "speed lettering" scheme, which first appeared in April 1991, combined the traditional SP gray and scarlet with D&RGW's flying Rio Grande lettering style. Between April and October 1995, SP took delivery of 279 examples of General Electric's state-of-the-art 4,400-horsepower model AC4400CW locomotives. Diesel Era collection

8. Denver & Rio Grande Western

In December 1880, Dr. William Bell, a Utah resident and friend and close business associate of General William J. Palmer, organized the Sevier Valley Railway. This was the opening round of events that brought Rio Grande to Utah. General Palmer had organized his Denver & Rio Grande Railway in 1870, and by 1872 it had reached Pueblo, Colo. In 1878, Palmer lost his battle with Santa Fe for a route south from Colorado to El Paso, Texas, and turned his sights west to Utah. His route west was along the Arkansas River through the Royal Gorge, and as any good rival would do, Santa Fe soon began building along the same route. The renowned Royal Gorge Railroad War commenced, only to be settled in late 1878 when AT&SF won by leasing the narrow-gauge Denver & Rio Grande.

In early 1880, through a series of court battles, Palmer regained control of his D&RG and commenced construction toward Utah. Within six months, the road had completed its route over Marshall Pass and was headed for Gunnison, Colo. With Utah getting closer, Palmer began looking for the best means to get there without too much trouble and expense. He decided to organize a separate company, Sevier Valley Railway, to build the line in Utah and connect with D&RG at the Colorado border. The intended route recorded for Sevier Valley Railway was to run south from Ogden to the north boundary of Arizona Territory, by way of Salt Lake City, Provo, Nephi, Salt Creek Canyon, and Salina. The new company was also to build east from Salina to the west boundary of Colorado to meet Palmer's westward-building narrow-gauge Denver & Rio Grande Railway. Nothing came of the Sevier Valley Railway due

to financial problems, but it was included in the July 1881 organization of the Denver & Rio Grande Western Railway, which Palmer incorporated to build into almost all locations in Utah that a railroad could be built. The extensive routes represented Palmer's attempt at covering all of his bases, trying to keep his rivals out of Utah. The grandiose, state-wide plans were never acted on and in June 1882, D&RGW completed its route into Salt Lake City.

The route completed ran west from the Colorado-Utah border, through eastern Utah, west up the Price River Canyon and over Soldier's Summit to a connection with the Utah & Pleasant Valley Railway, which operated between Provo and the Pleasant Valley coal mines at Winter Quarters and Scofield. The Utah & Pleasant Valley had been organized in December 1875 but didn't actually begin laying track until August 1878. The line was finished between the coal mines and Springville in late 1879, and was extended to Provo in late 1880. D&RGW purchased control of U&PV in June 1882, and used its 60 miles of tracks in Spanish Fork Canyon to extend its reach into Utah Valley and Provo. New construction between Provo and Salt Lake City was completed in June 1882.

It took another nine months, until March 1883, for a through route between Salt Lake City and Denver to be completed, when a connection was made west of Green River, Utah, between the construction crews of D&RGW (the Utah company) and those of D&RG (the Colorado company). Any distinction between the Utah company and the Colorado company was by this time trivial; on April 3, 1882, the Utah lines were officially leased to the Colorado company for the purposes of single-line operation of the two properties.

The next goal for Rio Grande was to extend its line north to Ogden, and a connection with Central Pacific. As Rio Grande's D. C. Dodge was quoted as saying, "to build to Salt Lake without going to Ogden would be half finishing the road."

Ogden's strategic and central location became apparent almost immediately after the completion of the transcontinental railroad in 1869. Throughout the 1870s and 1880s, Central Pacific and Union Pacific were almost constantly bickering over something, especially over the interchange of traffic at Ogden. As Union Pacific historian Maury Klein put it, the two were condemned "to a perpetual life as Siamese twins, joined at Ogden while struggling awkwardly to lurch off in other directions." Rail traffic in the west and along the new transcontinental line was captive to a monopoly held by UP and CP, at least until the Santa Fe completed its line from Chicago to Southern California in 1884, and Northern Pacific finished its northern route across Montana and Idaho to Pasco, Wash., in 1883. The narrow-gauge D&RGW was completed to Ogden in May 1883, giving Central Pacific an outlet to the east, shutting out its sibling Union Pacific. The completion of the UP subsidiary Oregon Short Line to the Pacific Northwest port of Portland in 1885 gave UP an outlet to the west, shutting out its sibling CP.

Union Pacific and Central Pacific shared the joint yard at Ogden, and UP was determined to prevent D&RGW, its rival for the Colorado mining traffic, from entering town. In addition to being UP's rival for the Colorado traffic, the combined D&RG/D&RGW connected at Denver with the Burlington, and at Pueblo with the Santa Fe, both of which were very interested in extending their lines west to connect with Central Pacific. Cooperation with Rio Grande would give them the connection, another plan UP wanted to thwart.

On the stormy evening of May 12, 1883, Rio Grande construction crews completed pre-assembled sections of rails and ties connected together as a portable unit, carried the track on their shoulders across the Central Pacific property line, and began laying it in the direction of the Ogden passenger depot. Their trick was soon discovered and a Union Pacific switcher and a length of heavy chain was used to dismantle the new narrow-gauge trackage. During the days following, D&RGW made arrangements with Central Pacific to lay narrow-gauge rails inside of its standard-gauge rails, and Rio Grande began operating trains into Ogden on May 17, after the bridge over the Weber River was completed. With the completion of Rio Grande tracks into Ogden, Central Pacific announced in June 1883 that it would lay a standard-gauge third rail on D&RGW's narrow-gauge route from Salt Lake City to Ogden, for the Salt Lake-bound Central Pacific traffic, but UP relented and the threat came to nothing.

D&RGW finally gained access to the Ogden passenger facilities by sharing a Central Pacific track to cross the original Utah Central line, adding a third rail inside the CP standard-gauge crossing to allow the three-foot-gauge D&RGW trains to use the same crossing. After using the three-rail crossing, D&RGW had a turnout that branched its narrow-gauge tracks away from the Central Pacific's standard-gauge tracks. This arrangement allowed D&RGW to directly serve

the joint Ogden passenger station of UP, CP, Utah Central, and Utah & Northern. D&RGW's freight trains into Ogden terminated west of Central Pacific's tracks. The railroad built its first yard on land south of its line entering Ogden, in the area between the Central Pacific tracks and the Weber River. Rio Grande gained access to CP's original roundhouse by use of a single track of 40-pound steel rail to the CP turntable, along with interchange tracks and transfer sheds adjacent to CP tracks.

Central Pacific and Rio Grande also laid joint three-rail trackage to serve the original stockyards. D&RGW soon completed a two-stall enginehouse, located just west of the CP main line. That early enginehouse was replaced in about 1885 with a four-stall brick roundhouse, torn down in about 1955, and served by an 80-foot turntable. The roundhouse was east of the Central Pacific (later SP) tracks, adjacent to D&RGW's 90-degree crossing of the Central Pacific's main line at 20th Street. That same 90-degree crossing is shown on an 1885 map, which also shows the narrow-gauge D&RGW tracks interchanging with the narrow-gauge Utah & Northern, all in the vicinity of 20th Street west of Wall Avenue. But the narrow-gauge interchange was about to change.

Ogden was at the far western end of a two-company Rio Grande system of narrow-gauge rail-roads that started in Denver. Rivalries between various factions within the two companies during the remainder of the 1880s forced both into court-appointed receiverships. They emerged in the late 1880s as better managed companies, but still narrow-gauge, very aware of the standard-gauge competition all around them. The company that ran into Ogden was reorganized from the original Denver & Rio Grande Western to the new Rio Grande Western Railway (originally proposed as the Utah & Colorado Railway), dropping the Denver part of its name to reflect its newly found independence from D&RG in Colorado, an independence that lasted another 10 years. At the eastern end of the system, D&RG connected with Santa Fe and Missouri Pacific at Pueblo, Colo., Rock Island at Colorado Springs, Colo., and Burlington at Denver. These companies were clamoring for access to the mines and other lucrative traffic of western Colorado and Utah, along with a connection with Central Pacific at Ogden, and they had their own surveying parties climbing all over western Colorado showing just how serious their interests and intents were. To keep

these invaders out of what they jealously considered to be their own territory, the two Rio Grande lines needed to convert to standard-gauge. It was not a question of if, but a question of when. If they didn't, their competitors would surely make good on their intents and build their own routes into the Salt Lake region.

The Salt Lake City-to-Ogden line of the Rio Grande Western Railway, as the July 1889 successor to D&RGW, was changed to standard-gauge on March 6, 1890. On June 10, 1890, RGW completed conversion of its tracks between Ogden and Grand Junction, Colo., from narrow-gauge to standard-gauge. In Colorado, D&RG did not complete its newly constructed standard-gauge connection, via Tennessee Pass and Glenwood Springs, until mid November 1890, by-passing the original narrow-gauge route to the south. On November 17, 1890, the first standard-gauge through train from Denver entered Salt Lake City.

In Ogden, the narrow-gauge tracks of UP subsidiary Oregon Short Line & Utah Northern were changed to standard-gauge in October 1890, seven months after RGW made the change in March. Just a year before, the new union depot of Ogden Union Railway & Depot Co. had been completed. Rio Grande made peace with Union Pacific, and signed an agreement with OUR&D that gave it direct access to the new Ogden depot. The changes for OUR&D are shown on a map dated 1890, and included access to Ogden's new union passenger depot for Rio Grande passenger trains by a new "RGW Connection" that crossed the Central Pacific main line between 20th and 21st streets. This connected with Central Pacific's own passenger line, and was in addition to the Rio Grande freight 90-degree crossing already in place. Later, Rio Grande constructed a new yard west of the 90-degree crossing, giving Rio Grande a freight yard both east and west of its crossing of Central Pacific's main line, by this time leased to Southern Pacific. Even though the east yard remained in place into the late 1960s, less and less direct D&RGW traffic was moving to and from businesses in Ogden, and the West Yard grew in importance due to increased interchange with Southern Pacific.

Union Pacific's resistance to Rio Grande's entering Ogden was only temporary. After Central Pacific allowed D&RGW to use its tracks to reach the passenger depot, UP must have resigned itself to the fact that Rio Grande was there to stay. In May 1892, Rio Grande signed an agreement for the use and partial lease "of the railroad, tracks, switches, passenger depot building, offices and all passenger terminal facilities" of the Ogden Union Railway & Depot Co. The lease also allowed Rio Grande to maintain a passenger agent and baggage-handling facilities at the depot. At the time, Union Pacific, Southern Pacific, and Oregon Short Line & Utah Northern also shared equal use of the depot and its facilities. The lease ran for a four-year period, and Rio Grande paid $18,000 annual rent. The lease was never renewed, but Rio Grande continued to pay the same annual rent, and was allowed continued use of the depot.

The death of Collis P. Huntington in August 1900 changed railroading in Ogden for the next 70 years. Huntington's death put his controlling shares of Southern Pacific, and its leased Central Pacific line, onto the market, where E. H. Harriman almost immediately snapped them up, thereby controlling

both UP and SP, effectively shutting out the Rio Grande in Ogden. [In 1908 RGW was absorbed by D&RG, along with several other companies, and in 1921, D&RG was reorganized as the Denver & Rio Grande Western Railroad.] UP and SP met and exchanged trains at Ogden, making it difficult for Rio Grande to solicit traffic to and from the West. Harriman's consolidation of his two railroads, and Rio Grande's difficulty in winning through traffic at Ogden, was the opening round of what became known as the "Ogden Gateway" case, a series of court decisions, and rulings by the Interstate Commerce Commission that dragged out for 45 years, from 1923 to 1968.

The Ogden Gateway case involved all three railroads. It dealt with the relationship between Union Pacific and Southern Pacific, how they treated each other, and how they in turn treated Rio Grande. Under Harriman's influence, there was no return to the early years, when D&RGW (and later the RGW), was regularly being either favored or ignored, depending on relations between Union Pacific and Central Pacific/Southern Pacific at the time, although most traffic to and from the east still went over UP. If the bickering became serious, Union Pacific had the advantage of diverting West Coast traffic to the Northwest, and SP had its connection with Rio Grande. By the turn of the century, D&RG in Colorado and RGW in Utah were both controlled by George Gould, who was building his own railroad empire that included the two Rio Grandes and their Missouri Pacific connection at Pueblo. Harriman's control of the SP, and the need for a dependable connection for the Rio Grande to the West Coast were the major reasons Gould built the Western Pacific Railway west from Salt Lake City, started in 1906 (with D&RG backing) and completed in 1909.

The Ogden Gateway case began in 1923 when the ICC was deciding whether SP had the right to control the Central Pacific. In its decision, ICC stated that the Ogden Gateway was exclusively for interchange between UP and SP, and with this support from the federal government, traffic agreements were made between the two companies that continued to shut D&RGW out of sharing in cross-country rail traffic. In one round of the Ogden Gateway case, D&RGW in August 1949 filed a complaint with the ICC for full joint rates for all east- and westbound traffic at Ogden. In January 1952, the ICC issued an order that only partially opened the gateway, and then for only 10 commodities, still shutting D&RGW out of the lucrative Pacific Northwest traffic. The 1952 decision allowed UP to solicit traffic for SP from as far east as Oklahoma and Pittsburgh, and permitted SP to solicit traffic for UP throughout California. In response to the January 1952 order, D&RGW in October 1953 filed a suit in U. S. District Court in Denver calling the ICC ruling "unlawful, arbitrary, and capricious." The suit was expected to reach the Supreme Court for a final decision. In January 1955 the District Court returned the entire case to the ICC for re-hearing, putting the question back into the hands of the ICC, where it had begun six years before.

The issue of freight traffic routing continued to be openly debated both in the courts and at hearings of the Interstate Commerce Commission. By the mid-1960s, both Union Pacific and Southern Pacific could see that the interchange at Ogden by way of the jointly owned Ogden Union Railway & Depot Co. had outlived its usefulness. Traffic on the Overland Route had declined significantly, especially the seasonal trains of perishable goods. This, and changes in the Utah tax code led to a severe reduction in OUR&D operations. The ICC held hearings in the mid-1960s to consider curtailment of OUR&D operations, and in October 1967 the ICC gave its blessing. Soon after, D&RGW and SP began direct interchange without OUR&D switching, and the Ogden Gateway case was closed.

Throughout the years of court battles, Rio Grande continued to keep its Salt Lake City-to-Ogden line well maintained and up to date. During the late 1940s and early 1950s, Rio Grande kept one its small General Electric 44-ton center-cab switchers in Ogden to switch the local industries. D&RGW's yard office at Ogden was replaced by a $40,000 building in September 1951, at a location known as Transfer, where D&RGW trains were handed over to Southern Pacific. The new building replaced an old boxcar that had been serving as an office for many years. The 13 office employees who had been working in the old boxcar now had a modern, air-conditioned office. It also included radio communications via loudspeakers located in the yard. Floodlights had been installed a year earlier. In February 1953, D&RGW announced that as part of a $20 million improvement program, it would spend $88,000 to improve the interchange facilities with Southern Pacific. In August 1953, D&RGW purchased 35 acres between its present Ogden yards and the Ogden River for future industrial development.

In anticipation of settlement of the Ogden Gateway case, during late 1960 D&RGW began a $2 million expansion and upgrading of its line between Salt Lake City and Ogden. Most of the improvements were along the line itself, including heavier rail and better ballast, along with extension of the Woods Cross and Clearfield passing tracks. The improvement project also included a new 109-foot bridge across the Weber River at the west end of the Ogden yards, and 21,000 feet of additional tracks in the Ogden yard.

During the late 1960s, America's railroads went through numerous corporate changes. Most of the major lines were sold to newly organized corporate holding companies that carried with them many attractive tax advantages, and which were not subject to regulation by the ICC. In early 1969, Union Pacific Corp. began operating the Union Pacific Railroad as a corporate subsidiary. Likewise, Denver & Rio Grande Western Railroad in 1969 came under the corporate control of Rio Grande Industries, a holding company organized for that purpose in 1968. Competition with Union Pacific to the north, and Santa Fe to the south, proved at times to be a formidable challenge for the small independent road. Even with the settlement of the Ogden Gateway case, the continued cooperation of SP and UP made competition difficult. Changes were many, both good and bad, and at times to the railroad's employees it seemed that the railroad was of but minor interest to the parent company. The last shoe dropped in late 1982 with the merger of the Union Pacific and Western Pacific railroads. Revenues continued to fall and in late 1983, Rio Grande Industries began selling off its non-railroad interests, including Rio Grande Motorways. The railroad was also for sale. On October 29, 1984, Rio Grande Industries, and

its D&RGW railroad subsidiary, was sold to Anschutz Corp., a Denver-based oil and land development company. The sale did not affect the daily operations, other than to give employees a morale boost, and to provide a stable future.

With the waters of the Great Salt Lake slowly rising during 1983 and 1984, D&RGW began temporarily detouring its trains over Union Pacific's paralleling, double-track line between Salt Lake City and Ogden. An agreement was reached on October 22, 1985 that gave D&RGW (and run-through Southern Pacific trains) long-term access to Union Pacific's high-speed line in return for Union Pacific gaining access to D&RGW's nearly level and easier route between Salt Lake City and Provo. When D&RGW quit using its Salt Lake to Ogden line, the signals and grade crossing protection were removed to save maintenance costs. Many local cities assumed that the tracks were abandoned and paved over many grade crossings. In addition, several local real estate agents and subdivision developers continued spreading the abandonment myth to persuade prospective home buyers to locate near the "abandoned" tracks. In mid-December 1991, Southern Pacific, as successor to D&RGW, reminded local residents through the media of newspapers and television that the tracks were only inactive, not abandoned, and that trains could begin operating along the route should rail business increase to a level that would exceed the capacity of the UP line to handle all of the Union Pacific traffic along with the Southern Pacific/D&RGW traffic.

After the attempt to merge the Santa Fe and Southern Pacific railroads failed in its final appeal in June 1987, the Interstate Commerce Commission ordered that the already merged parent corporation sell one of its two railroads. On September 25, 1987, Rio Grande Industries and Santa Fe Southern Pacific Corp. announced that Rio Grande Industries would

During the 1980s, D&RGW operated a daily freight between Salt Lake City and Ogden, in addition to the occasional SP trains that traveled directly through Ogden to Rio Grande's Roper yard in Salt Lake City. At other times, SP would interchange complete trains with Rio Grande at Ogden. On this cold March day in 1982, two D&RGW GP30s and a single GP40 cross over the Rio Grande double track at the far west end of its Ogden yard to couple onto a Salt Lake-bound train that has just arrived off the SP. (D. B. Harrop)

Standard motive power for Southern Pacific's trains into Ogden during the 1970s and early 1980s was GM-EMD model SD45s, with their 3,600-horsepower, 20-cylinder diesel engines. Here, three of these haulers prepare to head west with a train of regular carload freight. In the foreground is Rio Grande's 90-degree crossing of SP's yard lead tracks at 21st Street. The crossing was in place as early as 1885, after the standard-gauge Central Pacific agreed to allow the narrow-gauge D&RGW to cross its tracks and establish its own freight yard closer to Ogden's business district. To the left in this view is Rio Grande's main (but still small) Ogden yard. To the right is Transfer and the newer west yard, established in the mid-1950s to support increased interchange with SP. The 90-degree crossing was removed about 1970. (Emil Albrecht, James W. Watson Collection)

purchase the SP and merge its existing railroad, the D&RGW, into it. The ICC approved the sale on August 9, 1988, with the actual merger taking place on October 13, 1988.

By the time of the merger, D&RGW's facilities in Ogden consisted mostly of interchange tracks with Southern Pacific. Over the previous years since the settlement of the Ogden Gateway case, the two companies had been cooperating more and more. The 90-degree crossing of the SP main line and yard tracks at 20th Street was removed in about 1969. In 1970, SP and Rio Grande had begun to interchange complete trains through Ogden, with SP crews and locomotives going through to Salt Lake City. The mid-1980s saw more Southern Pacific trains by-passing SP's own yard at Ogden, destined for direct interchange with Rio Grande at Salt Lake City. With these changes already in place, the 1988 merger had little effect on their operations. Because trains were using UP tracks, the former interchange track at Transfer was shut down and many tracks in the West Yard were removed as D&RGW's presence was cut back even more. In early 1992, a local switching road called Utah Central, began operations serving grain storage facilities situated in Rio Grande's former West Yard, along with other industries located along the inactive Rio Grande main line into Ogden. Today there is little trace, except to the trained eye, of the operations Rio Grande once had in Ogden. ✪

9. Ogden's Rail-served Industries

With the development of the large railroad terminal in Ogden in the mid- and late-1870s, business and industry soon took advantage of the availability of cheaper rail transportation. Other than the mining industry, one of the first major industries served by railroads in Utah was the shipment of salt from the shores of Great Salt Lake. In addition to being used by farmers and ranchers throughout the region, salt was needed in the silver reduction mills of Montana, and increasingly in Utah, as flux for their ores. Among the earliest salt plants, in 1880, was George Payne's, located in Syracuse, named for the salt-industry center of the same name in New York state. The shipment of salt started with the use of wagons to haul dry salt from the lake shore to the new Utah Central line completed between Ogden and Salt Lake City in 1870. The salt traffic soon grew to such proportions, about 20,000 tons per year (90,000 tons for the entire eastern shore by 1891), that Union Pacific began thinking of building a branch directly to the salt plants on the lake shore. In February 1887 the Ogden & Syracuse Railway was organized to build that branch line, although actual construction had already begun in January. This line was completed between Syracuse Junction (the name was later changed to Clearfield) and Syracuse, almost six miles to the west, on the lake shore. However, the combined effects of the silver collapse of 1893 (with a resulting decrease in silver mill market) and a low cycle of natural changes in lake level caused a cutback in salt production. Traffic on the branch soon depended almost solely on visitors to the Lake Shore resort, built adjacent to the salt works. The Ogden & Syracuse Railway was one of the companies that merged to form the Oregon Short Line & Utah Northern in July 1889, and the line became the OSL&UN's (and later OSL's) Syracuse Branch. It remained in operation until the salt works failed completely and the receding lake shore brought about the closing of the resort. The branch remained intact until March 1906 when it was shortened by about one mile. The rest of the Syracuse Branch stayed in service, mostly for sugar beet service, until August 1955, when it was cut back to its present three mile length, ending in east Syracuse at the C. H. Dredge warehouse on 2000 West.

Other early industries served by Ogden-area railroads included agricultural products for sale outside of the immediate vicinity. One of the first was the export

The original Pacific Fruit Express ice plant was built by Union Pacific in 1889. It was expanded in 1897 to its final, four-storage-galleries version. All ice used by this facility was shipped from natural ice ponds at Evanston, Wyo., and Carlin, Nev. The entire facility was destroyed by fire in August 1919. This design was very similar to those built by Union Pacific at both Evanston and Laramie, Wyo. (Pacific Fruit Express, California State Railroad Museum Collection)

of eggs from Cache Valley by Adams & Vandyke, an Ogden freighting firm. From 1869 to 1871, many shipments of eggs, along with butter, went to the mining and railroad towns in Nevada, and further west to San Francisco. At the same time, Adams & Vandyke encouraged local farmers to grow crops for cash sale. The most successful of these was potatoes, with "car-loads upon car-loads" being sent to Colorado and California, starting a demand for Utah potatoes and a "potato boom" that lasted from the 1870s until at least the late 1880s.

Wheat was also an early Utah commodity that was shipped by rail. In 1879, the ship "Ivy" sailed from San Francisco bound for Europe with 66,000 bushels (1,905 tons, or about 63 30-ton carloads) of Utah wheat. The grain had been gathered at Ogden by Zions Co-operative Mercantile Institute and sent to San Francisco by rail over the Central Pacific. Carload shipments of Utah peaches, plums, and pears also made their way by rail to markets in California. Beginning in 1881, H. L. Griffin began shipping fruits and produce from Utah to markets throughout the West, and sent many shipments of potatoes to Illinois, Ohio, Tennessee, and Texas. In 1887 alone, he shipped 165 carloads, along with 85,000 dozen eggs. David Kay acted as broker for more than 800 carloads of grain, dried fruit, seeds, and potatoes to almost every state, from California in the west to New York in the east.

Ogden Union Stock Yards and the meat packing industry

The railroad stock car was developed as one of the first special-design freight cars, to handle live cattle from the open ranges of the West to the markets of the East and Midwest. The much-romanticized cowboys and cattle drives of the 1860s to 1880s that brought Texas beef to the railheads at Dodge City and Wichita, Kansas, became possible only with the availability of the stock car. Ogden, too, was a shipment point for livestock. Maps from 1874 show a large "horse corral" and large stockyards served by Central Pacific. By 1889, large stockyards and horse corrals were located on Central Pacific land between the CP tracks and the Weber River. These stockyards were jointly served by both standard-gauge roads, Union Pacific and CP, as well as by the narrow-gauge D&RGW (and later

standard-gauge Rio Grande Western). In May 1898, both Rio Grande Western and Oregon Short Line signed an agreement with UP that allowed the two companies access to the "Stockyard or Stock Corral." The annual fee was set at $350 for each company.

As the livestock industry in Utah continued to grow, so, too, did the livestock handling facilities, culminating in the giant Ogden Union Stock Yards, completed in 1917. A year previously, as shown on a map dating from 1916, the need for a new location was evident by the extensive stockyards crowded in between the SP yards, the old Utah Central main line, and the 1897-built UP roundhouse. In addition to handling beef cattle, Ogden soon developed into the sheep center of the West, and later became the home for the largest lamb slaughtering industry in the nation. The location on West 24th Street near the Weber River of the Ogden Packing & Provisioning Co.'s slaughterhouse (later the American Packing & Provisioning Co., then Swift & Co.) was dependent on the adjacent stockyards.

A need for better transportation facilities became more apparent as the nation's livestock and meat industry continued to grow. Federal law, in effect since 1905, requires that livestock be fed and watered at least every 36 hours while in transit. Because of its inter-change location between Southern Pacific and Union Pacific, Ogden was an ideal location for a much-expanded and improved stock handling facility to fulfill this requirement. The need for expansion made it obvious that the stockyards could not remain at their pre-1917 site east of the Weber River, among the railroads' mechanical repair buildings. A new site was selected across the Weber River and operations of the new Ogden Union Stock Yards began on April 1, 1917. Ogden Union Railway & Depot built a spur that crossed the river north of the Ogden Packing & Provisioning plant. Growth was steady, and by 1929, Ogden was the largest livestock market west of Denver. The daily number of cars was said to be 250 carloads of cattle, 200 carloads of sheep, and 100 carloads of hogs.

To promote this industry and the city's growing stature in that field with the completion of the stockyards, the Ogden Livestock Show was organized in 1918 as a new auctioning center for the region's ranchers, growers, and livestock brokers. A specialized auction facility, known as the Golden Spike Coliseum, was completed in 1923, and the Ogden Livestock Show was re-named the Golden Spike National Livestock Show. An office building located at the stockyards, known as the Exchange Building, was completed in 1930 as a central location for transacting livestock business.

The Ogden Union Stock Yards and the Swift & Co. plant, and to some degree the operations of Wilson & Co. on Wilson Lane, were the focus of the area's livestock industry. The Swift plant was first operated by the Ogden Packing & Provisioning Co., which was a February 1906 outgrowth of the Ogden Packing Co., itself organized in 1901. The Ogden Packing & Provisioning Co. became the American Packing & Provisioning Co. ("Mountain Brand Products") in July 1924, at which time it purchased control of the Ogden Union Stock Yards Co.. The packing company and the stockyards remained under common control until a federal court decision in 1935 prohibited any packing house in

"Stockyards Caballeros." Ogden Union Stock Yards was switched by the crews of the Ogden Union Railway & Depot Co., using locomotives leased from UP and SP. Here, in 1941, the crew of the stockyards switcher, Cleve "Smitty" Smith and Lawrence "Mitch" Mitchell mug for the photographer, while their foreman, Charley Nate, looks on. The photographer, Ken Knowles, was secretary-treasurer of the stockyards company until its closure in 1971. (Kenneth R. Knowles, Mrs. Doris Knowles Collection)

the nation from owning or having interest in any stock yard. In January 1936, the stockyards were sold to the Denver Union Stock Yards Co., which remained in control until they were closed in January 1971. American Packing & Provisioning Co. was sold to Swift & Co. on July 24, 1949. Swift & Co. maintained a large lamb processing facility at Ogden that shipped whole lamb carcasses, hung in specially equipped Pacific Fruit Express iced refrigerator cars to the primary lamb markets in New York and Philadelphia. After completing a new facility in Sacramento, Calif., Swift & Co. closed its Ogden plant on November 13, 1970.

When the word livestock is used, many will think of cattle. At the Ogden stockyards, livestock meant sheep. The total numbers of sheep that passed through Ogden was always at least three times the numbers for cattle, and in some years it was four times. The peak year for numbers of animals was 1945, with almost 1.8 million head of sheep, 300,000 head of cattle, and 350,000 hogs. The year 1945 was also the peak year for livestock-related rail traffic, with 20,000 cars of sheep, 19,000 cars of cattle, and 6,000 cars of hogs being either unloaded at Ogden, or loaded after sale, or re-loaded after the prescribed four-hour rest period. Sheep and the processing of lamb and mutton was the reason Swift & Co. purchased the American Packing & Provisioning Co.'s plant in Ogden in 1949. The Swift plant in Ogden furnished almost all of that company's

Thousands of stock cars were loaded and unloaded every year at Ogden Union Stock Yards, which were a significant source of traffic for the city's three major railroads. Most of the traffic consisted of the shipment of sheep, as shown here by this string of all-wooden stock cars being loaded at the stockyards' Sheep Division. (Mrs. Doris Knowles Collection)

Ogden Union Stock Yards was a landmark industry in West Ogden from its construction in 1917 to its closure in 1971, and its gradual removal throughout the 1980s. The original stockyards are shown here during the 1940s. At lower left is the Sheep Division, completed in 1934. At lower center is the Horse Division, and at upper center is the Golden Spike Coliseum, home of the annual Golden Spike Livestock Show. The Exchange Building stands by itself near the Horse Division. At top, just left of center, is the large packing plant of Swift & Co., the largest sheep and lamb processing plant in the nation. (Utah State Historical Society)

Ogden Union Stock Yards handled an average of three times as many sheep as cattle. An entire Sheep Division was completed in 1934 to allow separate handling of the booming sheep business. In this 1939 photo, stockyard workers are shown "counting off" a full trainload of Idaho lambs.
(Mrs. Doris Knowles Collection)

lamb and mutton meat for Eastern markets.

In addition to Swift & Co., other firms served the meat packing industry. These included Wilson Packing Co. and Ogden Dressed Meat Co. Wilson Packing (later, Wilson & Co.) was located at about 900 West on 21st Street, and was sold to W. C. Parke & Sons in about 1943. Parke & Sons closed its operation in 1970. Other livestock-associated companies large enough to warrant railroad service included the Western Livestock Feed yard on Wilson Lane, and Utah By-Products Co., which was first located at the stockyards and later in the former Utah Canning Co.'s building on 29th Street.

The Ogden union stockyards were served almost solely by Union Pacific from the east side. A limited service was provided by D&RGW from the west side. At first, UP (actually OUR&D) served the stockyards over a single track bridge that crossed the Weber River. In December 1930, a second lead was added and the river bridge was widened to two tracks.

D&RGW's 1951 Traffic Guide shows Ogden Union Stock Yards as having 356 pens for all livestock, and 214 low pens for hogs only. The yards had 19 loading chutes for single-deck cars and 14 loading chutes for either single-deck or double-deck cars. (Because of their shorter height, sheep and hogs were usually shipped in double-deck railroad cars.) In comparison, facilities at Denver were roughly three times the size of those at Ogden, with 1,000 pens and 79 loading chutes. On D&RGW, only Denver was larger than Ogden in livestock handling capacity.

The peak year for the Ogden Union Stock Yards was 1949, with revenue of $87 million. The peak years for sheep sales were between 1936 and 1944. In the late 1940s and early 1950s, the meat packers began buying directly from the growers, reducing the participation of the stockyards and livestock brokers (the middlemen). The availability of good roads and bigger trucks made it possible to use trucks to ship livestock direct from growers (and the then-new feed lots), to packing houses, cutting the railroads out of the rapidly changing meat-packing industry. To cut transportation costs even more, packing houses were soon moved near the feed lots, replacing large plants in urban areas with smaller and more numerous packing plants in rural areas, redesigned to be more efficient. By 1960, all of the large meat packing plants in Chicago were closed. The largest stock-handling facility in the world, the Chicago Union Stock Yards, closed in 1970 due to lack of business. The combination of direct sales and trucks soon significantly cut the numbers of animals moving through the Ogden stockyards. While the ratios between sheep, cattle and hogs stayed the same, the volume changed from the 1945 peak of 2.4 million head to 594,000 head in 1960, to just 168,000 (a more than 90 percent reduction from 1945) in 1970, the stockyards' final full year.

Throughout their entire history, livestock sales at Ogden Union Stock Yards were conducted both by public auction and by what was called "private treaty," or closed-commission sales. Changes affecting the meat-packing industry nationwide also affected Ogden. The auction activity slowly declined in the decade prior to the late 1960s, and closed-commission sales ended at Ogden in December 1967. The stockyards closed on January 31, 1971. Within a year, the stockyards and all adjacent property, including the Coliseum and Exchange buildings, were sold to Weber County by the parent company, Denver Union Stock Yards. On January 4, 1972, a new company, the Weber Livestock Auction Co., began auction sales on a much smaller scale at the Ogden stockyards, leasing the facilities from Weber County. The sale of sheep remained for another couple years, with Southern Pacific moving its last carloads of sheep in April 1973.

Pacific Fruit Express

Soon after the completion of the transcontinental rail line through Ogden, the route became the home of the first shipment of perishable goods (fruits and vegetables) from California growers to markets in the East. At first, shipments were sent in ventilated boxcars, called "fruit cars," some of which are visible in the early photos of Promontory. The first shipment, said to be a load of grapes and pears, went east in November 1869. By the mid-1870s, annual shipments of fruit had grown to at least 115 carloads from California alone. By 1895, the car fleets of both Union Pacific and Central Pacific/Southern Pacific included as many as 1,800 cars dedicated to the shipment of perishables. In the previous decade, the two companies had organized the California Fast Freight Line, specifically to move California fruits.

By the mid-1890s, several private car lines and shippers owned and operated fleets of specialized cars, the largest of which was the Armour Packing Co. The total fleet of refrigerator cars was just over 1,000 in 1880 and more than 6,000 in 1885. Within 15 years, by the turn of the century, the fleet grew to more than 68,000 cars, 20,000 of which belonged to Armour alone, giving the company control of a third of the private refrigerator cars in the country. Much of this traffic moved via the Overland Route, through Ogden.

Armour and the other companies (including Swift & Co., Cudahy, and Schwarzchild & Sulzberger, which later became Wilson & Co.) had started with the shipments of dressed meat from their various packing houses. Their shipments soon included fruits and other perishables. Along with the meat packers, private companies that shipped perishables, likely through Ogden, included Continental Fruit Express, Goodell Line, Kansas City Fruit Express, California Fruit Express, and Fruit Dealers Dispatch. The shipments over the private car lines exceeded those in the railroads' own cars.

To better preserve the perishables, ice was added to keep the shipments cool, thus giving birth to iced refrigerator cars. The first really successful refrigerator car was the Tiffany car of the late 1860s, which used ice in separate boxes stacked on the boxes of the perishable load. The first recorded shipment of California strawberries to New York was in an iced Tiffany car in 1888, although it is not known if the shipment was through Ogden on the Overland Route, or by way of Southern Pacific's just-completed Sunset Route. Later, the ice was placed in special compartments (bunkers) suspended from the car roof, or at the end of the car.

To furnish ice for these refrigerator cars, large supplies of natural ice were needed. Ice was harvested during winter and stored in heavily insulated (with sawdust) icehouses located along the routes that the cars took. The major refrigerator car shipper through Ogden was the Armour Co., which handled perishable traffic under contract for both Union Pacific and Central Pacific. Wintertime harvesting and storage of ice for summer use was not new, but what the car companies needed was a reliable and consistent supply of it. This became doubly important when Union Pacific and Southern Pacific formed the jointly owned Pacific Fruit Express Co. in 1906. During its first year,

PFE continued to use the facilities that had been used by the Armour Co., including facilities at Donner Lake, Calif., Carlin, Nev., and Evanston, Wyo. In 1907, PFE purchased the Armour facilities and began a program to increase its natural, and later, manufactured, ice capability. The extensive ice ponds, and harvesting and storage facilities at Evanston, built by UP in 1887, were a focus of PFE operations in the region. With the formation of PFE in 1906, the UP icehouse in Ogden (completed in 1889, and matching the one just completed at Evanston) was leased to the new jointly owned company. The Ogden plant's icehouse had a storage capacity of 35,000 tons, enough to supply approximately 7,000 railroad refrigerator cars, each of which

After fire destroyed the four original ice houses in 1919, Pacific Fruit Express replaced them in 1921 with this all-concrete Ice Manufacturing Plant. It had a production capacity of 375 tons per day, and a storage capacity of 14,600 tons, enough to completely re-ice more than 2,900 refrigerator cars, at five tons each. (Pacific Fruit Express, California State Railroad Museum Collection)

Shown here are the three ice docks of Pacific Fruit Express. The ice dock along the right side of the photo, shown without a roof, was used mainly for perishable traffic originating at Ogden, and was served by a stub-end track. In the distance are the Albers Brothers Milling Co. mill and the Sperry Flour Co.'s mill, both major rail customers. (Pacific Fruit Express, California State Railroad Museum Collection)

used about five tons of ice when fully re-iced. The Evanston natural ice plant was closed in 1921 after PFE completed a new ice manufacturing plant at Ogden.

But Ogden was already important to Pacific Fruit Express operations in 1906 because it was the interchange point between SP and UP, thus requiring re-icing of cars. The original icehouse at Ogden was what PFE called an Ice Transfer Plant, a facility that received its ice from the natural ice plants at both Evanston and Carlin, storing it for use year-round. Maps of Ogden yard dated 1904 show both an original icehouse and a newer icehouse, built in 1889. The original icehouse measured 32 feet by 140 feet, located perpendicular to a seven-foot by 120-foot car icing platform, all situated at about 27th Street, west of the yard tracks. The newer facility, measuring 98 feet by 200 feet, was located between the original Union Pacific roundhouse and the OUR&D yard tracks, at about 26th Street. Facilities almost identical to those completed by UP at Ogden in 1889 were also built by UP at the turn of the century at both Laramie, Wyo., and Grand Island, Neb. By 1916, the larger storage house had been moved to the original site and had doubled in size. The UP icehouse at Ogden was made up of four attached but separate buildings, all of which stored ice. Insulation to keep the ice solid year-round came from double walls with sawdust between. On August 5, 1919, all four PFE icehouses were destroyed by fire. A replacement was not completed until 1921, at the same site on 26th Street, but with re-arranged trackage to allow easier access for through trains. The former-PFE building that stands today was constructed by PFE in 1921 as an Ice Manufacturing Plant. Built entirely of concrete, it had a daily capacity of 375 tons of ice, later increased to 500 tons. By this time, refrigeration technology was advanced enough to allow ice to be manufactured, rather than harvested, thus increasing the capability of PFE's iced refrigerator car fleet and the "protective services" that the company marketed.

In addition to the new ice manufacturing plant, Pacific Fruit Express in 1921 also built a single island-type icing platform, which forced the demolition of the nearby 1897-built UP roundhouse. The new platform was 2,000 feet long with two adjacent service tracks, and could service 46 cars along each side. In 1927 a second, 70-car island-type platform was added, and the original 46-car platform was extended to 66-car capacity. Both platforms were of PFE's standard covered-island design.

The 1927 changes allowed longer Southern Pacific trains to directly enter the icing platform tracks from the north for re-icing, without having to break the trains in two. This was possible because of the extension, completed in July 1927, of the 24th Street viaduct directly west to the high ground of West Ogden. Before this, the viaduct (completed in 1904) had ended about a block east of the Weber River and automobiles crossed the river via a bridge adjacent to the railroad bridge for UP's Evona Branch. The road crossing for 24th Street at the base of the old viaduct made earlier extension of the icing platforms impossible. Sometime after 1928, an adjacent, uncovered 15-car dock was added, served by stub-ended double tracks for the initial icing of shipments of fruits and vegetables originating in Ogden. The platforms for through trains gave a combined capacity for re-icing up to 272 cars at any one time. PFE continued to expand its facilities in Ogden, and by 1929, the ice plant had a capacity of 400 tons of ice daily. During that year, 82,302 refrigerator cars were iced at Ogden.

In 1954 the icing plant was upgraded and became the most modern ice manufacturing plant on the PFE

In 1954, Pacific Fruit Express completed its Riverdale Ice Manufacturing Plant. This new 700-ton facility was built along with other expansion features in East Yard, located between 33rd Street and 50th Street. It was located at the south (railroad east) end of the newly expanded yard, and included a new double-track, 110-car ice dock with mechanical icing machines.
(Pacific Fruit Express, California State Railroad Museum Collection)

system. A new ice manufacturing plant and 110-car icing platform were constructed in Riverdale Yard and in August 1954, PFE added the ability for automatic icing with the installation of three Preco-brand mechanical icing machines, also at Riverdale. Prior to 1954, the PFE tracks in Riverdale Yard had been used only for cleaning and storage of westbound (empty) cars. The new plant was capable of producing 700 tons of ice per day, in the form of 4,750 cakes of ice, each measuring about 11 inches by 22 inches by 42 inches. A bridge conveyor took these ice cakes overhead to the new mile-long ice platform, built to re-ice two 110-car trains at the same time, giving PFE the capacity to service 352 cars at a time. With the completion of this platform, the original 70-car platform in the old main yard was retired, leaving only the remaining original 66-car platform in place. This 1954 expansion gave PFE two separate facilities at Ogden: the original 66-car platform and 1921-built, 500-ton ice manufacturing plant in the main yard (at 26th Street); and the new 700-ton ice manufacturing plant and 110-car mechanized icing platform at Riverdale. A 1992 comprehensive history of Pacific Fruit Express shows that in 1943, both original platforms in the Ogden main yard were extended by 33 car-lengths to accommodate trains lengths of 100 cars. This information may have been gleaned from a proposal retained as part of PFE records, as there is no other evidence of this expansion. This proposal may have been associated with the expansion of OUR&D's Ogden yard, which included the construction of the new Riverdale East Yard in 1942.

The 1954 expansion of icing facilities reflected the booming nature of PFE's traffic. Perishable traffic through Ogden originated on SP, from throughout Oregon and from a myriad of sources in California, north of Santa Margarita in accordance with the 1923 agreement that assured traffic over the Overland Route through Ogden. All of SP's perishable traffic from points in the Central Valley north of Bakersfield, and from the Salinas Valley north of Santa Margarita moved east by way of Ogden. The perishable traffic during World War II for PFE alone was in the range of 350,000 cars per year. During the harvest season in California and Oregon, solid trains of PFE refrigerator cars moved east through Ogden, averaging 700 to 800 cars a day. PFE's peak years for carloadings, with almost 500,000 cars loaded per year, were between 1950 and 1953, with only slightly less, but still more than 400,000 cars per year, throughout the mid-1950s. A steady decline in carloadings throughout the 1960s was a reflection of both the development of larger mechanical refrigerator cars and increasing competition from refrigerated highway trucks.

In mid-1953, Pacific Fruit Express placed its first mechanical (non-iced) refrigerator car into service, part of a group of 25 cars built that year. The fleet grew rapidly through the remainder of the decade, and in 1960, the company owned more than 2,700 mechanical cars, comprising nine percent of PFE's 28,600-car fleet. By 1970, the quantity of mechanical cars had grown to more than 12,400 cars, 68 percent of a fleet of 18,200 cars. The last season for iced refrigerator cars through Ogden was in 1972, and the last iced car on all of PFE was operated in September 1973, when PFE eliminated all icing facilities.

The new Pacific Fruit Express ice dock at Riverdale stretched almost the entire length of the yard. Shown here along the left center of this photo in September 1954, the ice dock was just recently completed. Also visible at right center is the new Union Pacific car repair track at Riverdale. (Union Pacific Museum Collection, Negative 37492)

Competition from refrigerated highway trucks began in the early 1950s, at the same time that mechanical refrigeration was first used by the railroads. By the late 1960s only a third of the perishable produce was moving by rail, and by 1979, the railroads' share fell to only 10 percent of all produce traffic. As mechanical refrigerator cars continued to replace iced refrigerator cars, the need for extensive icing facilities diminished, until the early 1970s, when they stood unused. The icing platforms at the original location were retired during the early 1960s, and the platforms in Ogden at Riverdale remained until the early 1970s. During the summer of 1974, the Riverdale icing platforms were removed as a potential fire hazard, at about the same time as the icing platforms in Roseville, California (also on the Overland Route), which were demolished in March 1974. Pacific Fruit Express retained employees locally to maintain its fleet of mechanical refrigerator cars, both at the car repair track at Riverdale and on the many through trains handed over between SP and UP. The breakup of Pacific Fruit Express in April 1978, with its remaining assets being split between UP and SP, illustrated the general decline of transcontinental rail shipment of perishable goods.

Grain Elevators, Grain Mills, and Flour Mills

Another major source of traffic for railroads in Ogden was the grain storage, grain milling, and flour milling business. Since its early, pioneer days, the city has been the location of flour-producing gristmills. And the industry continues today, with Cargill, Inc. and Cereal Food Processors being important suppliers for flour and bran in the western United States.

Three large flour mill and grain elevator operations are located in the area: the Sperry mill (now Cereal Food Processors) on 29th Street and Pacific Avenue, and two mills in West Ogden, the Globe mill (now Cargill) and the Farmer's Grain Co-operative mill. Other companies milling flour included the Albers Brothers Milling Co. on 27th Street, and the Hilton Flour Mills. By 1929, Ogden had become the grain and flour milling center of the West, with 15,000 cars of grain moving through the local yards.

The Ogden mill and storage bins of Sperry Flour Co. were completed about 1920. Within 10-15 years, the number of bins was doubled, with the Sperry name being spelled out in just a single line, and the large grain storage facility became a landmark of railroading in Ogden. The plant was later operated by General Mills, Sperry's parent company, and remains in operation today as Cereal Food Processors, Inc. *(Colorado Historical Society)*

The Sperry Flour Company mill and storage bins in their final configuration, shown here in March 1947. *(Emil Albrecht, James W. Watson Collection)*

The Sperry mill was one of Sperry Flour Co.'s many mills in the West, which included facilities in California, Washington, Oregon, and Idaho. Sperry got its start in 1852, when Austin Sperry and George Lyon erected their first mill in Stockton, Calif. By 1936, the Sperry company had five mills, with a total daily capacity of 13,800 barrels of flour and 1,850 tons of feed grains. The storage silos at Ogden were part of a network that included five mills and 88 associated county elevators throughout the West, with a combined capacity of 13 million bushels. In 1928, Sperry was included in gigantic merger of milling, cereal, and elevator companies that formed General Mills, Inc.

Sperry remained separate until General Mills consolidated its operations. Prior to that, the General Mills organization was mainly a centralized marketing and research operation, but as the market that it served continued to change and grow, a more centralized control of milling required that the General Mills name be applied to all of its milling operations. General Mills closed its Ogden mill in early 1967.

The plant fell silent and the silos remained empty until July 1967 when Colorado Milling and Elevator Co. took them over. The plant was later sold to The Peavey Co., which merged with agricultural giant ConAgra in July 1982. By a consent agreement between the two companies and the Federal Trade Commission, the merger was allowed with the stipulation that ConAgra would divest itself of four western milling operations. The Ogden plant was chosen as one of the four, and it was sold in April 1984 to ConAgra's competitor, Cereal Food Processors. It continues to mill both hard flour and soft flour, with a daily capacity of 13,000 hundred-weight (100-pound bags, or cwt). Its wheat comes by rail from the Midwest. The mill uses soft wheat and hard wheat, received in an average of 10 cars per day. Some soft wheat comes by truck from Idaho.

The Globe mill in West Ogden was built in 1920 by the Globe Milling Co. It was sold to the Pillsbury Co. in 1941, along with Globe mills in Colton, San Diego, Sacramento, San Francisco, and Los Angeles, all in California. Also at Los Angeles were Globe's feed mill, feed lot, cottonseed operation, and macaroni factory. The original Globe mill in Ogden had a flour-making capacity of 4,000 cwt. per day. A typical 40-ton-capacity railroad boxcar could hold 800 cwt. By 1950, Pillsbury had increased the plant's output to 5,000 cwt., and, by the mid-1960s, to 7,500 cwt. In 1973, the plant could produce 10,500 cwt. of hard flour (for macaroni) and 9,000 cwt. of soft flour (for breads and cakes). Much of Pillsbury's Ogden "grind" went to furnish the California flour market, competing with mills in Washington, Oregon, and Kansas City.

The cost of transportation was, and still is, a great factor in keeping Ogden mills open, furnishing flour and grains for sale in the West. In 1971, the Santa Fe railroad made a favorable change in its rate to move finished flour from Kansas to California, which also shut out Ogden's flour completely from the Phoenix, Ariz., flour market. Pillsbury's Ogden mill furnished all of the flour for the company's "Gold Medal" flour market west of the Rockies, keeping supermarkets supplied from a wholesale warehouse in Clearfield, Utah. In addition to producing flour of all types and grades, Pillsbury's Ogden mill and its adjacent 2.5-million-bushel elevator served as a storage facility for wheat and barley that Pillsbury bought from local growers and sold all over the West.

Pillsbury sold the former Globe mill to Cargill, Inc. in 1991. Cargill made some changes in capability, converting it to a "swing mill" that can produce either 10,000 cwt. of soft flour, or an equal quantity of hard flour. Although Cargill has stopped producing flour made from hard Durham wheat (used for macaroni and pasta), it still produces large quantities of heavy bran. Grain for Cargill arrives either by rail or by truck, and finished flour and grain products leave by bulk rail car, by bulk truck, or in bags and sacks protected inside trucks and boxcars.

The factory of Utah Canning Co. was a landmark at 29th Street from its organization in 1897 (its predecessor company opened in 1888) until its closure and sale to Utah By-Products in 1972. Union Pacific's GTE (Gas-Turbine Electric) locomotives came to the railroad beginning in 1952, and by 1959 the design grew to the three-unit, 10,000-horsepower type represented by Union Pacific number 3 on September 2, 1962. A sister locomotive, UP number 26, is today preserved at Ogden Union Station. (Emil Albrecht, James W. Watson Collection)

Sugar Beets and the West Ogden sugar factory

Between 1895 and 1940, before the widespread use of trucks, railroads were the most efficient way to transport Utah's sugar beets to the factories. Because sugar beets are such a low-density item, many of them are needed to produce profitable amounts of sugar. Making sugar from sugar beets required large quantities of other raw materials, including coal, coke, and lime. Finished sugar was shipped from Amalgamated Sugar's West Ogden and other sugar factories in 100-pound bags. For 15 tons of finished, granulated sugar (300 100-pound bags) to be produced, the sugar factory required the delivery of 100 tons of sugar beets, nine tons of coal, and five tons each of coke and lime rock. To put these numbers in more visible terms, for each average 40-foot boxcar-load of finished sugar (1,000 100-pound bags), the West Ogden sugar factory would need six carloads of beets and partial carloads each of coal, coke and lime. The sugar factory in West Ogden, built by Ogden Sugar Co. in 1898 as the second sugar factory in the state, was the destination of many carloads of sugar beets. By 1900, it was one of 30 factories operating in the nation. During its first season of operation, it produced 1,280 tons of pure white beet sugar. In 1902, the company became the Amalgamated Sugar Co., with the West Ogden factory remaining in operation until September 1941, when it was closed due to decrease in local sugar beet growing capacity. It's machinery was moved to a new factory completed in Nampa, Idaho. The West Ogden buildings remained for use as warehouse facilities, and later by a liquid-sugar-making plant. The factory is today served by trackage formerly owned jointly by Union Pacific and Rio Grande. UP gains access through a connection to the former Rio Grande main line through West Ogden, from the west end of its Evona Branch (the remains of the original Utah Central's 1870 line to Salt Lake City).

Canneries

During the mid-1930s, Utah's canning industry was the eighth-ranked producer of canned goods in the nation. Over the span of years that canneries were active in Utah, from 1885 to the mid 1970s, fewer than 15 canneries were truly successful and were able to remain in business year-round. Railroads, and the low-cost transportation they offered, were important to the canneries and each of these successful canning factories was located on a railroad spur, which allowed direct shipment of canned goods to market. Del Monte's West Ogden plant was the largest in the state. It was built in 1900 by the Adams Nursery and Tin Can Manufacturing Co., which was reorganized in 1903 as the Wasatch Gardens and Orchard Canning Co. In 1914, the plant was purchased by William "Jake" Parker and became the center of his operations in Utah. Four years later, Parker sold his entire Utah operation to the Utah Packing Co., a newly organized subsidiary of California Packing Co. (also known as CalPac), which in 1968 became Del Monte, Inc., taking the name of one of its most popular brand name labels. Del Monte's West Ogden canning factory was closed in 1974. The building was then used by a lumber dealer for about 10 years, and in about 1986 the property was purchased by Grant Brothers for use in its livestock and trucking business.

Other canneries located along Union Pacific's main line through Ogden, each with its own spur, were the pioneering Utah Canning Co. at 29th Street and Pacific Avenue, and two others located east of UP's main line adjacent to Riverdale Yard: Sunshine Canning Co. on 31st Street, and Riverdale Canning Co. on Riverdale Road.

In 1914, to support the canning industry in Utah and other western states, the American Can Co. built in Ogden one of the largest can manufacturing facilities in the West. Between 1915 and 1979, when the plant was closed, American Can, located on 20th Street between Lincoln and Grant, shipped many boxcars filled with new, empty cans to canneries all over the state and the region. The factory was served by three of Ogden's railroads: Union Pacific, D&RGW, and Bamberger (from about 1947 to 1951). The large American Can smokestack, and the adjacent factory building, remain today as a testament to Ogden's past as a supplier to the region's canning industry. ✴

Bamberger Railroad's freight motor 525 awaits its next job as the railroad's Ogden switcher. The 525 was rebuilt by Bamberger's shop forces in 1920 using components of passenger motor 304, which was destroyed in the 1918 Ogden car barn fire. The railroad fabricated a new body following the design of the GE-built body of number 528. Number 525 was scrapped in 1952 when the railroad converted to diesel power. August 27, 1949. *(William A. Gibson Sr., William A. Gibson Jr. Collection)*

As part of the 1939 reorganization from financial receivership, Bamberger purchased five "Little Cars" secondhand from a car builder J. G. Brill Co. The cars had been built in 1931 but were returned to Brill after their original owner, the Fonda, Johnstown & Gloversville Railroad, a small railroad near Albany, N. Y., was abandoned. These five high-speed, lightweight cars were capable of 75 mph on their runs between Ogden and Salt Lake City, and at times continuing through to the end of operations in 1952, the little cars regularly attained these speeds. Here car 126 is shown loading passengers at Ogden on June 26, 1940. *(John F. Humiston)*

10. Electric and Interurban Railroads

Ogden was served by two separate electric railroads: the Bamberger Railroad and the Utah Idaho Central Railroad. Bamberger operated between Ogden and Salt Lake City. Utah Idaho Central operated between Ogden and its northern terminal of Preston, Idaho, at the north end of Cache Valley.

Bamberger Railroad

The trains of the Bamberger Railroad first came to Ogden under the banner of a predecessor company, the Salt Lake & Ogden Railway. SL&O was itself an extension of Simon Bamberger's Great Salt Lake & Hot Springs Railway, a suburban line built in 1891 between downtown Salt Lake City and Beck's Hot Springs, north of the city.

Within a year of the completion of the line to Hot Springs in 1891, Bamberger expanded his vision with plans to extend his Great Salt Lake & Hot Springs line to serve his coal mine at Coalville (paralleling Union Pacific east up Weber Canyon), with a 10-mile branch line to Ogden. In addition to transporting coal from his mine, Bamberger wanted to provide service for the local business traveler, providing more frequent service than either Union Pacific or Rio Grande, which did not offer conveniently timed passenger service between Ogden and Salt Lake City. Construction of the new extension began north from Beck's Hot Springs, four miles north of Salt Lake City, and the railroad reached Bountiful in 1892, Centerville in 1894 and Farmington in 1895. Financial difficulties followed, and the company was reorganized in October 1896 as the Salt Lake & Ogden Railway. To provide a destination for travelers while the company was recovering financially,

Bamberger purchased a swampy area just north of Farmington, drained it and built the Lagoon Resort, for residents of Salt Lake City who sought recreation outside of the city. (Lagoon remains today as one of the largest resort parks in the West.) The end of track remained at Lagoon from 1896 through 1902, when construction resumed, with Kaysville as the goal. Kaysville and Layton were reached in 1906, Kaysville on May 30 and Layton on September 4. The plans for

The interurban terminal was the focus of Bamberger Railroad operations in Ogden. In this photo taken on September 6, 1937, several Bamberger cars are visible, along with two Bamberger freight locomotives. (William A. Gibson, Sr., William A. Gibson Jr. Collection)

The steam trains of the Salt Lake & Ogden Railway arrived in Ogden for the first time in August 1908. Within two years, in May 1910, the railroad had converted to electric, self-propelled cars. Here we see SL&O number 315 waiting at the new-in-1915 Ogden terminal beside Ogden Rapid Transit car 103. The SL&O car is ready to take Train 14 south to Salt Lake City. The Ogden Rapid Transit car is ready to take Route 9 north to Hot Springs. (Gordon Cardall Collection)

serving the Coalville coal mines were soon dropped due to a business slump in 1907, but SL&O construction crews finished the line to Ogden in late July 1908, with passenger service between Salt Lake City and Ogden beginning on August 8, 1908. The depot was located at 31st Street and Lincoln Avenue. Although the Salt Lake & Ogden Railway was powered by large steam locomotives, it was still known as "the Dummy Line" because of its 1890s start with dummy streetcars, small steam locomotives that were built with bodies that resembled regular electric streetcars.

From the very beginning, Bamberger knew that if he wanted to compete with the much larger Union Pacific and D&RGW for high-speed passenger movements between Salt Lake and Ogden, and for freight traffic that would generate needed revenue, he would have to operate a first-class, well-engineered railroad. He constructed his railroad to steam-railroad standards, with wide sweeping curves and the lowest possible rate of climb, using standard 85-pound rail, gravel ballast, and standard-length pine ties. It was expensive to build the railroad with large curves and a relatively easy ascending grade of 1.1 percent (1.1 feet of rise for every 100 feet of route). To construct a railroad with these engineering features, many large cuts and fills were needed. But Bamberger knew that these high initial costs would be repaid many times over by his locomotives being able to pull more cars, at higher speeds. He also avoided the expedient use of franchises that would allow him to locate the railroad along public roads and highways. This feature alone would later save the company much grief and money by not having to move its tracks when these same public roads were widened and paved. Of course, these same improvements would eventually spell the death of the line, and its privately maintained right-of-way, as trucks and automobiles soon took away both its passenger and freight traffic, using right-of-way built and maintained entirely by public funds.

With the completion of the line in 1908, Bamberger began giving thought to joining the wave of interurban railroads (railroads that inter-connect large urban areas) that were modernizing their lines by electrifying them, using electric power to replace steam locomotives. The Salt Lake & Ogden Railway seemingly had all the requirements for a profitable interurban railroad: large cities at either end of the line (with large central city terminals) to provide both passengers and freight; a prosperous rural countryside between to supply more of both; and a well-engineered route that would allow operation of high-speed, electric interurban trains. In 1910, the electrification was completed by stringing overhead trolley wire and purchasing new equipment, along with constructing electrical substations along the line. Since Bamberger also owned several coal mines, it seemed proper to also construct a coal-fired power plant, and one was built at Farmington to furnish all of the needed current for the railroad. The first day of electric operation was May 28, 1910.

SL&O's first electrically powered cars came from the Jewett Car Co. of Newark, Ohio. Later in 1910, Bamberger purchased three trailers secondhand from Washington, Baltimore & Annapolis, which had recently upgraded its system and no longer needed the unpowered cars. Other trailer cars were purchased from the Niles Co. The electric cars were modern and fast. Bamberger adopted the slogan, "Every Hour, On The Hour, In An Hour," reflecting the high speeds which the cars were capable of. When electrification was completed, there were 10 trains running in each direction every day, all of which stopped at every station between Ogden and Salt Lake City.

The original Bamberger depot was located at 31st Street, where passengers found it necessary to seek other means to get themselves downtown, six blocks north. With the conversion to electric operation, Salt

The steel Bamberger bridge was a landmark of railroading in Ogden from its completion in 1914 until it was dismantled in 1977. Photographer Emil Albrecht took this view in 1946 of one of his favorite vantage points, from which he exposed many of his excellent photographs of railroading.
(Emil Albrecht, James W. Watson Collection)

Lake & Ogden received a franchise to construct a double-track line along Lincoln Avenue from 31st Street to the site of the new station yards just north of 24th Street. This brought SL&O cars to within two blocks of the heart of the business district and greatly increased the new railroad's popularity. In 1914, SL&O made an agreement with the newly built Utah Idaho Central Railroad that allowed the new terminal facilities to be shared by both interurbans; UIC then erected a station building which was used jointly. Also in 1914, Salt Lake & Ogden rebuilt its route into Ogden. The new line was raised high enough to cross over the Union Pacific tracks at 31st Street, and included new steel bridges over the Weber River and over the UP tracks.

Throughout its early years, the Salt Lake & Ogden Railway was known as "the Bamberger." In August 1917, the name was changed officially to the Bamberger Electric Railroad, accepting the road's nickname. Also in 1917, Simon Bamberger was elected governor as the Progressive Party candidate. Ironically, it was the improved road and highway system that he developed while in office that brought about the eventual demise of the interurban railroad system in Utah, from the Cache Valley on the north to Payson on the south, with his own Bamberger line in between. As people became more mobile and better able to get around in their own cars, they were less prone to take Bamberger's electric-powered trains. The publicly funded road system also allowed bus companies to offer passenger service, and allowed the trucking companies to offer more competitive rates, and they gradually took the lucrative package express business away from the interurban lines. To better compete with these rising new motor carriers that used the public roads, Bamberger on May 15, 1927 started a subsidiary bus service between Salt Lake City and Ogden under the name of the Bamberger Transportation Co. Beginning in 1927, the Bamberger was able to compete with the truck lines by offering its own trucking services for door-to-door delivery between the same cities that they also served with electrified railroad service.

On May 7, 1918, flames consumed the entire Ogden car house and adjoining substation. Twenty-one cars were destroyed, more than half the company's roster – a blow that was doubly crippling at the time because of wartime restrictions on obtaining critical materials needed for rebuilding the car fleet. The company recovered and began the struggle to repair the $500,000 damage. Slowly over the next couple years, the less severely damaged cars were repaired and returned to service, but it was a long time before the Bamberger line regained all the ground lost because of the fire.

When the federal government's United States Railway Administration took over operations of the nation's railroads in 1919, it swept aside the established practices that kept much of the steam road freight traffic off the Bamberger's line. From this time on, Bamberger became an important freight hauler for business between Salt Lake City and Ogden. From World War I until the end of its passenger operations in 1952, freight revenues always exceeded passenger revenues. The freight included coal that was interchanged at Salt Lake City with the Salt Lake & Utah interurban line, bound for points on the Utah Idaho Central. In 1924, both Union Pacific and Rio Grande accepted the existence of the 36-mile road and published joint freight rates for points on the Bamberger's line. During 1938, the railroad handled a total of 6,695 cars (just over 18 cars per day), 1,548 of which were coal, along with 3,672 cars of manufactured goods, 829 cars of agricultural products, 621 cars of forest products, and 25 cars of animals and animal by-products. Between 1934 and 1938, 65 percent of all revenue was derived from freight. Of the 37,464 carloads handled during that four year period, 92 percent was interchanged with connecting lines.

In 1933, the railroad was forced into bankruptcy, emerging in 1939 as the reorganized Bamberger Railroad, dropping the word "Electric" from its name. When it was built, the route of the Bamberger was nearly all double track between Ogden and Salt Lake City. Much of the second track was removed in the late 1930s as part of the belt-tightening following the reorganization. This move saved the railroad $9,000 per year in maintenance costs. At the same time, the railroad adopted a limited number of automatic block signals. During the 1939 reorganization, Bamberger owned 84 freight cars, four freight locomotives, 29 passenger cars, two express cars, a line work car, and two highway buses. In March 1939 the company purchased five high-speed, streamlined cars that were capable of 75 miles per hour. The new cars were quickly dubbed the "Little Cars," comparing them to the "Big Cars," the full-sized, heavy cars that Bamberger was operating. The electric cars of the Bamberger were always known for their speed. As late as September 1950, in a speed test, one of the little cars was clocked at 75 miles per hour, proving that 10 years later, they could still do it. The military build-up in 1940 and 1941 to support America's allies in the war in Europe saw the construction of several War Department facilities in Utah, including the Naval Supply Depot at Clearfield, along with the Ogden Arsenal, and Hill Army Air Field, both of which were located directly on Bamberger's route. The construction of these military installations made for a considerable increase in its freight traffic.

The increased military traffic included troop

With a growing amount of traffic stemming from the war in Europe, and the general military buildup in 1940 in the United States, the Bamberger Railroad went looking for more motive power. A surplus electric locomotive, number 1025, was found on the San Diego Electric Railway. It soon arrived in Utah, and is shown here on January 23, 1941 on its first day of operation as Bamberger's newest locomotive. Second from left is Julian Bamberger, president of the railroad. (Shipler Photo, Utah State Historical Society)

As a regular part of its extensive freight operations, Bamberger Railroad received, at least twice a week, a white Merchants Despatch Transportation (MDT) refrigerator car from Union Pacific. The shipment contained dry ice (solidified carbon dioxide) bound for Mariani & Sons in Ogden, the only wholesale source for dry ice in the region. In this view, Bamberger's Alco RS-1 number 570 is switching the Union Pacific/ Bamberger interchange on May 20, 1949. (Emil Albrecht, James W. Watson Collection)

trains that were operated by Bamberger into the Ogden Ordnance Depot (Ogden Arsenal) and Hill Army Air Field (Hill Field, also known as the Ogden Air Depot). At first, the Bamberger used its electric locomotives as motive power. But during the winter, when steam was needed to heat the passenger cars, the road borrowed a small steam locomotive from Union Pacific, most likely a 2-8-0. The 1940 construction of railroad trackage on the military bases at the Arsenal and at Hill Field, for which Bamberger would be doing the on-base switching, did not include the overhead wire needed for Bamberger's electrified operations. The government's own small diesel switcher locomotives were not large enough to pull an entire troop train, so Bamberger went shopping for an appropriate locomotive. In his search, Julian M. Bamberger, the railroad's president (and Simon's son), was looking for a locomotive with 1,000 horsepower, enough power that could be used on both the freight trains and the troop trains being run over his 36-mile railroad. To fill the need for a more powerful

locomotive for the new government traffic, Bamberger initially made arrangements to purchase Illinois Terminal Railroad four-truck Class D locomotive number 70. But the big puller would have been too much for the line's system of power substations, including the three newly installed, secondhand automatic substations. With the added costs of upgrading its entire power system, the plans to purchase the IT locomotive were shelved, and the company began looking at the purchase of an appropriate diesel locomotive.

Bamberger's first stop was the Electro-Motive Division of General Motors, because he owned stock in GM and preferred GM products. Unfortunately, EMD didn't make a 1,000-horsepower road switcher, so Bamberger had to settle for a model RS-1 from the American Locomotive Co. (Alco). Because of the high priority military traffic Bamberger would be moving, the Office of Defense Transportation gave the railroad authorization to buy two RS-1s, but the production of RS-1s was soon commandeered to operate the Trans-Iranian Railway in the Middle East. With this limitation, Bamberger was able to purchase just a single example of Alco's highly successful 1,000 horsepower road switcher. To satisfy the need for a steam generator to provide steam heat for the troop trains, the railroad had purchased an oil-fired steam generator when there were still plans to buy the Illinois Terminal all-electric locomotive. After the RS-1 was delivered on June 1, 1943, this steam generator was installed in its short hood, with the steam being furnished to adjacent cars by means of a hose through the end door of the locomotive.

This new locomotive, painted orange and given road number 570, would modernize the line's freight operations, being capable of pulling 40 loaded freight cars at a time. The railroad was justifiably proud of its new $100,000 purchase, putting it on display at Salt Lake City on June 1 and at Ogden on June 2. The next day, the new Alco went to work. According to the local press, the diesel was purchased to take care of growing amounts of freight traffic, without having to rebuild the company's already overloaded electrical system, needed by its fleet of electric cars that were used on passenger trains. With the arrival of the diesel, the Bamberger was able to return its interurban cars and eight overworked electric locomotives to their normal duties, the diesel being used to provide any service required by the military bases.

Locomotive 570 sported a feature unusual to diesel units – it was equipped with a trolley pole at each end to trip the Nachod-type traffic-controlling block signals that were actuated through the trolley wire. The block signals were used along two stretches of single track, between Centerville and Farmington and between Layton and Clearfield. (The other pieces of single track on the railroad were controlled by automatic block signals, actuated through the track.) During World War II, the railroad was well known for its five- and eight-car "Arsenal" trains, hauling war workers from Ogden to the station at Arsenal, adjacent to the west gate of today's Hill Air Force Base.

Another effect of World War II was the federal Office of Defense Transportation's suspension of all Bamberger Transportation Co. bus services, forcing even more passengers onto the trains. Bus service resumed after the war.

During World War II, Bamberger operated commuter trains for the Army's Ordnance Department. They ran between the interurban terminal in downtown Ogden and the Army's Ogden Arsenal (the location of the West Area of today's Hill Air Force Base). The Army purchased five large all-steel cars secondhand from Southern Pacific's Oakland Electric operation. Bamberger used its own locomotives to move the trains, which were lighted with current from a electric generator rigged to a small gasoline engine in the baggage compartment of one of the cars. Stoves were added for heating, and large sliding gates were added to the exit doors for safety. In this view, Ogden Arsenal (OA) car 104 is shown arriving at the Ogden interurban terminal. The arsenal trains continued to run until the end of the war, by which time the cars had lost the cumbersome exit gates and had been repainted from khaki green with light blue lettering to dark blue with white lettering. The trains started up again during the Korean war and ran until December 1952, three months after Bamberger itself stopped operating its own passenger trains. (Gordon Cardall)

In 1946, because of the heavy usage that number 570 saw during World War II, the locomotive needed a complete overhaul, which the road performed itself in its own shops at North Salt Lake. After the rebuilding, the Alco returned to road freight service between Salt Lake and Ogden. After another four years, the unit needed rebuilding again. The first overhaul for 570 had been difficult for the little road to do itself, so Bamberger approached General Motors about converting the locomotive to an Electro-Motive product. EMD agreed to do the conversion. The Bamberger unit was EMD's third repowering job at its factory in La Grange, Ill., in suburban Chicago. While the 570 was away being rebuilt, the Bamberger Railroad operated two of its electric locomotives, numbers 525 and 526, normally the Ogden switchers, in multiple-unit configuration for a combination of 900 horsepower. At times, Bamberger's number 550 was also used, depending on the number of cars to be moved. When the 570 returned from EMD in December 1951, it still had its 1,000 horsepower, but used an EMD diesel engine rather than the original Alco diesel engine. The EMD factory representative who delivered the locomotive informed Bamberger that it had the best of both worlds, EMD's diesel engine connected to the Alco's original General Electric electrical gear.

The rebuilding worked out so well that in June 1952, Bamberger purchased two additional diesel locomotives, and gave the business to EMD. They were 800-horsepower model SW8 locomotives, given road numbers 601 and 602. One of them, number 601, was equipped with a single trolley pole so that it could serve as stand-in for the 570, the regular road engine, whenever it was out of service for regular maintenance. The other SW8, number 602, was assigned as the switcher in Salt Lake City, and did not require a trolley pole.

On March 11, 1952, fire struck the Bamberger again. This time it was the North Salt Lake shops, where all of the company's repair work was done. The fire destroyed only repair machinery, but only after several pieces of rolling stock was successfully removed from harm's way. During mid-April, just a month after the fire, the company applied to the state Public Service Commission to abandon all passenger railcar service, which operated just three round-trips between Salt Lake City and Ogden, reduced on March 30 from the 11 trips per day before the fire. Bamberger proposed to replace all rail passenger service with bus service. The March 30 "emergency" schedule change had increased the number of bus runs to 20, four of which were "stub" runs, or one-way trips. On April 19, after many protests by Davis County residents, the PSC ordered the Bamberger to increase its railroad operations to five trains per day, and reduce its bus runs to 18, including three one-way trips per day.

The railroad continued to pursue changing its passenger service from trains to buses. On July 10, 1952, Bamberger formally applied to state authorities for permission to abandon all of its rail passenger service. In the application and later public hearing, the railroad said that although it had earlier denied that it planned to abandon rail service, the cost of rebuilding the North Salt Lake shops, together with a recent fire adjacent to its facilities in Ogden (at the Royal Canning Co.) made the expense of continued passen-

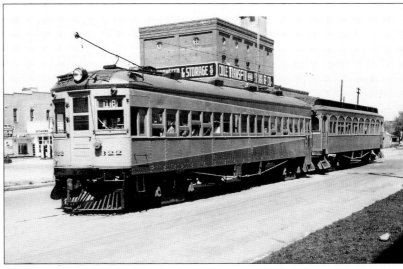

ger operations simply too high. The change was needed, the company argued, "in the public interest." On August 21, the state Public Service Commission agreed. To support the expected changes, the railroad had purchased for its subsidiary, Bamberger Transportation Co., 17 new, modern buses. The buses came in two configurations: 33 seats and 45 seats, nicknamed by the crews as "little buses and big buses," much the same way that the original rail cars were the "big cars," and the five streamlined cars of 1939 were the "little cars." The company stated that the public would be better served by the bus routes, with 78 potential stops, than by the railroad, with its 27 stops. In the hearing, the costs of both rail operations and bus operations were given, with 85 cents per mile for rail and a bit less than 42 cents per mile for bus. Throughout the abandonment proceedings, Bamberger stated that freight operations would remain unchanged, except that they would be operated solely with diesel power rather than using the electric locomotives.

The last day of electric passenger operations came on September 6, 1952, when Bamberger passenger car 322 and trailer 436 left the Salt Lake City depot bound for Ogden. Among those on board were the motorman, James Nelson, and Julian Bamberger, along with his wife, and his married daughter. The opposing final run between Ogden and Salt Lake City used car 351, with motorman Gordon Cardall at the controls. After already driving two bus round-trips that day, Cardall had swapped assignments with a fellow employee in order to operate that last Ogden-to-Salt Lake run. The return leg of the schedule put Cardall in the driver's seat of one of Bamberger's buses. While this was the end of scheduled rail passenger operations, Bamberger continued to operate for another three months a daily, two-car train between Ogden and Arsenal in the mornings and return in the evenings for defense workers at the Ogden Arsenal and Hill Air Force Base.

In a move to continue narrowing its focus on freight operations, Bamberger Railroad on June 26, 1953, sold its bus subsidiary, Bamberger Transportation Co., to the Lake Shore Motor Coach Lines Co., newly organized for the purpose. Lake Shore's president and organizer, Dale Barratt, was general manager of Salt Lake City Lines, the local bus company that had taken over the streetcar lines in Salt Lake City. Barratt was also regional director of the parent

The trains of the Bamberger Railroad entered Ogden along Lincoln Avenue and traveled north to the interurban terminal between 23rd Street and 24th Street. In this view, Bamberger cars 322 and 401 head south along Lincoln in April 1943, having just crossed 24th Street, bound for Salt Lake City. (Gordon Cardall)

company, National City Lines. The sale became effective on July 3, when Lake Shore took ownership of Bamberger's 17 buses. In a side note about later bus operations, Barratt sold Lake Shore to Salt Lake City Lines in 1965 and left Utah. In August 1968, Barratt returned and purchased all interests in Salt Lake City lines, which he sold to the new Utah Transit Authority in August 1970. The former Lake Shore (ex-Bamberger) operations were split off from Salt Lake City Lines in May 1969 and sold to Cook Transportation of Logan.

Some historians of the Bamberger and its operations lament the loss of the electric passenger trains, saying that there was plenty of patronage to support continued operation. The truth most likely was that the cost of continued electric operations was rising, and passenger revenues were falling, due to the paralleling public highways. Only the freight traffic held any potential for growth. The electric freight locomotives were old, expensive to operate, and were all in need of serious rebuilding to make them more powerful. The end of electric passenger operations, caused in part by the losses of the North Salt Lake shops fire, allowed the Bamberger to replace its electric locomotives with diesel versions, remove the electric wire, and concentrate on freight operations as a regular short line railroad. Julian Bamberger was, at the time, vice president of the American Short Line Railroad Association. The future of the railroad was on the horizon. With the North Salt Lake fire, as convenient as it may have been in bringing on abandonment of passenger operations, Julian Bamberger, president, and Hugh L. Balser, vice president and general manager (and Bamberger's brother-in-law), took the opportunity to improve their company and ensure its future.

Unfortunately, even with the changes that took place in 1952, revenues did not meet expectations. Julian Bamberger was reaching retirement age (he retired in August 1956), and had devoted his entire adult life to operating the railroad. In 1910, he had been asked by his father, Simon Bamberger, to take the place of his brother, Sidney Bamberger (who had died unexpectedly) in managing the railroad. By 1956, and after 46 years of service (40 years as president), it was time for Julian to end his involvement while he and the other owners still could benefit financially. In a sale that was effective on August 23, 1956, the Bamberger Railroad was sold to the Murmanill Corp. of Dallas, Texas. The new owners announced that no changes would take place in the operation of the now-all-freight railroad, which was operating three daily trains between Salt Lake City and Ogden. The decision to sell was not up to Julian alone. The railroad was, and always had been, a family operation. Julian's father, Simon Bamberger, had built it, and by the time of the sale in 1956, two of Julian's sisters still held considerable interests. The Bamberger heirs (Simon Bamberger died in October 1926) held 66-2/3 percent share in the company, with 140 other stockholders holding the rest. Murmanill paid a reported $2.5 million for 100 percent interest in the line. The Murmanill name was a combination of the company's principle owners: Clint Murchison and Gerald C. Mann, both of Dallas. Murchison was a wealthy a Texas oilman and industrialist.

There was open speculation in the local press that the Murmanill Corp. was working closely with other Texas investors to acquire control of the Missouri Pacific and Western Pacific railroads (which had once jointly owned Rio Grande) to aid New York investor Robert R. Young in expanding his newly acquired New York Central into a transcontinental operation. The Bamberger would provide a connection between Salt Lake City and Ogden for this new group of railroads. At the very least, it would be a sought-after prize should Southern Pacific decide to expand south to Salt Lake City, or Western Pacific expand north to Ogden.

Whatever the reason for the purchase by the Texas investors, they soon started to sell off pieces and parts of the railroad to regain their investment. First to go, in February 1957, was the Ogden freight depot, located at the interurban terminal that stood between 23rd and 24th streets, and between Lincoln and Grant. It was sold to the Ogden Iron Works, which planned to construct a steel warehouse on the property. The new Bamberger owners announced that they planned to erect a replacement freight depot on property the company owned at 31st Street and Grant. By the end of the year, negotiations were under way to sell major portions of the railroad at Ogden to Union Pacific, and other portions in north Salt Lake City to D&RGW. The then-president of the Bamberger, Lee Aikin, stated that the principle reason the new owners were disposing of the historic rail property was "that it wasn't making any money." He further said, "As you know, railroad revenues generally are off some 16 percent in the nation. The Bamberger cannot exist under its present revenues. We bought this railroad to operate it. But the past year and three months we have lost money. We have done everything in our power to make money."

In early December 1958, the Interstate Commerce Commission approved the sale of portions of the Bamberger to UP and Rio Grande. The middle 25 miles would be abandoned and torn up. Union Pacific purchased the northern 13 miles, between Ogden and Hill Air Force Base, including the re-engined locomotive 570. D&RGW purchased the southern seven miles between Salt Lake City and "refinery row" at 20th North. Both sales were reported to be for a half million dollars each. The last run over the portion to be abandoned took place on December 31, 1958. The last train left Salt Lake City at 1 p.m., arriving in Ogden at 31st Street and Grant Avenue at 5:25 p.m., pulling a string of about 20 rail cars picked up on the way north. Goodbyes and farewells were said by a large group of business and community leaders upon its arrival. It then returned to Salt Lake City, picking up empty cars, including the last coal cars at Smith Milling in Bountiful and the empty car that had held the last shipment of automobiles to Bountiful. The eulogy given by the *Salt Lake Tribune* the next morning was that "The Bamberger Railroad died yesterday, the victim of a collision with the family automobile," perpetuating the myth that Bamberger's sole source of revenue had been its passenger operations.

In February 1959, the remainder of the railroad, including the two remaining switchers and all of the remaining rail, track hardware, and rolling stock and equipment, were sold for $300,000 for salvage to Morse Brothers Machinery of Denver, and Commercial Metals Co. of Dallas. Removal of rail began immediately. From Clearfield, the salvage crews moved south at the rate of two miles per day. By mid-March 1959, just over 25 miles of rail had been removed and stacked in rows in Salt Lake City, just south of the Beck Street overpass. Because it was directly in the path of the planned Interstate Highway 15, the depot and adjacent right-of-way at Clearfield was sold to the Utah State Road Commission, and the depot was demolished during December 1959.

After the Bamberger ended operations on December 31, 1958, locomotives 601 and 602 were sold. Both survive today [1997] after passing through a couple of different ownerships. As noted, Union Pacific bought locomotive 570, along with the portion of the line between Ogden and Hill Air Force Base. Union Pacific moved the locomotive to its Omaha, Neb., shops, and repainted and renumbered it as UP 1270. The unit was used by UP for another 12 or so years in the Omaha area and other points in Nebraska until it was retired and traded to EMD on an order for SD40-2 road diesels in 1972.

Street Railroads

In addition to its extensive system of electric interurban railroads, at one time Utah also had an extensive system of electric street railways, popularly known as "trolleys." Streetcar lines were built in Ogden, Brigham City, Logan, Salt Lake City, and, for six short years, in Provo. Six streetcar routes operated in Ogden, with a total length of about 24 miles. Between 1900 and 1914, streetcars were operated by the Ogden Rapid Transit Co. and streetcars in Logan was operated by the Logan Rapid Transit Co. These two companies combined in 1914 to form the Ogden, Logan & Idaho Railway, which became the Utah Idaho Central Railroad in 1918, as will be noted later. Ogden, Logan & Idaho (and the later UIC) continued to operate streetcar service in both cities until the cities began paving their streets. At that time, many of the lines were removed because the railroad couldn't pay its share of the paving costs. In Logan there were three lines, totaling just over eight miles, and by 1926, the Logan streetcars were replaced by buses.

Street railroads started in Ogden in 1883 with the formation of the Ogden City Railway on August 23 of that year. Its purpose was to build a mule-powered rail line in Fourth and Fifth streets (today's 24th and 25th streets) from Wall Street east to the city limits. Another line was to intersect the first two at Main Street (later Washington Avenue, then Washington Boulevard) and extend from the south limits to the north limits of the city, which were then at the Ogden River – for a total of five miles of street railway. By late 1888, this company had completed only two miles of track and owned only a few cars and mules. In late 1888 it was purchased by investors, led by Will R. Swan, who also owned the Swan Land & Livestock Co. The new owners within a year expanded the system to 10 miles, operating it with steam-powered "motors" (also known as "dummies"), and "a great number of cars, horses, and mules." The line also included operations to the Hot Springs health resort, northwest of Ogden, over the line of the newly organized Ogden & Hot Springs Railroad and Health Resort Co., both the resort and the railroad being owned by the same Swan interests. This line ran along Washington Avenue to North Ogden, then west to Hot Springs.

In addition to the steam dummies, Ogden City Railway, in July 1890, purchased a small Shay locomotive, an unusual design of steam locomotive with a geared drive train that allowed it to travel over uneven streets and turn the sharp corners found on typical street railways. The Shay was sold in January 1891 to the Oregon Lumber Co. (owned by David Eccles), and may have spent a brief time as plant switcher at Eccles' sawmill in Baker City, Ore. The locomotive was later sold to the Salt Lake & Mercur Railroad in October 1894. The SL&M used it as its number 1, operating a mountain mining railroad that crossed the backbone of the Oquirrh Mountains in western Utah County. After SL&M shut down in 1918, the little locomotive was sold, and ended its career working for the Mowry Lumber Co. in Glenwood, Ore.

Ogden City Railway went bankrupt in late 1890 and was purchased by the Ogden Electric Railway Co., controlled by the Jarvis-Conklin Co., an investment firm in Kansas City. This company comprised investors from Kansas City, Omaha, and Sioux City, Iowa, who were looking to start an electrical generating enterprise, and needed a street railway to invest in and electrify. They found the small Ogden City Railway in trouble, and available. Ogden Electric Railway was organized on November 28, 1890, for the purpose of operating a street railway "along, upon and through the streets and public thoroughfares of Ogden City, and along, over, and upon the public highways of Weber County." The company soon made preparations to electrify its newly acquired system.

The new company succeeded in building only a single electric line, and accumulated a heavy debt doing it. Ogden residents David Eccles and Thomas Dee became concerned about the condition of their city's deteriorating street railway and offered to purchase the company from its Midwestern owners. In May 1900, Eccles and Dee organized Ogden Rapid Transit Co. to acquire and operate the properties of the Ogden Electric Railway Co. At the time, Ogden

Street railroading started with the Ogden City Railway, a mule-car company organized in 1883. That pioneering company was replaced in 1888 by the electrified Ogden City Street Railway, whose car number 150 is shown here on 25th Street at Washington, bound for the steam railroad depot. Ogden City Street Railway ran until 1890, when it was replaced by the Ogden Electric Railway Co., which itself replaced in 1900 by the Ogden Rapid Transit Co. (Ogden Union Station Collection)

The cars of Ogden Rapid Transit operated between Union Station and downtown Ogden, and along Washington from the south city limits to North Ogden, and on west to Hot Springs. The company also ran excursion trains to the mouth of Ogden Canyon, to a sanitarium that later became better known as Rainbow Gardens. Ogden Rapid Transit took over the operations of the bankrupt Ogden City Street Railway in 1900, and in 1914 was combined with its sister (also Eccles-owned) company, Logan Rapid Transit Co., becoming Ogden, Logan & Idaho Railway. (Ogden Union Station Collection)

Electric Railway was operating only two cars - one on Washington Avenue and the other on 25th Street. The company's other cars were not fit for service. At midnight on Saturday, May 19, 1900, the Ogden Rapid Transit Co. took over the operation of the former Ogden Electric Railway.

The Ogden Rapid Transit Co. was an Eccles company. David Eccles, head of the Eccles family and one of the wealthiest men in Utah, was the founder and heaviest investor. Throughout the history of Ogden Rapid Transit, and the later Ogden, Logan & Idaho Railway (after 1918, the Utah Idaho Central Railway), the name Eccles was never missing from the board of directors. Ogden Rapid Transit rapidly put the street-car lines into first-class condition. The main line was along Washington Avenue, which in July 1900 was double-tracked between 19th and 23rd streets. A branch was built to Glenwood Park, and later extended up into Ogden Canyon.

By March 1909, the routes of Ogden Rapid Transit included six distinct lines: the Washington Line, along Washington Avenue from the north city limits south to 36th Street (4.8 miles); the 25th Street Line, from Union Station east to its eastern end at Polk Avenue (1.7 miles); the 23rd Street Line, from a connection with the Washington Line at 23rd Street, to its eastern end at Harrison Avenue (one mile); the Mouth of Canyon Line, from a connection with the Washington Line at Canyon Road, east to the Canyon Mouth (2.4 miles); the Hot Springs Line, from the north city limits to Hot Springs (6.9 miles); and the Fair Grounds Line, from a connection with the Washington Line at 17th Street, west to the Fair-grounds (0.4 mile); plus another 6.8 miles of second track along Washington Avenue and 25th Street, making a total of 24 miles.

Within a year after David Eccles and his associates organized the Ogden Rapid Transit Co. in 1900, they soon owned another railroad in the area, this one running north from Ogden. In September 1889, Will Swan and his associates had organized the Ogden & Hot Springs Railroad to build from the Ogden north city limits, and a connection with their newly acquired (in August 1889) Ogden Electric Railway, north along Washington Avenue to North Ogden, then west to the

Hot Springs health resort, which they had organized on the same day, as the Ogden & Hot Springs Health Resort Co. They must have had other plans for their railroad before its actual organization, as its original name was to have been the Ogden Belt Railroad, but a handwritten name change to the Ogden & Hot Springs Railroad was added to the typed incorporation papers at the time of its filing. To make financing easier, the two companies were combined two months later as the Ogden & Hot Springs Railroad and Health Resort Co. In 1901, Eccles bought the Swan properties, both the railroad and the health resort. The railroad and health resort were separated in October 1903, and Eccles and his associates organized the Ogden & Northwestern Railroad to operate the Hot Springs line and extend it to Brigham City. The line was completed to Brigham City in 1907, and electrified at the same time. The Ogden & Northwestern also built a branch to Plain City. This 8.5-mile branch line was completed in 1909 with new construction that left the Ogden Rapid Transit Washington line at Five Points (Second Street). The new route headed northwest to Harrisville, then meandered in a general westerly direction to Plain City, all at an initial cost of $48,000. For the first seven years, the motive power on the Plain City Branch was by steam dummies (a roundhouse was built at 19th Street). The line was used mainly for freight traffic to serve the agricultural area north and west of Ogden. In 1916 the Plain City line was electrified, and in 1918, it was extended to Warren. In June 1911, the entire Ogden & Northwestern Railroad line from the Ogden north city limits to Brigham, and the line from Five Points to Plain City, was sold to Ogden Rapid Transit, both companies being controlled by Eccles.

Ogden Rapid Transit completed its line from Ogden to Huntsville in the Ogden Valley in 1915, after first extending its Canyon Mouth (Sanitarium) Line up-canyon to The Hermitage resort in 1909. The *Electric Railway Journal* of November 12, 1910, wrote:

> "The most interesting portion of the system [Ogden Rapid Transit] is the line that was put in service a year ago last summer in the canyon of the Ogden River. This canyon has long been famed among tourists as well as among the residents of Utah for its exceptional scenic features. The lower end of the canyon is particularly rugged and picturesque and the few spots where it widens out have been utilized for resorts, camping sites and summer homes. About two years ago, officials of ORT, realizing the possibilities of the canyon as a revenue producer, began the construction of a line to The Hermitage, a popular hotel and resort in the canyon.

> "The company was already operating a branch to a sanitarium near the mouth of the canyon. This line was extended along the bank of the river and for the most part on the side opposite the wagon road. For the greater portion of the distance the roadbed had to be blasted out of solid rock, and concrete banks and walls had to be built to hold the grade. Nearly all the post holes for the trolley line also had to be prepared by blasting. A fair idea of the heavy construction necessary may be gained from the fact that the three miles of line in the canyon cost $100,000.

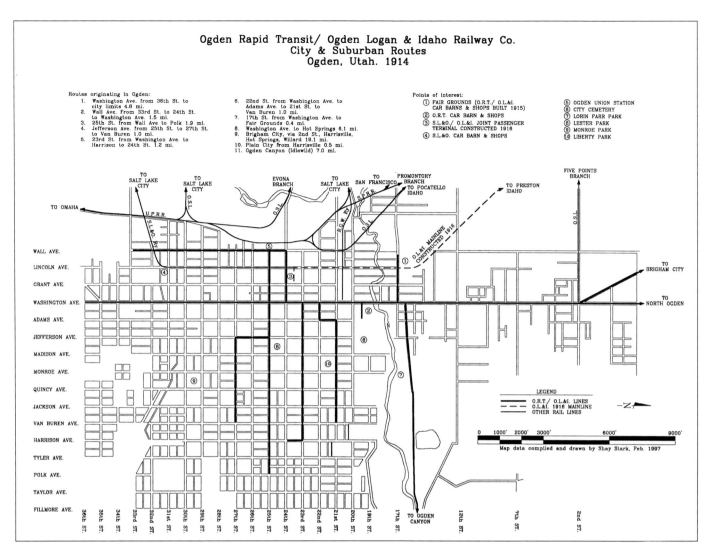

Ogden Rapid Transit/ Ogden Logan & Idaho Railway Co.
City & Suburban Routes
Ogden, Utah. 1914

Routes originating in Ogden:
1. Washington Ave. from 36th St. to city limits 4.8 mi.
2. Wall Ave. From 33rd St. to 24th St. to Washington Ave. 1.5 mi.
3. 25th St. from Wall Ave to Polk 1.9 mi.
4. Jefferson Ave. from 25th St. to 27th St. to Van Buren 1.0 mi.
5. 23rd St. from Washington Ave. to Harrison to 24th St. 1.2 mi.

6. 22nd St. from Washington Ave. to Adams Ave. to 21st St. to Van Buren 1.0 mi.
7. 17th St. from Washington Ave. to Fair Grounds 0.4 mi.
8. Washington Ave. to Hot Springs 6.1 mi.
9. Brigham City, via 2nd St., Harrisville, Hot Springs, Willard 19.1 mi.
10. Plain City from Harrisville 0.5 mi.
11. Ogden Canyon (Idlewild) 7.0 mi.

Points of interest:
① FAIR GROUNDS (O.R.T./ O.L.&I. CAR BARNS & SHOPS BUILT 1915)
② O.R.T. CAR BARN & SHOPS
③ S.L.&O./ O.L.&I. JOINT PASSENGER TERMINAL CONSTRUCTED 1916
④ S.L.&O. CAR BARN & SHOPS

⑤ OGDEN UNION STATION
⑥ CITY CEMETERY
⑦ LORIN FARR PARK
⑧ LESTER PARK
⑨ MONROE PARK
⑩ LIBERTY PARK

LEGEND
O.R.T./ O.L.&I. LINES
O.L.&I. 1916 MAINLINE
OTHER RAIL LINES

0   1000' 2000' 3000'   6000'   9000'
Map data compiled and drawn by Shay Stark, Feb. 1997

"The total length of the line from the Union Depot in Ogden is seven miles and in that distance the road rises 700 feet to a 5000-foot elevation at the upper end [at The Hermitage]. The maximum grade is 4 percent, and this extends for a distance of about 2000 feet. The prevailing grade is 2-3/4 percent, and the maximum curvature is 30 degrees. There are not many cuts in the line, but such as have been made have also required fills of rock, the deepest of them being about 16 feet. The line crosses the river three different times in the canyon, at one point by means of an 80-foot, steel plate girder bridge. Rails weighing 48 pounds [per yard] are used, and five sidings are provided so that a 10-minute headway can be maintained if desired."

Simon Bamberger, who owned The Hermitage, also wanted to build a rail line to his resort hotel; as did the Ogden Rapid Transit Co., backed by the Eccles family. Bamberger acted by surveying and grading an extension from his Lincoln Avenue line in Ogden eastward toward the canyon's mouth. Ogden Rapid Transit started its extension from its line already in service to a sanitarium near the mouth of the canyon. Eccles got started first, and was closer, so Bamberger reluctantly withdrew, abandoning his virtually completed grade, which later became part of the public highway into the canyon.

With the completion of the Ogden Canyon Line, Ogden Rapid Transit took delivery of four new

"suburban" cars from St. Louis Car Co. to operate the new route. These cars were much larger and heavier than anything the company had previously operated. They were equipped with smoking compartments and toilets, and seated 46 passengers. Three years later, in 1913, the company rebuilt two of its older cars, numbers 16 and 17, as unique open-roof observation cars for use in the canyon. The Independence Day holiday of 1910 saw 7,000 passengers carried over the new line, making one think that a trip to The Hermitage and its adjacent picnic grounds must have been "the" thing to do that weekend. The average Sunday and holiday travel numbers were about 1,800 passengers, with half that number on weekdays. These figures were for the months of June, July, and August, during which a car was operated every 20 minutes. During winter, the schedule was cut back to a car every one hour and 20 minutes.

The streetcar lines of Ogden were included in Ogden Rapid Transit's merger with Logan Rapid Transit that formed the Ogden, Logan & Idaho Railway in May 1914. By that date, the streetcars were also operating over Wall Avenue from 33rd Street, north to 24th Street and east to Washington, a distance of 1.5 miles. There were also other lines: along Jefferson Avenue from 25th Street to 27th Street, then along 27th Street to Van Buren Avenue (one mile); the 22nd Street Line had been shifted at Adams, north to 21st Street, then east along 21st to Van Buren (the tracks were

One of the first streetcar routes ran from the city's railroad depot, east to downtown, along Fifth Street, which within a few years became 25th Street. This view shows 25th Street at Wall Avenue about 1900, as seen from the clock tower of Union Station. (Utah State Historical Society)

removed along 22nd Street east of Adams); and the 23rd Street Line had been added from Washington to Harrison Avenue and along Harrison to 24th Street (1.2 miles).

Also included in the Ogden, Logan & Idaho merger was Ogden Rapid Transit's suburban line along Washington to North Ogden, through Pleasant View and west to Hot Springs and Brigham City. This was the former Ogden & Northwestern line between Ogden and Brigham City, built by the Ogden & Hot Springs company in 1889, sold to Ogden & Northwestern in 1903; and re-sold to Ogden Rapid Transit in June 1911. The Ogden, Logan & Idaho company immediately built a new line from the Fairgrounds, at 17th Street and Wall Avenue, northwest to Harrisville, then north to Hot Springs, and a connection with Ogden Rapid Transit's original O&NW line to Brigham City via North Ogden. Ogden, Logan & Idaho Railway changed its name and became the Utah Idaho Central Railway in January 1918.

The streetcar lines within Ogden were separated from Utah Idaho Central in January 1920, under the new name of the Utah Rapid Transit Co. At that point, URT's property consisted of 39 miles of trackage: 31.25 miles of single track; 5.81 miles of second track; and 2.05 miles of spur tracks. There were also 44 motor cars, three trailers, and five work cars. In addition to the streetcar lines in Ogden, the new Utah Rapid Transit took over the line through Ogden Canyon to Huntsville.

During May 1928, Utah Rapid Transit discontinued streetcar service over the former Ogden & Northwestern's original Plain City line, built in 1914, along Harrisville Avenue, from Five Points to the crossing with the newer Utah Idaho Central line north to Harrisville. At the point of the former crossing, a connection was made that allowed UIC trains to operate directly over the Plain City Branch.

During the summer of 1932, several floods in Ogden Canyon damaged the tracks of Utah Rapid Transit's line to Huntsville. In September, URT received regulatory approval to discontinue railroad service, to remove its tracks from the route between Ogden and Huntsville, and to substitute buses and light trucks over the well maintained public highway that paralleled the entire route through Ogden Canyon.

Just two months later, Utah Rapid Transit received additional regulatory approval to remove its agent and to close the station at Huntsville, but the regulators asked that the bus arrive 15 minutes earlier than before, at 7:45 a.m., to provide the 33 students in Huntsville with someplace warm to wait until the bus departed at 8 a.m. Other stations in the area functioned like this, with school trains that waited to provide shelter for the students, on Utah Idaho Central in Cache Valley, at Wellsville, Millville, Providence, and Hyde Park. The school trains of UIC and URT were an unusual operation in interurban passenger service, especially in the West.

The tracks in Ogden Canyon weren't actually removed until 1934, when Pine View Dam was under construction, and then only between Black Rock Point and Huntsville. The tracks from Ogden to Black Rock Point were used to supply materials to build the dam. In early November 1940, Utah Rapid Transit's successor company, a new bus-only carrier named Ogden Transit Co., received approval to cancel the entire Ogden Canyon bus route.

The removal of streetcar tracks in Ogden began in mid-June 1933, when Utah Rapid Transit received approval to discontinue service along 28th Street. The route ran east along 28th from Washington Avenue to Jefferson Avenue, then south along Jefferson Avenue to 33rd Street.

Two years later, on August 5, 1935, the state Public Service Commission approved URT's request to replace all of its streetcar service with gasoline bus service, and to abandon and remove all tracks from the city's streets. Fifteen months later, on December 16, 1936, all rights of the Utah Rapid Transit Co. were transferred to the new Ogden Transit Co. In May 1947, the company purchased the Ogden car barns of the bankrupt Utah Idaho Central Railroad, situated at 17th Street and Lincoln Avenue, for use as a garage for its buses.

Ogden was the home of important defense-related installations during World War II, and Ogden Transit prospered because of it. During the war, OT purchased 32 buses to support the increased ridership. But the boom lasted only for the duration. As cars, gasoline, and tires again became available after the war, more and more residents stopped riding buses. The end of private bus operation in Ogden came during mid-January 1952, when the Public Service Commission authorized the firm to discontinue its bus operations, effective May 19, 1952. Total annual ridership had declined from 8.5 million in 1945 (just over 23,000 per day) to 4.5 million in 1950, and to 3.4 million in 1951 (9,315 per day); the decline was, naturally, attributed to the increased use of private automobiles. The end of private bus operation also brought an end to the involvement of the Eccles family in public transit in Ogden, which had begun in 1900. The company was replaced by Ogden Bus Lines, a city franchise for operation of municipal bus service. Ogden Bus Lines continued to operate city service into the 1970s, under a variety of contract operators. In 1974, Weber County residents voted an increase in sales tax and Utah Transit Authority took over the operation of bus service in Ogden.

Utah Idaho Central

The Utah Idaho Central Railroad began as the Ogden, Logan & Idaho Railroad. The earlier road had merged the streetcar and suburban lines of two companies organized by David Eccles and his associates, Ogden Rapid Transit Co. and Logan Rapid Transit Co., in both of those cities in 1914, and connected the two by way of Brigham City in 1915. Logan Rapid Transit had in 1912 completed its line north to Preston, Idaho. Preston was to remain the northern end of a network of electric interurban railroads extended along the Wasatch Front from Cache Valley in the north, south to Payson, at the southern end of the Utah Valley. David Eccles died of an apparent heart attack while hurrying to catch a train in Salt Lake City on December 5, 1912, but his sons and associates kept his numerous business interests going with the same vision and concern.

As already noted, Ogden Rapid Transit had its roots in 1883 as the street railroad in Ogden. By 1907, the line had been extended to Brigham City, under the auspices of a new Eccles company, the Ogden & Northwestern Railroad, which also built a line to Plain City in 1909. The Ogden & Northwestern lines were sold in 1911 to Ogden Rapid Transit, which had also completed a line into Ogden Canyon to The Hermitage resort in 1909. When these two rapid transit companies merged on October 17, 1914, the new company was made up of the streetcar lines in Ogden, the line up Ogden canyon to The Hermitage, the line through North Ogden to Hot Springs and Brigham City, and

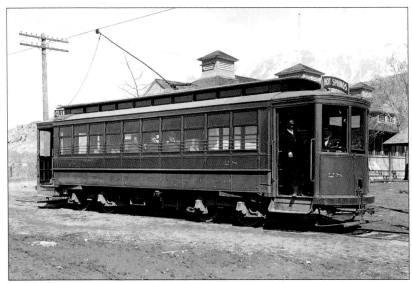

The mineral hot springs west of Pleasant View and North Ogden became a favorite destination for area residents soon after the city was settled. The location took the name Hot Springs with the completion of Utah Northern's narrow-gauge line in 1874. In 1888, a health resort was completed and the same businessmen built a railroad to bring people to the resort, offering special Sunday excursion trains. In 1900, Ogden Rapid Transit Co. began operating its streetcars to Hot Springs, and ORT's successors Ogden, Logan & Idaho and Utah Idaho Central continued to offer service to Hot Springs until the UIC was shut down in 1947. Here, Ogden Rapid Transit car 28 waits at Hot Springs on March 11, 1908.
(Utah State Historical Society)

the former O&NW branch to Plain City, along with Logan Rapid Transit streetcar lines in Logan, and LRT lines north from Logan to Smithfield, and south from Logan to Providence. The Smithfield line was extended to Preston, Idaho, and Providence line was extended to Wellsville, in 1915 by the new Ogden, Logan & Idaho Railroad.

Soon after the organization of the Ogden, Logan & Idaho, the two predecessor lines were connected via new construction between Brigham City and Wellsville, via Collinston Summit (route of today's Utah Highway 30 between Garland and Logan). The line over Collinston was completed by renovating the abandoned right-of-way of the narrow-gauge Utah Northern, built in 1873 and abandoned in 1890. The right-of-way north from Brigham City was planned as early as May 1910 when Ogden Rapid Transit had pur-

The Utah Idaho Central Railroad came into existence in 1918 when the Ogden Logan, & Idaho Railroad changed its name. The OL&I was organized in 1915 to operate the combined routes of the Ogden Rapid Transit and Logan Rapid Transit companies. Throughout its early years, UIC called itself the Cache Valley Route, a reflection of its service to the entire Cache Valley of northern Utah and southeastern Idaho. Transportation wasn't the only use for the railroad's electric cars. Here, UIC car 504 (built in 1915) serves as a source of compressed air for track workers as they repair a spur that served an Ogden coal dealer. September 6, 1937.
(William A. Gibson, Sr., William A Gibson Jr. Collection)

chased property along the "Old County Road."

The connection was completed in mid-October 1915, and the first train between Ogden and Preston was operated on October 14. The new line was officially opened on October 27, 1915. At first, the company ran 16 passenger trains a day in each direction between Ogden and Preston, and another two between Ogden and Brigham City. The trip to Preston took five hours northbound, and 10 minutes less for the return to Ogden.

Providing freight service was an important source of revenue for the Utah Idaho Central since its earliest days as Ogden Rapid Transit. That early traffic, in the link-and-pin coupler days, was operated with ORT's Number 1 steam locomotive from the Oregon Short Line interchange at Five Points, north along the North Ogden Line to the cannery in North Ogden. Coal and fruit was also moved to Brigham City. Freight traffic grew until freight revenues exceeded passenger revenues by a considerable margin. Utah Idaho Central participated in both local and national freight tariff rates and maintained freight interchanges at Ogden with D&RGW, Southern Pacific, OSL, and Bamberger, with OSL at Dewey, and with OSL's Cache Valley Branch at Hyrum and Logan, Utah, and Preston, Idaho. UIC provided free pick-up and delivery of less-than-carload (LCL) freight traffic at all of its agency stations, and provided next-morning delivery of both carload and LCL shipments between the Cache Valley and Ogden, and Salt Lake City via interchange with Bamberger. Express service was offered, using the Railway Express Agency from all stations along the UIC. LCL and express business was handled along the UIC by two rebuilt passenger motors, car numbers 505 and 510, which provided speedy and efficient movement for these light shipments during both daytime hours and as the overnight merchandiser.

Along the Ogden Canyon line, freight traffic going between Ogden and Huntsville and surrounding communities consisted of sheep and sugar beets, and other farm products, along with clay. From the earliest, former Ogden Rapid Transit days, full carloads of coal were moved up Ogden Canyon to The Hermitage resort. Materials and equipment for the construction of Pine View Dam were shipped into the canyon before the branch was abandoned in 1932. The main line, between Ogden and Preston, Idaho, handled such items as coal, peas, fruit, milk and other dairy products, cement, gravel, sugar beets, automobiles, brick, and livestock. The Plain City Branch also handled this same variety of freight commodities.

The completion of improved roads, using both local and national tax dollars, brought competing truck lines into all of UIC's service area. As more highways were completed, UIC's freight business slowly dwindled until it depended almost entirely on bulk items, such as gravel and coal.

In addition to using cars interchanged with connecting railroads, Utah Idaho Central had its own fleet of freight cars. Among them were wooden boxcars, wooden refrigerator cars purchased secondhand in 1916 from American Refrigerated Transportation in St. Louis, former OSL wooden stock cars purchased secondhand from Union Pacific in 1916, wooden gondolas used for coal and brick service, wooden flat cars, wooden center-dump cars used for sugar beet service, and small wooden dump cars for clay service. In 1921, the railroad bought 100 new steel gondolas from Ralston Steel Car Co., and in 1939 it purchased three ex-Pacific Fruit Express refrigerator cars which it used as dry box cars. Many of UIC's cars saw more than 20 years of on-line and interchange service and were retired by 1938. The road's caboose fleet consisted of three wooden cars, numbers 401 to 403, built by predecessor road Ogden, Logan & Idaho in its own shops in 1916.

By mid-1918, electric railroads were already feeling the pressure of competition from the automobile. There were enough residents of Ogden, Logan, and Brigham City now driving to work, rather than riding

Utah Idaho Central car 503 is about to leave Ogden, bound for the railroad's northern terminal at Preston, Idaho. But first, the Railway Express Agency must load its packages. The package express business (similar to today's United Parcel Service and Federal Express) represented a major part of UIC's profitable business, and the railroad operated regular single- and double-car trains to ensure the timely arrival of the express and other small packages. June 1940.
(John F. Humiston)

the electric cars, that UIC applied to the Public Service Commission of Utah for relief from having separate commuter rates for these three cities. On July 16, 1918, PSC approved the railroad's request. By this time the streetcar line in Brigham City was seeing only intermittent service provided by just one car.

In August 1919, UIC received regulatory approval to discontinue and dismantle its streetcar line in Brigham City. That line was a single track from the Union Pacific (OSL) depot, east along Forest Avenue to Main Street, then south along Main and U. S. Highway 89 for about three miles to Fruitdale, this part of the line being the remaining portion of the old Ogden Rapid Transit line between Ogden and Brigham City.

The diminishing numbers of passengers on the local and suburban lines continued to keep revenues lower than expected. This decline was blamed on the growing numbers of automobiles. The most obvious declining numbers were coming from the Ogden streetcar lines, which were broken off as a separate operation in January 1920, calling itself Utah Rapid Transit, and also controlled by the Eccles family interests. The main benefit would be that management could now focus on streetcar operations, and not have to worry about inter-city passenger operations and the growing freight traffic. Likewise, Utah Idaho Central could now focus on improving its operations, without concern for Ogden's streetcars.

UIC retained the Plain City Branch because of its significant freight operations. Another freight branch was the Quinney Branch in Cache Valley, built by the Eccles' Cache Valley Railroad to serve the new sugar factory of Amalgamated Sugar Co. (also an Eccles company) at Quinney (later Amalga). Built in 1916, it served mainly to transport sugar beets to the sugar factory.

Utah Idaho Central possibly had the lowest population density for an large interurban system in the nation, fewer than 400 people per square mile. Because of the low population density, and therefore very large school districts, the railroad contracted with the districts to furnish school trains, which in later years accounted for more than 80 percent of the railroad's passenger revenue. During 1919, six daily trains ran between Preston and Ogden, with a Saturday through Monday train between Preston and Wellsville, and a stub daily train between Ogden and Dewey. The only passenger service offered on the Quinney Branch was a two-car school train.

As the nation's highways were slowly being improved, the amount of local passenger traffic for the interurban railroad slowly declined. Also, the cities began improving and paving their streets. With the Utah Idaho Central's tracks in place down its streets, Logan City expected the railroad to pay its share of the paving costs. Revenues derived from streetcar operations in Logan did not justify sharing in the paving expense, so UIC sought to abandon the streetcar service, retaining only its main line on Main Street, and its freight connection to OSL along Third South. In early September 1926, Utah Idaho Central received state Public Service Commission approval to abandon its streetcar line in Logan, and replace the service with gasoline buses. The company was already operating two Mack buses between Ogden and Preston, since August 1924.

The changes in 1926 put two buses on the streets

of Logan, with three more small buses added in 1935 and 1936. In 1938, several other buses were purchased. A single bus was added in 1940, and two more in 1945. All revenues continued to fall and in June 1947, Utah Idaho Central's bus operations were sold to Burlington Transportation Co. At the time, Union Pacific Stages and Fastway Lines were also operating over the same routes. Fastway Lines was owned and operated by Vern Cook of Logan, who sold his Salt Lake City-Cache Valley routes to Burlington in February 1948 in exchange for Burlington's local ex-UIC routes between Wellsville and Logan, along with the former UIC Logan city service. In 1969, Cook purchased the former Bamberger bus routes of Lake Shore Lines from Salt Lake City Lines and combined them with his former UIC Ogden to Cache Valley routes, all under the name of Cook Transportation Co.

An excellent description of Utah Idaho Central was filed with federal regulatory agencies in 1936, in a case to determine the company's status as a common carrier. In that document, the railroad was shown to be 94.63 miles in length, with two branch lines, one at seven miles (the Plain City Branch) and the other at 14 miles (the Quinney Branch). The line included 36 miles of spurs and yard tracks, making for a total of more than 152 miles of trackage, all in Utah, except for about seven miles in Idaho. Principle cities served were: Ogden, population 40,272; Brigham City, population 5,093; Logan, population 9,979; and Preston, population 3,381. There were 80 miles of 70-pound rail and 11 miles of 65-pound rail, with the remainder ranging from 40 pounds per yard to 85 pounds per yard. The ties were 6 inches by 8 inches and eight feet long. Only 11 miles of the line had tie plates, allowing accelerated chafing and wear between the wooden ties and the steel rail on the remaining trackage. The grade (rate of climb) of the line varied between level and almost 19 miles of 2 percent (2 feet of climb per 100 feet of track), most of which was over the Collinston Divide between Bear River Valley and Cache Valley. The maximum grade was in Logan, where a short stretch of 4.77 percent was needed because of the in-street running along Main Street at about 100 South. Most of the curves were at 12 degrees or less, but there were some spurs with 60 degrees of curvature (100-foot radius), which were so tight that they required boxcars to be switched one at a time.

UIC passenger trains in 1936 usually consisted of just one car, with a second car at times, making an average of 1.1 cars per train for the year. The adjacent steam roads were operating passenger trains of between seven and 11 cars each. There were 73 stops along the line, of which 52 were flag stops. Of the total of 408,634 passengers, 175,599 were students going to and from the public schools at the public expense. The average fare was 20 cents.

Freight traffic consisted of agricultural products, such as sugar beets, milk, tomatoes, and peas moving to factories, canneries, or processing plants along the line, and manufactured goods moving to connecting railroads. Because of the special nature of this raw agricultural traffic, many of the trains were only one or two cars in length. A daily express and package train operated with refrigeration facilities during summer and heating during winter. During the year, freight trains along the main line averaged 6.2 cars each, and the number of trains varied from 4.4 during March, to 14.7 during the harvest in October, making for an annual average of 7.7 trains per day, compared to 45 to 63 cars per day on the nearby steam roads. During 1934, Utah Idaho Central handled 6,354 carloads, of which 2,226 were local and 4,017 were interchanged with other carriers. Of the interchange traffic, 2,075 cars were moved to points in Utah, and the other 1,942 were moved to points in other states. During that same year, the railroad delivered traffic (including beets, coal, sand, gravel, gasoline, ties, lumber, poles and tin cans for the canneries) from 31 states, and shipped goods bound for 26 states (including beets, sugar, potatoes, sand, gravel, milk, canned goods, tomatoes, sheep, tin cans, and cattle).

Freight revenue always exceeded passenger revenue on the Utah Idaho Central. During 1933 and 1934, freight revenue was six times that of the passenger business, and throughout the 1920s and 1930s it was always at least twice, and usually three or four times passenger revenues. The company owned five 50-ton electric locomotives and two 35-ton electric locomotives. Three self-propelled cars hauled package freight, and they could pull other cars as needed. The largest locomotives could pull 1,000 tons, or an average of 12 to 14 cars of 45 tons each. Occasionally, a helper locomotive was needed over Collinston Divide. At times, entire trains of empty cars were operated, but these were limited to 35 cars due to air brake considerations. The company owned 100 gondola cars (the 1921-built steel cars), 22 ballast cars, 18 boxcars, 14 flat cars, 12 stock cars, and seven refrigerator cars. But UIC admitted that only the gondola cars were suitable for interchange with connecting carriers. The one fact that becomes apparent from this 1936 description of the railroad was that the Utah Idaho Central was a freight railroad that also hauled passengers, 42 percent of whom were school children handled under contract with the local school districts.

In 1939 and 1940, the company reorganized and restructured its financial debt, with no change in actual ownership, mainly members of both the Eccles and Browning families. Throughout these years, the railroad always met its expenses, with revenues exceeding expenses by between 20 and 30 percent. In the reorganization papers, it showed that it operated 160.08 miles of track, consisting of 94.63 miles of mainline, 26.04 miles of branch line, and 39.41 miles of sidings and spurs. The company also owned 15 self-propelled passenger cars, seven passenger trailers, seven freight locomotives, four self-propelled express cars, two self-propelled work cars, 176 freight cars, and five motor buses. The same individuals also owned the Salt Lake & Utah Railroad, which operated an interurban railroad between Salt Lake City and Payson, at the south end of Utah Valley, along with the Utah Rapid Transit Co., operators of the buses within Ogden City.

As noted earlier, in the discussion of Oregon Short Line, OSL predecessor Oregon Short Line & Utah Northern in 1892 built a one-mile branch line from its main line, east along Second Street to Washington Avenue, where it interchanged with Ogden & Hot Springs Railroad and its line to North Ogden. In September 1942, as part of preparations for construction of the U. S. Army's Quartermaster Corps' Utah General Depot (now Defense Depot Ogden), Ogden City took the franchise away for the OSL branch along Second Street, and ordered UP to remove its tracks. Rail access to the depot was to be by way of UP's remaining five-mile stub of the original 1869 transcontinental line.

Union Pacific fought the loss of the Second Street franchise all the way to the Utah State Supreme Court, but lost in February 1943. A time extension was given, but UP finally removed its tracks along Second Street, from its main line to Washington Boulevard. This also cut Utah Idaho Central's access to its 3.55-mile long North Ogden Line, which it reached by trackage rights over the UP branch line between the branch's crossing of the UIC main line and Washington Boulevard, then north along the boulevard to North Ogden. In October 1944, Utah Idaho Central applied to abandon its North Ogden Line. The proposed abandonment was protested by Ben Lomond Orchard Co., North Ogden Canning Co., North Ogden Fruit Exchange, and North Ogden Town itself. The only spur on the line served North Ogden Canning Co. A fruit loading track in North Ogden was used by the other protestors. Aside from the fact that UIC had lost access to the line, it showed that expenses far exceeded any potential revenue from continued operations and in December 1944, it was allowed to abandon and remove its trackage along Washington Boulevard.

A decline of local passenger and freight traffic following the end of World War II dealt the death blow to an already ailing Utah Idaho Central. The lifting of wartime restrictions on fuel and "unnecessary" travel saw the rise of private auto travel, along with the growth of trucks moving less-than-carload freight traffic over the publicly funded and maintained highway that paralleled the entire Utah Idaho Central route between Ogden and Cache Valley.

During the peak year of 1945, Utah Idaho Central handled 238,702 passengers, an average of 653 passengers per day, together with 136,272 passengers in its motor coaches along the paralleling highways. A peak year for freight traffic was 1942, when 478,486 tons were handled in 10,746 cars (about 30 cars a day).

The declining traffic, both freight and passenger, soon led the railroad into difficulties with its shareholders and bondholders. One of the company's major shippers had always been the Amalgamated Sugar Co. Utah Idaho Central was the major source of transportation for the sugar company, moving freshly harvested sugar beets from trackside loaders to the firm's

Throughout its history, Utah Idaho Central was a freight railroad, with freight revenue regularly contributing more to the company's profits than passenger revenue. The last revenue freight run took place in February 1947, two weeks after the final passenger train. Five freight locomotives were delivered between 1915 and 1917, with number 901, shown here at Preston on June 24, 1940, being the first to arrive. All five freight locomotives were scrapped during 1947 after abandonment.
(John F. Humiston)

sugar factory at Lewiston, and moving the finished product to both regional and national markets. After other, unsuccessful, alternatives were explored, a last-resort appeal on the part of the railroad was made to the board of directors of Amalgamated to assume the management and direction of the railroad's affairs. The board accepted, and on January 1, 1945, Amalgamated Sugar Co. took 96 percent ownership of the railroad. Financial difficulties continued, and UIC declared formal bankruptcy in December 1946.

On January 31, 1947, Utah Idaho Central applied to the Interstate Commerce Commission to abandon of its entire railroad. The major reason given was due to its economic condition, the railroad had been forced to continually defer maintenance, and at the time, it would require an expenditure of $350,000 to bring the railroad up to minimal operational standards. The deferred maintenance had been in its ties, ballast, rail, roadbed drainage, fences, gates, cattle guards, overhead wire and structure, and all of its rolling equipment. A high percentage of its ties were old and decayed. Many rails were surface-bent and had battered joints, especially in the cities and towns, and on the curves. At many locations, the track had sunk below water level due to inadequate ballast and roadbed drainage. The salvage value of all property was put at $640,000.

During its final days, the railroad exchanged freight traffic with Union Pacific, Southern Pacific, Rio Grande, and Bamberger, all at Ogden. It did the same with Union Pacific at Brigham City, Dewey, Hyrum, Logan, and Lewiston. As 1947 began, two round-trip passenger trains ran daily, including No. 1 and No. 4, the daily mail train. But on January 5, 1947, the second train, numbers 2 and 3, stopped running between Logan and Ogden. This change left only a single passenger train in each direction each day between Preston, Idaho, and Ogden, which also carried mail and express items. During the previous five years, the company had eliminated one stub run between Logan and Preston, along with another stub run between Logan and Mendon. In addition, it had eliminated two school trains between Logan and Mendon, and one daily trip each way between Ogden and Preston, along with a scheduled freight and less-than-carload train in each direction.

The last run for the Utah Idaho Central came on Saturday, February 15, 1947, after a federal judge issued an order on February 13 suspending the line's operations. The court order had come at the request of the line's trustee, First Security Corporation (organized in June 1928 as a consolidation of several Eccles- and Browning-owned banks), which had held the financial "paper" on the railroad since the 1939 reorganization. The complaint stated that the railroad had used its profits to pay only interest on its debt and had been unable to pay down any of the actual principal amount owed from the 1939 loan of $452,000. The complaint also stated that all maintenance on the line had been deferred in favor of interest payments. Between 1942 and 1946, UIC had run at a loss, showing a debt of more than $289,000 – unable to make money even carrying wartime loads, the opposite of almost every other railroad in America. The end of railroad operations brought all of the line's freight and passenger equipment to a standstill, including nine locomotives, 16 passenger cars, nine miscellaneous cars, and 15 other freight cars. The shutdown idled 190 employees. Even though trains stopped running, UIC buses continued to run between Ogden and Preston three times daily. In June 1947, Utah Idaho Central's bus operations were sold to Burlington Transportation Co. and operated by Burlington Trailways, and later by Cook Transportation Co.

In May 1947, the Ogden car barns at 17th Street and Lincoln Avenue were sold to the Ogden Transit Co. (successor to Ogden-streetcar operator, Utah Rapid Transit Co.) for use as a garage for its gasoline buses. The brick car barns measured 90 feet by 325 feet, and had been completed in 1915 by the predecessor line, Ogden, Logan & Idaho, and was known as one of the largest and most modern car shops in the west. The shops consisted of six brick buildings, including the car barn, the machine, blacksmith and truck shop, the paint and carpenter shop, the substation (added in 1918), and the boiler house. After the transit company ended its bus operations, the buildings were used by the Mormon church as a storehouse.

As one of its final acts of bankruptcy, UIC in February 1948 sold its right-of-way between Hot Springs and Collinston to the Utah State Road Commission for $22,193.

Ogden Interurban Terminal

The Ogden Terminal of Utah Idaho Central and Bamberger was a combination passenger-freight yard that originally had nine tracks; Tracks 1-5 were normally used by passenger trains, while Tracks 6-9 accommodated freight cars. Access for passengers was via the south side from a long, narrow brick building that fronted on 24th Street. Serving as waiting room, ticket office, baggage room, and snack bar, the building also housed UIC's operating offices. It was rushed to completion in time for Ogden, Logan & Idaho's January 1, 1915, start-up date. Although it was recognized as being too small almost from the start, plans for a larger, more imposing station were postponed time and again, and were never completed.

The facility was a joint operation, with the two railroads each owning components of the terminal. Utah Idaho Central owned the station building and the trolley wire, while Bamberger owned the land, the freight platform, and tracks to 23rd Street. UIC handled day-to-day terminal operations. Trains entered and departed via Lincoln Avenue, between 23rd and 24th streets, on jointly owned trackage that used Bamberger's 750 volts d.c., with UIC changing over from its standard 1,500 volts at 23rd Street.

When Utah Idaho Central shut down its operations in 1947, Bamberger took over the terminal and built a new, well-designed bus terminal that fronted on Grant Avenue, occupying the space formerly held by the old terminal tracks 3, 4, and 5. The original terminal building, having been owned by UIC, was sold as part of its liquidation. Bamberger buses, along with buses of other companies such as Trailways, began using part of the train yard after the tracks were either paved over, or removed altogether. After Bamberger abandoned its passenger operations in 1952, all tracks were removed except a track to the freight depot, one team track, and trackage serving Fuller Paint Co. and Cramer Coal Co. ✴

85

Trains arrived and departed the Ogden interurban terminal on trackage along Lincoln Avenue, on the west side of the terminal block. In this view taken on the afternoon of June 24, 1940, Bamberger "Little Car" number 125 takes Train 18 south to Salt Lake City. Entering Lincoln Avenue, it is passing Cramer Coal Co.'s billboard advertising the fuel dealer as a source for King Coal-brand coal, from United States Fuel Co.'s large mine at Hiawatha, Utah. In the distance, a Utah Idaho Central green and silver car loads at the terminal's freight house. (John F. Humiston)

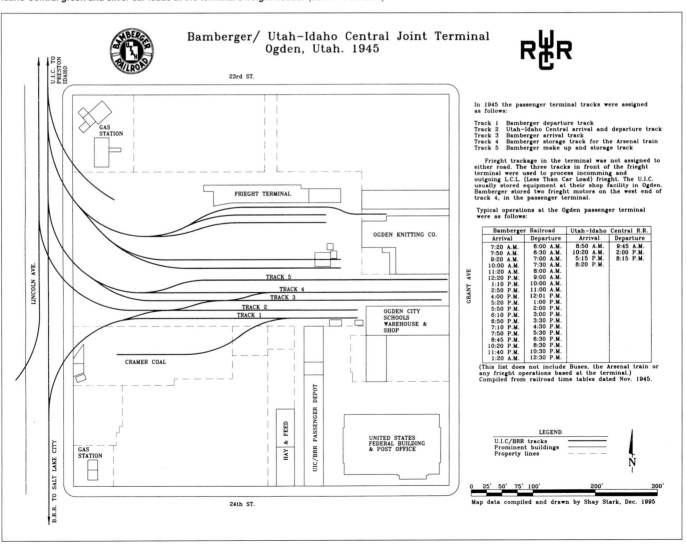

Bamberger/ Utah–Idaho Central Joint Terminal
Ogden, Utah. 1945

In 1945 the passenger terminal tracks were assigned as follows:

Track 1   Bamberger departure track
Track 2   Utah–Idaho Central arrival and departure track
Track 3   Bamberger arrival track
Track 4   Bamberger storage track for the Arsenal train
Track 5   Bamberger make up and storage track

Frieght trackage in the terminal was not assigned to either road. The three tracks in front of the frieght terminal were used to process incomming and outgoing L.C.L. (Less Than Car Load) frieght. The U.I.C. usually stored equipment at their shop facility in Ogden. Bamberger stored two frieght motors on the west end of track 4, in the passenger terminal.

Typical operations at the Ogden passenger terminal were as follows:

Bamberger Railroad		Utah–Idaho Central R.R.	
Arrival	Departure	Arrival	Departure
7:20 A.M.	6:00 A.M.	8:50 A.M.	9:45 A.M.
7:50 A.M.	6:30 A.M.	10:20 A.M.	2:00 P.M.
9:20 A.M.	7:00 A.M.	5:15 P.M.	8:15 P.M.
10:00 A.M.	7:30 A.M.	8:20 P.M.	
11:20 A.M.	8:00 A.M.		
12:20 P.M.	9:00 A.M.		
1:10 P.M.	10:00 A.M.		
2:50 P.M.	11:00 A.M.		
4:00 P.M.	12:01 P.M.		
5:20 P.M.	1:00 P.M.		
5:50 P.M.	2:00 P.M.		
6:10 P.M.	3:00 P.M.		
6:50 P.M.	3:30 P.M.		
7:10 P.M.	4:30 P.M.		
7:50 P.M.	5:30 P.M.		
8:45 P.M.	6:30 P.M.		
10:20 P.M.	8:30 P.M.		
11:40 P.M.	10:30 P.M.		
1:20 A.M.	12:30 P.M.		

(This list does not include Buses, the Arsenal train or any frieght operations based at the terminal.)
Compiled from railroad time tables dated Nov. 1945.

LEGEND
U.I.C/BRR tracks
Prominent buildings
Property lines

N

0 25' 50' 75' 100'   200'   300'

Map data compiled and drawn by Shay Stark, Dec. 1995

Map labels: U.I.C. TO PRESTON IDAHO — 23rd ST. — GAS STATION — FRIEGHT TERMINAL — OGDEN KNITTING CO. — TRACK 5 — TRACK 4 — TRACK 3 — TRACK 2 — TRACK 1 — OGDEN CITY SCHOOLS WAREHOUSE & SHOP — LINCOLN AVE. — GRANT AVE. — CRAMER COAL — HAY & FEED — UIC/BRR PASSENGER DEPOT — UNITED STATES FEDERAL BUILDING & POST OFFICE — GAS STATION — B.R.R. TO SALT LAKE CITY — 24th ST.

11. Utah State Railroad Museum at Ogden Union Station

The original plans to turn Ogden Union Station into a museum and convention center were first presented to officials of both Union Pacific and Southern Pacific at the celebration of the Golden Spike Centennial in 1969. In December 1971, after the May 1971 takeover by Amtrak of all passenger trains through the city, the first formal proposal for a railroad museum in the Ogden Union Station was presented in a letter to the president of Ogden Union Railway & Depot Co. in San Francisco. The letter, from Ogden Mayor Bart Wolthuis, asked that the empty building be donated to the city for use by the Golden Spike Empire as a museum. It took a couple years for the proposal to be taken seriously, and more time for negotiations to be completed, but Ogden's city fathers were persistent. In 1973, the city organized the Union Station Development Corp. to manage and operate the hoped-for prize, and by June 1975, Ogden Mayor Stephen Dirks announced that a general agreement had been reached for the city to acquire the station, with details of the sale still to be worked out. By early 1977, all parties were agreed and the vacant station was turned over to the city to become a tourist and convention center. Renovation work began immediately, under the direction of Elizabeth "Teddy" Griffith, who as a volunteer for the Junior League of Ogden, had finished a study of the building's history that placed it on the National Register of Historic Places. (Teddy Griffith stayed on as Union Station's director until her retirement in October 1993.)

Renovation continued and by mid-1978, a dedication ceremony was scheduled. To celebrate, Union Pacific operated its widely known 1944-built 4-8-4 steam locomotive number 8444 and a special train from Cheyenne. The train arrived a week early and was held ready at Salt Lake City, awaiting the big day. On October 21, 1978, the train left Salt Lake City with Utah Governor Scott M. Matheson and UP President John C. Kenefick in the locomotive cab for the quick run to Ogden.

In an earlier attempt at railroad preservation, on July 18, 1959, two retired 0-6-0 steam switching locomotives were dedicated in Ogden's John Affleck Park on Wall Avenue. Union Pacific 4436, a 1918 Baldwin, and Southern Pacific 1297, a 1908 Alco-Brooks engine, were donated by the railroads and displayed nose to nose (similar to the 1869 Golden Spike ceremony), with a granite stone and bronze plaque between. The many years of display were not kind to these two little workhorses, and they were finally removed in 1993. They remain part of the Ogden Union Station museum collection.

Union Station was designated as the official Utah State Railroad Museum on February 26, 1988. When the station was dedicated in 1978, UP donated a retired steam derrick, and a steam rotary snowplow, two of the last pieces of steam-powered equipment remaining on the railroad. To build a collection, other donations were sought from Ogden's railroads and from other corporations. In October 1985, Union Pacific donated one of its retired EMD Model DDA40X 6,600-horsepower Centennial diesel road locomotives, number 6916.

In 1986, Continental Engineering of North Kansas City, Mo., donated Union Pacific gas-turbine

Union Pacific's earliest gas-turbine locomotives entered service in 1952 as 4,500-horsepower units. An updated, 8,500 horsepower, three-unit design entered service in 1958. Upgraded 10,000 horsepower during the mid-1960s, these 30 units stayed in service until 1968-1970. Turbine 26, shown here on September 28, 1968, entered service in February 1961, was retired in February 1970, and was sold in September 1971. After initial plans to use the turbine as a stationary power plant fell through, the unit languished in a Kansas City scrap yard until July 1987, when it was donated to Ogden Union Station. Given a full cosmetic restoration, the unit is today displayed to commemorate the Gas Turbines and the role they played in UP's operations in Ogden. (A. J. Wolff)

locomotive number 26-26B. It had been stored at Continental's facility for 13 years, ever since UP had sold the retired units in 1970. The gas-turbines were powerful locomotives that operated regularly out of Ogden throughout their service lives, from 1958 until their retirement in 1970. Turbine 26-26B arrived in Ogden on July 10, 1987, and was repainted and cosmetically restored by volunteers of the local Golden Spike Chapter of the Railway & Locomotive Historical Society. In September 1987, Southern Pacific donated its GP9E 3769, a 1,750-horsepower EMD road switcher from the 1950s, which it had retired in late 1986, along with caboose 1555.

During 1991, the museum acquired from the United States Air Force at Hill Air Force Base a collection of 35 former military cars and locomotives. Included were four specially constructed training cars used to train bomber crews for the Strategic Air Command. Of the 35 pieces of rolling stock, 12 were in better condition and were retained for the historic collection, with the remaining 23 pieces being sold for their scrap value, and the proceeds going to renovate the remaining pieces.

A project to operate tourist trains between Ogden and the Promontory site of the driving of the Golden Spike was announced in February 1992, under the name of the Ogden-Promontory Tourist Rail Line. The proposal called for the operation of a tourist line from Ogden Union Station to Corinne on Union Pacific tracks. There, the passengers would transfer to 1920s-era railroad equipment and continue their journey to the National Parks Service's Golden Spike National Historic Site at Promontory. Running trains between Corinne and Promontory would require re-laying part of SP's Promontory Branch (abandoned and torn up in 1942) – the route of the original 1869 transcontinental railroad. The feasibility of the tourist operation was confirmed by a 1991 study funded by a $10,000 grant from Ogden City. A resolution, sponsored by Weber County Senator Winn Richards, and passed by the Utah State Legislature in February 1992, asked the federal government to provide $300,000 for a more detailed study. The 1991 study confirmed that the operation of tourist trains along the route would just barely pay operating expenses, but would never recover the expected construction cost of $12 million. Local public officials continue to search for ways to fully fund the project.

D&RGW narrow-gauge 2-8-0 No. 223

Denver & Rio Grande Western Railroad narrow-gauge 2-8-0 locomotive number 223 is the sole surviving engine built by the Grant Locomotive Works. It operated in Utah between 1881 (when it was built) until 1890, when the D&RGW tracks in Utah were changed from narrow, three-foot gauge to standard, 4 feet 8-1/2 inches gauge. Number 223 remained in service on Rio Grande's other three-foot gauge routes in Colorado until its retirement in 1940. D&RGW loaned the locomotive to the people of Salt Lake City as part of the city's Pioneer Day celebration on July 24, 1941, and after participating in the parade down Main Street (mounted on a highway trailer), it was placed on display in Liberty Park. It was formally donated to the city in 1952. Years later, Salt Lake City wanted to expand a playground adjacent to the locomotive's display site, and on January 11, 1979, the city gave the engine to the State of Utah. The Utah State Division of History accepted it with intentions of displaying it at the former Salt Lake City Union Station of D&RGW and Western Pacific, the future home of the Utah State Historical Society.

The locomotive remained at Liberty Park, near the carousel, until March 27, 1980, when it was gingerly lifted from its resting place of 28 years onto a heavy-duty flatbed trailer and moved across town to a new location west of the former Rio Grande station. There the little locomotive sat for 12 years, suffering from varying degrees of bureaucratic and budgetary concern and neglect.

After many proposals were floated to either restore the locomotive or sell it to other interested groups, in June 1989, the State History Office consulted with a professional restoration specialist on possible alternatives. Costs varied from $88,000 for simple stabilization for continued display to $1 million to make Number 223 fully operational. A public meeting was held on December 7, 1989, seeking input for the locomotive's disposition. Due mostly to lack of funding from the state legislature, the 223 project languished until 1991. In the meantime, the museum at Ogden Union Station was designated by the Legislature as the Utah State Railroad Museum. D&RGW 223 was given to the Utah State Railroad Museum and moved to Ogden Union Station in 1992. At that time efforts were begun by the Golden Spike Chapter of the Railway & Locomotive Historical Society to restore the little locomotive, possibly to operating condition, and those efforts continue today. ☆

In an early effort to preserve railroad history, Union Pacific and Southern Pacific in July 1959, each donated a retired 0-6-0 steam switching locomotive to the City of Ogden. They were set up for display at the new John Affleck Park on Wall Avenue. Union Pacific number 4436 was UP's contribution. Awaiting its donation, UP 4436 is shown here at UP's Ogden roundhouse in 1958. (Emil Albrecht, James W. Watson Collection)

Ogden's Riverdale Yard received eastbound trains from SP, and from Salt Lake City and southern California, along with a few trains from UP's Oregon Short Line subsidiary. Here, a "Short Line" train arrives at Ogden during the late 1950s. Passing the storage silos of the former Sperry Flour Co., it is about to enter Riverdale Yard. The train's motive power is a typical set of EMD cab units in their A-B-B-A configuration, meaning a controlling A-unit at each end, with two booster B-units between. (Emil Albrecht, James W. Watson Collection)

Bibliography

Books

Abdill, George B. *Pacific Slope Railroads, From 1854 to 1900.* (New York: Bonanza Books) By arrangement with Superior Publishing Co. Copyright 1959 by Superior Publishing Co., Seattle.

Ames, Charles Edgar. *Pioneering The Union Pacific, A Reappraisal of the Builders of the Railroad.* (New York: Appleton-Century-Crofts Division, Meredith Corp., 1969).

Arrington, Leonard J. *Brigham Young: American Moses.* (Champaign-Urbana, Ill.: University of Illinois Press, 1985) Illini Books edition, 1986.

_____, *David Eccles, Pioneer Western Industrialist.* (Logan, Utah: Utah State University, 1975)

_____, *Great Basin Kingdom.* (Lincoln, Nebraska: University of Nebraska Press, 1966) Reprint of 1958 Harvard edition.

Athearn, Robert G. *The Denver and Rio Grande Western Railroad, Rebel of the Rockies.* (Lincoln, Neb.: Bison Books, University of Nebraska Press, 1977) Reprint of *Rebel of the Rockies: A History of the Denver and Rio Grande Western Railroad,* Yale University Press, 1962.

_____, *Union Pacific Country.* (Lincoln, Neb.: Bison Books, University of Nebraska Press, 1976) Reprint of Rand McNally & Co., 1971.

Bachman, J. R. *Story of The Amalgamated Sugar Co., 1897-1961* (Caldwell, Idaho: Caxton Printers, Ltd., 1962) Copyright The Amalgamated Sugar Co., Ogden, Utah.

Bancroft, Herbert Howe. *History Of Utah* (Salt Lake City, Utah: Bookcraft, Inc., 1964) Reprint of 1886 book.

Beal, Merrill D. *Intermountain Railroads.* (Caldwell, Idaho: Caxton Printers, Ltd., 1962).

Bliss, Jonathan. *Merchants and Miners in Utah: The Walker Brothers and Their Bank.* (Salt Lake City: Western Epics, 1983).

Carr, Stephen L. and Robert W. Edwards. *Utah Ghost Rails.* (Salt Lake City: Western Epics, 1989).

Carter, Kate B., compiler. *Heart Throbs of the West,* Volume 2. (Salt Lake City: Daughters of Utah Pioneers, 1940).

Collett, Carol Ivins. *Kaysville - Our Town, A History.* (Kaysville, Utah: Kaysville City, 1976).

Daughters of Utah Pioneers. *East of Antelope Island.* (Salt Lake City: Publishers Press, 1948) Fourth Edition, 1971.

Drury, George H., comp., *The Train-Watcher's Guide to North American Railroads.* (Milwaukee: Kalmbach Publishing Co., 1992) Railroad Reference Series No. 11, 2nd edition.

Farnham, Wallace D. "Shadows From The Gilded Age" in *The Golden Spike*, David E. Miller, ed., Utah State Historical Society and The University of Utah Press. (Salt Lake City: The University of Utah Press, 1973)

Galloway, John Debo, C. E. *The First Transcontinental Railroad, Central Pacific, Union Pacific.* (New York: Simmons-Boardman Publishing Corp., 1950).

Griswold, Wesley S. *A Work of Giants, Building the First Transcontinental Railroad.* (New York: McGraw-Hill Book Co., 1962).

Hemphill, Mark W. *Union Pacific Salt Lake Route.* (Erin, Ontario: The Boston Mills Press, 1995).

Hilton, George W. and John F. Due. *The Electric Interurban Railways In America.* (Stanford, Calif.: Stanford University Press, 1960).

Hofsommer, Don L. *The Southern Pacific, 1901-1985.* (College Station, Texas: Texas A&M University Press, 1986).

Hunter, Milton R., comp. and ed. *Beneath Ben Lomond's Peak, A History of Weber County 1824-1900*, by Weber County Chapter, Daughters of Utah Pioneers. (Salt Lake City: The Deseret News Press, 1944).

Hyman, Sidney. *Marriner S. Eccles. Private Entrepreneur and Public Servant.* (Stanford, Calif.: Stanford University Graduate School of Business, 1976)

Kaysville-Layton Historical Society. *A History of the Bamberger Railroad.* (Kaysville-Layton Historical Society and Heritage Museum, 1990)

_____, *Layton, Utah, Historic Viewpoints.* (Kaysville-Layton Historical Society, 1985).

Klein, Maury. *Union Pacific, Volume I, Birth of a Railroad, 1862-1893.* (Garden City, N,Y,: Doubleday & Co., 1987).

_____, *Union Pacific, Volume II, The Rebirth, 1894-1969.* (New York: Doubleday & Co., 1989).

Koch, Michael. *The Shay Locomotive, Titan of the Timber.* (Denver: World Press, 1971).

Kraus, George. *High Road To Promontory: Building the Central Pacific (now Southern Pacific) across the High Sierra.* (Palo Alto, Calif.: American West Publishing Co., 1969).

LeMassena, Robert A. *Rio Grande...to the Pacific.* (Denver: Sundance Publications, Ltd., 1974) Third Printing, Second Edition, May 1979.

Madsen, Brigham D. *Corinne, The Gentile Capital of Utah.* (Salt Lake City: Utah State Historical Society, 1980).

Morgan, Dale L. *The Great Salt Lake.* (Albuquerque, N.M.: University of New Mexico Press, 1973, reprint of 1947)

Myrick, David F. "Refinancing And Rebuilding The Central Pacific: 1899-1910" in *The Golden Spike*, David E. Miller, ed., Utah State Historical Society, University of Utah Press. (Salt Lake City: University of Utah Press, 1973)

Pitchard, George E. *Newspaper Notes Project, Railroad Notes.* (Salt Lake City: George E. Pitchard, August 1987).

The completion, in December 1971, of UP's new run-through track along the west side of Riverdale Yard expedited the movement of increasing numbers of run-through trains moving through Ogden. Two years before, beginning in 1969, UP began receiving 47 EMD model DDA40X locomotives (christened as "Centennial" locomotives, to commemorate the 100th anniversary of the driving of the Golden Spike in 1969), along with many other state-of-the-art locomotives, to pull the company's time-sensitive trains. On June 10, 1975, Centennial locomotive 6940 is eastbound through Ogden, moving around the south leg of the 30th Street wye. The train will change crews at Riverdale and continue east, up Weber and Echo canyons into Wyoming. (D. B. Harrop)

Raymond, Anan S., and Richard E. Fike. *Rails East To Promontory, The Utah Stations,* Cultural Resource Series, No. 8, U. S. Department of the Interior, Bureau of Land Management, Utah, 1981.

Riegel, Robert Edgar. *The Story of the Western Railroads.* (Lincoln, Neb.: Bison Books, University of Nebraska Press, 1964) Reprint of Macmillian Co., 1926.

Roberts, Richard C. and Richard W. Sadler. *Ogden: Junction City.* (Northridge, Calif.: Windsor Publications, 1985, reprinted 1988).

Signor, John R. *Donner Pass, Southern Pacific's Sierra Crossing.* (San Marino, Calif.: Golden West Books, 1985).

_____, *The Los Angeles & Salt Lake Railroad: Union Pacific's Historic Salt Lake Route.* (San Marino, Calif.: Golden West Books, 1988).

Skaggs, Jimmy M. *Prime Cut, Livestock Raising and Meatpacking in the United States, 1607-1983* (College Station, Texas: Texas A&M University Press, 1986)

State of Utah, Department of Public Instruction. *Utah - Resources and Activities,* Supplement to the Utah State Courses of Study for Elementary and Secondary Schools. Salt Lake City: 1933.

Stewart, John J. *The Iron Trail to the Golden Spike.* (Salt Lake City: Deseret Book Co., 1969).

Strack, Don. "Utah's Canning Industry." In *Utah History Encyclopedia,* edited by Allen Kent Powell, pp. 67-70. (Salt Lake City: The University of Utah Press, 1994)

_____, "Railroads in Utah." In *Utah History Encyclopedia,* edited by Allen Kent Powell, pp. 450-455. (Salt Lake City: The University of Utah Press, 1994)

Strapac, Joseph A. *Southern Pacific Historic Diesels: Volume 3, E-Units and Passenger Fs.* (Bellflower, Calif.: Shade Tree Books, 1996)

_____, "Twenty-Eight Years of Alco Diesels" in *Southern Pacific 1967-1968 Motive Power Annual.* (Burlingame, Calif.: Chatham Publishing Co., 1968)

Sumsion, Oneita Burnside. *Thistle...Focus on Disaster.* (Springville, Utah: Art City Publishing Co., 1983)

Terry, William W. *William W. Terry Collection.* Weber State University, Special Collections, MS 116, Ogden, Utah.

Trottman, Nelson. *History of the Union Pacific, A financial and economic survey.* (New York: Augustus M. Kelley Publishers, 1966) Reprint of Sentry Press, 1923.

White, Henry K. *History of the Union Pacific.* (Clifton, New Jersey: Augustus M. Kelley Publishers, 1973) Reprint of University of Chicago Press, 1895.

White, John H., Jr. *The American Railroad Freight Car.* (Baltimore, Md.: The Johns Hopkins University Press, 1993).

Wilson, O. Meredith. *The Denver and Rio Grande Project, 1870-1901, A History of the First Thirty Years of the Denver and Rio Grande Railroad.* (Salt Lake City: Howe Brothers Publishing Co., 1981).

Video tape recordings

Morrison-Knudsen Co., Incorporated. "*Mariners In Hardhats*" (Pasadena, Calif.: Pentrex, 1993) Video recording of original M-K 30-minute film explaining construction features of Southern Pacific's Salt Lake causeway.

Newspapers

Deseret News
Deseret Evening News
Ogden Standard Examiner
Ogden Junction
Salt Lake Tribune

Dissertations

Adkins, Marlowe C., Jr. "A History of John W. Young's Utah Railroads, 1884-1894." MS Thesis. Utah State University, Logan, Utah, 1978.

Johnson, David F. "The History and Economics of Utah Railroads." MS Thesis. University of Utah, Salt Lake City, Utah, 1947.

Reeder, Clarence A., Jr. "The History of Utah's Railroads, 1869-1883." Ph.D. dissertation, University of Utah, Salt Lake City, Utah, 1970.

Periodicals

Anderson, H. V. "*New sampler speeds design of 31,000,000-cu yd fill,*" Civil Engineering, Volume 27 [December 1957] pp. 40-43.

Arrington, Leonard J. "The Transcontinental Railroad and Mormon Economic Policy.. *The Pacific Historical Review,* Volume 20, Number 2 [May 1951], pp.143-157.

_____, "Utah's Coal Road in the Age of Unregulated Competition." In *Utah Historical Quarterly,* January 1955, pp. 35-63.

Behrens, Peter. "Industrial Processing of Great Salt Lake Brines by Great Salt Lake Minerals & Chemicals Corp.," *Great Salt Lake, a Scientific, Historical and Economic Overview,* J. Wallace Gwynn, ed. (Utah Geological and Mineral Survey, Bulletin 116, June 1980)

Harrop, D.B. "*Rebuilding of a Legend*", CTC Board, Issue 103, January 1984, pp.12-19

Union Pacific's gas turbine locomotives were unique to that railroad, and the Ogden service tracks always seemed to hold several units awaiting their next assignment. The first example, a double-cab design, demonstrated on the railroad in 1948 and resulted in a 10-unit group of almost identical, single-cab locomotives four years later. A later group of 15 units, with exposed side walkways and known as Veranda turbines, as shown here by number 69 in May 1959, arrived in 1954.
(Emil Albrecht, James W. Watson Collection)

Jaekle, W. M. "*$49,000,000 project for Southern Pacific,*" Civil Engineering, Volume 27, December 1957, pp. 44-47

Mann, David, H. "The Undriving of the Golden Spike," in *The Last Spike Is Driven*, Utah Historical Quarterly, Volume 37, Number 1 [Winter 1969], Everett L. Cooley, editor, pp.124-134.

"*Abandonment Report: Bamberger Railroad,*" Short Line Railroader, Number 40, July 1959

"*Bamberger Railroad,*" Interurban Special No. 4, September 1946

"*Ogden: Gateway of the West,*" Utah Payroll Builder, Volume 19, Number 5, May 1930

Manuscripts
Austin, Richard L. *The Union Pacific Railroad: A Study Of Its First Entrance Into Utah With An Emphasis On Weber Canyon.* Unpublished manuscript on file at Ogden Union Station, Ogden, Utah. No date.

City of Ogden, Utah. *Minutes Of City Council, Ogden City, 1869-1872*; LDS Church Historical Department, MS 3720, folder 2.

Interstate Commerce Commission. *Southern Pacific Proposed Abandonment, Finance Docket 9791, proposed abandonment of portion of Promontory Branch between Kelton and Lucin, Utah. Application made on April 3, 1933, denied on June 11, 1934.* Published in Volume 199, Interstate Commerce Commission Reports, pp. 731-739 (199 ICC 731).

Rio Grande Western Railway. *Lease and Agreement for leasing the Ogden Union Depot facilities between The Ogden Union Railway & Depot Company and The Rio Grande Western Railway Co.* Treasurer's Contract No. 1890, May 1, 1892.

Rio Grande Western Railway. *Lease From The Union Pacific Railroad Company to The Rio Grande Western Railway Company and The Oregon Short Line Railroad Co. of the Stock Corral at Ogden.* Treasurer's Contract No. 1938, May 31, 1898.

Roberts, Richard C. *Ogden Union Station: as an Architectural Reflection of Ogden City History and Cultural Values*, unpublished manuscript in possession of Michael Burdett, Ogden, Utah. [no date, circa 1980]

State of Utah, Office of Secretary of State. *Articles of Incorporation, Ogden Union Railway and Depot Company*, Index number 486; also in index 4324

Terry, William W. *Weber County Is Worth Knowing.* [no publication information]

Union Pacific Railroad. *Corporate History of Oregon Short Line Railroad Company, As of June 30, 1916, prepared in compliance with requirements of ICC Valuation Order No. 20.*

Union Pacific Railroad. *Corporate History of Union Pacific Railroad Company, As of June 30, 1919, prepared in compliance with requirements of ICC Valuation Order No. 20.* ✭

Riverdale Yard was completed in 1942 (as East Yard), and expanded in 1954 (as Speedway Yard). This March 1957 view shows the south (railroad east) end of the yard as it appeared after the 1954 expansion, including the new PFE ice plant and icing dock. After the retirement of the two Baldwin heavy switchers in 1968, UP assigned three examples of EMD GP9s to do Ogden's heavy switching. These units were originally assigned to UP's eastern divisions, and were not equipped with dynamic braking, a feature required for road service in the west's mountainous terrain. More powerful switchers were needed at Riverdale because of the long strings of cars (at times complete trains), and the 0.5 percent grade down to 29th Street. (Emil Albrecht, James W. Watson Collection)

Index

Westbound trains left Ogden via SP, or via UP subsidiary Oregon Short Line to Pocatello, Idaho, or to Salt Lake City and possible destinations on another UP subsidiary, Los Angeles & Salt Lake. By the late 1950s, steam motive power was all but gone on Union Pacific west of Green River, Wyo. In steam's place, UP operated a large, 344-unit fleet of EMD GP9s, 175 of which were cabless B-units. Here, on November 29, 1958, UP 341 and four cabless units move around the south leg of the 30th Street wye, headed for Salt Lake City. As in many photographs of Ogden railroading, the silos and mill of the former Sperry Flour Co. are visible in the background. (Emil Albrecht, James W. Watson Collection)

Ogden Union Railway & Depot Co.'s new East (later Riverdale) Yard was put into operation in 1942. Until that time, many of the tracks of the main yard at Ogden were regularly filled with westbound empty Pacific Fruit Express refrigerator cars. As shown in this view from 1940, looking south and taken from the 24th Street viaduct, at least four tracks are filled with empty PFE cars.
(Emil Albrecht, James W. Watson Collection)